1970s Baseball

A History and Analysis of the Decade's Best Seasons, Teams, and Players

www.1970sBaseball.com

Introduction

In the history of our national pastime, few decades have provided more notable headlines, more milestones, and more intriguing seasons than the 1970s. Baseball changed quickly from the stodgy, buttoned up 50s and 60s product; divisional play, in its infancy after debuting in 1969, led to exciting races in the standings and gave us memorable League Championship Series in both leagues. And like it or not, the designated hitter, evening World Series games, and free agency emerged and were here for good by mid-decade.

How about the superstars who left their mark? Long before the internet, we met not only baseball icons but personalities with such star power that they became household names, many of whom are still well-known today. Pete Rose, Tom Seaver, Reggie Jackson, Nolan Ryan, Jim Palmer, Johnny Bench, Willie Stargell - all transcend the sport. Hallowed career records held for more than half a century by the likes of Babe Ruth and Ty Cobb were broken by Hank Aaron and Lou Brock, distinguished stars with unquestioned credentials in their own right. These men, along with others like Willie Mays, Harmon Killebrew, Ernie Banks, Bob Gibson, and Al Kaline wrapped up long Hall of Fame careers during the decade.

Just as quickly Fred Lynn, Lou Whitaker, Steve Garvey, Ron Guidry, Mike Schmidt, Dave Winfield, Jim Rice, Bruce Sutter, Dave Parker, George Brett, Robin Yount, Rich Gossage, and Paul Molitor became new heroes, and they excelled and thrilled us well into the next decade.

Great dynasties emerged, and then in some cases, crumbled before our eyes. We saw the baton of repeat/three-peat championships passed across the continent from the Swingin' Oakland A's to the Big Red Machine in Cincinnati and then all the way east to the Bronx Bombers in New York. Meanwhile, back out west, the Dodgers could not quite crack through for a World Series title. In the late 70s, Philadelphia and Kansas City dominated their divisions, only to continually fall just short of reaching the Fall Classic. The Pittsburgh Pirates' titles in '71 and '79 sandwiched the three 'dynasty franchises'; Pittsburgh closed the decade by staging their own repeat of sorts, eight years in the waiting, as the square-capped Fam-i-lee picked up where the early decade Lumber Company had left off - downing Earl Weaver's Orioles in 7 games. Like the Pirates and Reds, Baltimore, the decades' first World Champion, was a consistent contender, seeming to either win or come close to winning a title, pennant or division every year.

The book that follows is my attempt to sort out, categorize, and make sense of ten great years of baseball. This was the book I always wanted to read but could never find. I review each season, stopping along the way to mention divisional races, individual achievements of note, and post-season highlights. Then I created Top 10 rankings for every position, plus managers. In that regard, only a player/manager performance from 1970-79 is taken into consideration, and each player is only considered at a single position other than DH, which gets some attention in its own right later in the book.

I also rank top fielders by position, best clutch players, power-speed men, even the top tape measure blasts for the decade.

Then on to the franchise rankings, with reviews for each team as we rank them 1 through 26, and include a look at each club's Top 3 in 15 statistical categories. There we examine full decade standings, post-season results, and of course another ranking, this time for best rivalries. Again this is a decade ranking, not all-time. So a great historical rivalry like Dodgers-Giants was not particularly strong in the 70s, where for the most part San Francisco was not relevant, other than in their ability to trade talented outfielders away – for more on that feel free to skip ahead to the Giants team review (page 133).

Finally I rank the decade's Most Valuable Players from 1-10, and take a quick look at best individual seasons (for position players, starting pitchers, and relievers), before capping off the rankings with Top 10 Memorable Moments. We also set aside a bit of time to examine year-by-year All-Star game results and starters.

Sprinkled throughout the book, some in the season section, others mostly in the team section, are relevant articles of interest on issues like 4 man pitching rotations, free agency, strikeout pitchers, the 1973 MVP vote, features on notable players such as Roberto Clemente, Rusty Staub, Ralph Garr, and Jimmy Wynn, plus some notes on the 3000 hit club and 500 homer club, both of which were greatly represented in the decade.

And would any baseball book be complete without stats? I don't think so, thus in the appendix you can find Award winners, year-by-year leaders, plus single season and full decade Top 20s in 17 different categories.

Please enjoy the material your own way. For some small bites here and there will do the trick, keeping you busy with new tidbits throughout the winter, summer, and well into the fall chill. Others will gorge themselves as if eating a Thanksgiving feast. Either way, digest it all at your own pace, and I'd greatly appreciate if you send feedback.

As with any subjective listings, there will probably be some agreement, and even more disagreement. Let the debates begin!

Home Plate: Center of Controversy

One of my earliest baseball memories is the opening footage from the highlight film of the 1973 World Series between the Mets and A's. In super slow motion, Bud Harrelson of the Mets races down the inside of the third base line, passing Oakland's catcher Ray Fosse, who is a few feet up the line in foul territory grabbing the on-coming throw. Though it's impossible to tell 100%, every indication is that Fosse never made a tag as Harrelson squeezed past and crossed the plate. Home plate umpire Augie Donatelli is lying flat on his stomach and raises his fist to make the 'out' call. The footage moves back to regular speed as Harrelson and manager Yogi Berra rush toward home plate, arguing wildly while on-deck hitter Willie Mays drops to his knees pleading with Donatelli. Miraculously, no one is ejected.

The play happened with 1 out and the score tied 6-6 in the top of the 10th inning of Game 2 with the A's leading the series one game to none. Felix Milan had just flied to Joe Rudi in shallow left field and Harrelson tagged up and attempted to score the go-ahead run. Donatelli, expecting Harrelson to slide, wound up out of position behind the play and had a poor angle to tell if Harrelson is actually tagged as he passes Fosse en route to the plate. He most likely was never touched, and Mays, Harrelson, Berra, and Milan all went nuts.

Somewhat ironically, Harrelson went on the score New York's go ahead run in the 12th as the Mets rallied for a crazy 10-7 win. So while the high-profile call was incorrect, it had no bearing on the outcome of the Series that Oakland went on to win in 7 games.

Controversial plays at the plate were something of a tradition in World Series games during the 1970s.

In the 1975 Fall Classic, prior to becoming the Game 6 hero, Boston catcher Carlton Fisk was on the wrong end of a controversial call *near* home plate. In the 10th inning of Game 3 with a runner on first, Cincinnati's Ed Armbrister attempted a sacrifice bunt that bounced off the plate. Fisk reached up for the ball and temporarily collided with Armbrister, who was just making his way out of the batter's box toward first base. Fisk came free and then made an errant throw to second base. Boston manager Darrell Johnson argued with home plate umpire Larry Barnett that interference should have been called. Once order was restored, Joe Morgan singled to win the game, giving Cincinnati a 2-1 series lead - they took the Series in 7.

So the '73 call was 'probably' incorrect, but New York won the game anyway. The '75 call led to a game-winning run, but may or may not have been incorrect - it can be reasonably argued that Armbrister had a right to the baseline, and/or that the collision did not cause the errant throw anyway, as Fisk still separated from Armbrister and was able to plant his feet before throwing the ball away.

But in 1970 the outcome of a World Series game was tilted on a call that was clearly incorrect.

In the 6th inning of a 3-3 tie in Game 1 of the 1970 World Series between Baltimore and Cincinnati, the Red's Ty Cline chopped a ball in front of home plate with Bernie Carbo on third base. Oriole's catcher Elrod Hendricks scrambled after the ball, home plate umpire Ken Burkhart followed, and somehow wound up tangled between Hendricks and Carbo, who was making his way to the plate. Hendricks reached to tag the sliding Carbo and Burkhart was knocked down with his back to the play. Before Carbo reached the plate Hendricks tagged him with his mitt but still had the ball in his bare hand. Burkhart looked back to see Hendricks holding the baseball and called Carbo out, denying Cincinnati the potential go-ahead run. The O's eventually broke the tie and won 4-3, and eventually took the series 4 games to 1.

Years before instant replay video review rules, home plate umpires often found themselves on the hot seat during the Fall Classics of the 1970s.

Season Summaries

1970

The decade opened with several off the field controversies. Denny McClain, fresh off two straight Cy Young award seasons, was suspended three times and never regained his pitching form. St Louis' Curt Flood lost a court case in a bid to become a free-agent and sat out the year. The Seattle Pilots went bankrupt after one season and were moved to Milwaukee four days before opening day, and umpires staged a strike before the playoffs.

On the diamond, 1970 saw some of the most impressive single season hitting performances in recent memory. In the American League, standouts included Washington's Frank Howard (44 HR, 126 RBI, .283), Minnesota's Harmon Killebrew (41-113-.271), Carl Yastrzemski of Boston (40-102-.329) and Baltimore's league MVP Boog Powell (35-114-.297). The National League had stellar performances from Atlanta's Hank Aaron (38-118-.298) and batting champ Rico Carty (25-101-.366, 31 game hitting streak), Chicago's Billy Williams (37-122-.333), San Francisco's Willie McCovey (39-126-.289), plus Cincinnati's Tony Perez (40-129-.317) and MVP Johnny Bench (45-148-.293), who led the Reds to their first pennant since 1961.

NL Cy Young winner Bob Gibson of St Louis went 23-7 and tied San Francisco's Gaylord Perry for the league lead in wins. Ferguson Jenkins won 22 games and set a Cubs team record with 274 strikeouts. New York's 18-game winner Tom Seaver led the league with 283 strikeouts and a 2.82 ERA, and set a major league record against San Diego with 10 straight strikeouts and a record tying 19 in the game.

In the AL, Sam McDowell of Cleveland won 20 games and led the majors with 304 strikeouts. Cy Young winner Jim Perry led Minnesota to a division title with a 24-12 record. Two Orioles, Mike Cuellar and Dave McNally, tied Perry for the league lead in wins, while their teammate Jim Palmer won 20 games and led the Birds with a 2.70 ERA.

Veterans Hank Aaron and Willie Mays reached 3,000 hits, while Vida Blue (Oakland), Bill Singer (LA), Doc Ellis (Pittsburgh), and Clyde Wright (California) all threw no-hitters.

Pittsburgh won the NL East fueled by a powerful attack featuring Willie Stargell, Roberto Clemente, Bob Robertson and Manny Sanguillen, but the Reds, who had won the West by 14 games under rookie manager Sparky Anderson, held them to only 3 total runs and no home runs in a three game NLCS sweep. Baltimore, who won 108 games during the regular season, was just as convincing in the ALCS. The Birds batted .330 and made quick work of Minnesota for the second straight season; the Twins only held a lead for ½ an inning in the three games combined in 10-6, 11-3, and 6-1 dismantlings.

In the World Series Baltimore dominated the action, hammering 10 HRs, including 2 each from Powell, Frank Robinson, and series MVP Brooks Robinson. In Cincinnati, the O's fell behind 3-0 in Game 1 and 4-0 in Game 2 before roaring back to take both games, 4-3 and 6-5 respectively. When the action moved to Baltimore, the O's were in command of Game 3 all the way, winning 9-3, highlighted by Dave McNally's complete game victory and grand slam homerun. An eighth inning 3–run homer by Lee May helped the Reds to a comeback 6-5 win in Game 4, before Baltimore closed it out 9-3 in Game 5, with Mike Cuellar going all the way after being knocked out in the third inning of Game 2. Brooks Robinson hit .429 and played a fantastic third base, making several diving plays to squash Cincinnati rallies. In a season dominated by outstanding hitting, it was the man known as 'The Human Vacuum Cleaner' who led the way.

1971

Defending champion Baltimore continued on-course, winning over 100 games and the American League pennant for the third straight year. This time the pitching staff had not three, but four 20 game winners, with Pat Dobson (20-8) joining Mike Cuellar (20-9), Dave McNally (21-5), and Jim Palmer (20-9). Palmer again led the team in ERA (2.68). Baltimore's trademark pitching was backed by an airtight defense, including Gold Glovers 3B Brooks Robinson (who won 16 gold gloves in his career), CF Paul Blair (9), SS Mark Belanger (8), and 2B Dave Johnson (3).

Oakland began a run of 5 straight division titles, winning the AL West by 16 games. Catfish Hunter went 21-11 with a 2.96 ERA, but the biggest story of the season was 21 year old Vida Blue, who captured both the Cy Young Award and MVP Honors with a 24-8 record, 301 strikeouts, 8 shutouts, and a league leading 1.82 ERA. Detroit's Mickey Lolich led the league with 25 wins and 308 strikeouts, while Chicago's knuckleballer Wilbur Wood enjoyed an outstanding 22 win season with a 1.91 ERA.

In the National League, Pittsburgh repeated as NL East champs, fending off a late charge by the Cardinals and MVP Joe Torre, who took the batting title at .363, adding 24 HR and 137 RBI. Again the Bucs rode the torrid bats of Willie Stargell (48 HR, 125 RBI, .295Avg), Roberto Clemente (.341, 86 RBI) and catcher Manny Sanguillen (.319, 84 RBI), along with consistent pitching from All-Star Doc Ellis (19-9) and Steve Blass (15-8).

Chicago's Ferguson Jenkins took Cy Young honors and led the league with 24 wins, while New York's Tom Seaver won 20 games and led the majors with a 1.76 ERA.

Two top stars had their best seasons of the decade in 1971. Yankee centerfielder Bobby Murcer batted .331 with 25 HR, and Henry Aaron bombed 47 HR with 118 RBI, .327 batting average, and a major league best .669 slugging %.

San Francisco, riding the arms of Juan Marichal (18-11, 2.94) and Gaylord Perry (16-12, 2.76), and the overall outstanding play of Bobby Bonds (.288, 33 HR, 102 RBI), opened up an early 10 game lead in the NL West, then slumped to an 8-16 finish, barely edging out the Dodgers by a single game.

The Giants, with a complete game from Perry and a Willie McCovey HR, took Game 1 of the NLCS, only to lose the next three to the Pirates. The Pittsburgh bats outlasted a strong Giants staff with 8 HR in the Series, including 3 from Rob Robertson in Game 2. Robertson hit 4 NLCS HRs overall, and batted .438, with Dave Cash (8-19, .421) and Roberto Clemente (6-18, .333) adding support. Baltimore notched their third straight ALCS sweep, needing only 4 different pitchers (McNally, Cuellar, Palmer, plus 2 relief innings from Eddie Watt) to quiet Oakland's bats.

The World Series opened in Baltimore with the Orioles topping the Bucs 5-3 on the strength of 3 homeruns, and then enjoying an 11-3 trouncing in Game 2. The Pirates swept the next three at home - Steve Blass tossed a complete game and benefited from a Robertson 3-run homer as the Pirates took Game 3, and then the Bucs followed with 4-3 and 4-0 wins to take a 3-2 series lead. In Game 6 back in Baltimore, the O's overcame a 2-0 deficit to tie the game in the 7th inning and eventually pulled it out in the 10th. But Blass pitched another complete game gem in Game 7, allowing only 4 hits as the Pirates won 2-1, capturing their first Championship since 1960. Roberto Clemente hit safely in all 7 games and was the Series MVP with a .414 batting average and 2 HR.

1972

In the off-season the Washington Senators franchise moved to Arlington as the Texas Rangers. During spring training Mets manager Gil Hodges passed away, and a player strike wiped 86 games off the schedule.

Once play got underway it did not take long for Oakland and Cincinnati to establish their excellence and begin a collision course toward the World Series. The A's built on their 1971 success, overcoming a Vida Blue hold-out on the arms of starters Catfish Hunter (21-7, 2.04 ERA), Ken Holtzman (19-11, 2.51), and Blue Moon Odom (15-6, 2.51), relievers Rollie Fingers (11-9, 21 saves, 2.50 ERA) and Darold Knowles (5-1, 11 saves, 1.36 ERA), and the offense of Reggie Jackson (25 HR), Joe Rudi (.305), Mike Epstein (26 HR), and Bert Campaneris (52 steals). The A's won the division by 5 games, overcoming a strong challenge from surprising Chicago. The White Sox boasted league MVP Dick Allen, a .308 hitter who topped the league in HR (37), RBI (113), Slugging (.603), and On Base % (.422), and pitcher Wilbur Wood, a 24 game winner.

The AL East race was even closer, with Detroit, behind Mickey Lolich's 22 wins, edging Boston by ½ game, and Baltimore and New York by 5 and 6 ½ games respectively. Boston's Luis Tiant showed incredible versatility, compiling a 15-6 record, a major league leading 1.91 ERA, 12 complete games and 3 saves over 19 starts and 24 relief appearances. Cleveland's Gaylord Perry led the league with 24 wins and had a 1.92 ERA.

The Reds came back from a slumping season to regain their 1970 form and easily won the NL West behind the bats of MVP Johnny Bench (40HR, 125 RBI), Pete Rose (.307), Tony Perez (90 RBI), and newly acquired second baseman Joe Morgan (.292, 58 SB, league leading 122 runs scored) from Houston, plus the starting pitching led by ace Gary Nolan (15-5, 1.99 ERA). Reliever Clay Carroll set a major league record with 37 saves. The Pirates slugged their way to a third straight NL East crown; Willie Stargell led Pittsburgh with a 33 HR, 112 RBI, .293 season; in all 7 of 8 position player starters hit .282 or better. Chicago finished second by 11 games despite the efforts of batting champion Billy Williams (.333) who also tallied 37 HR and 122 RBI. The Mets finished in third place behind the pitching of Tom Seaver (21-12, 249 Ks), NL Rookie of the Year Jon Matlack (15 wins, 2.32 ERA), and bullpen ace Tug McGraw (27 saves, 1.70 ERA).

Two men from last place clubs did much of the heavy lifting for their teams. Cy Young Award winner Steve Carlton went 27-10 with a 1.97 ERA and 310 Ks for a Phillies team that won only 59 games. San Diego's Nate Colbert hit 38 HR, and his 111 RBI led the team by 64.

Both LCS went the distance, the first time this had happened in either league. Oakland took the first two games at home and then dropped the next two in Detroit, before finally edging the Tigers 2-1 in the deciding game. Blue Moon Odom won 2 games and gave up no runs in 14 innings of work, while Vida Blue tossed a total of 5 scoreless innings in 4 games out of the bullpen. Reggie Jackson was lost for the World Series after injuring his hamstring while stealing home. In the NLCS, Cincinnati fell behind 2 games to 1 before blowing out the Bucs 7-1 in Game 4. In the deciding game, Pittsburgh's Dave Guisti could not hold a one-run 9th inning lead. He surrendered a tying leadoff homer to Johnny Bench, and later in the same inning Bob Moose's wild scored pinch runner George Foster with the deciding run. Pete Rose batted .450 with 4 doubles in the series.

As they had done in the NLCS, the Reds fell behind in the World Series, with Oakland taking a 3 games to 1 lead. Cincinnati edged Oakland 5-4 in Game 5, with Pete Rose driving in the go-ahead run in the top of the 9th, and Joe Morgan throwing out a runner at the plate in the bottom half. The Reds followed that victory with an 8-1 win in Game 6, but Oakland's star reliever Rollie Fingers closed out a 3-2 nail biter in Game 7 to lock up the Championship for the A's. Catfish Hunter won 2 games and Gene Tenace hit .348 with 4 HR and 9 RBI to win the series MVP award.

On December 31, tragedy struck the baseball world as it had in spring training. Roberto Clemente, who collected his 3,000 hit during the season, died on a plane that crashed while flying supplies from his native Puerto Rico to earthquake victims in Nicaragua.

Year of the One-Man Show

1972 was a unique baseball season in many ways: Before a single regular season pitch was thrown the Washington Senators franchise had moved to Arlington as the Texas Rangers, Mets manager Gil Hodges passed away in spring training, and the first player strike in Major League history took place in April, resulting in a total of 86 lost games. Then the Oakland A's began a dynasty of three straight World Series championships, and on New Year's eve Pittsburgh Pirate great Roberto Clemente died in a plane crash.

The year will also will be remembered by outstanding performances from two players on last place clubs, both with statistically historic contributions to their teams.

During the early 1970s lefty Steve Carlton featured a curve, slider, and rising fastball that were all considered as good as any pitcher's in the majors. Pittsburgh's Willie Stargell said "Hitting against Steve Carlton is like eating soup with a fork". He was never more dominant in his Hall of Fame career than in 1972, when he went 27-10 with a 1.97 ERA in his first season as a Phillie after being acquired from St. Louis in a straight-up swap for Rick Wise. Carlton fanned 310 batters, the most in a National League season during the decade, and his 27 wins were the 70's most in either league. No pitcher has won more games in a season since. Carlton accomplished this for a Phillies team that finished dead last in the NL East with only 59 wins. He accounted for a major league record 45.8% of his team's victories - the first time in 50 years that a pitcher had more than 40% of his team's wins. Along the way, Carlton received little help from the Philadelphia bullpen; he went the distance in 30 of his 41 starts, and only 3 of his 27 wins were saved.

Meanwhile, in San Diego, the Padres struggled through their third year of existence in familiar territory - the National League West basement, where they would finish in each of their first 6 seasons. One of the Padres few bright spots in 1972 was their 6' 2", 190 pound slugging first baseman, Nate Colbert. Despite the Padres scoring a league-worst 488 runs, Colbert somehow drove in 111, 5th best in the majors. The next highest total for a Padre was Leon Lee - with 47! In essence if you were attending a Padres game back then it would have made sense to watch Nate hit and then make your way to the refreshment stand. Colbert WAS the San Diego offense; his 38 home runs were more than 3x better than team runner-up Lee's 12. He also led the team with 141 hits (30 more than Lee's 111), 87 runs (37 more than Lee's 50), 70 walks (29 better than second baseman Darrel Thomas' 41), and doubles (28).

Colbert only hit .250 and did strikeout 128 times, but imagine what the man could have done in a lineup with an actual table-setter or two in front of him (opening day leadoff man Enzo Hernandez hit .195 and #2 hitter Darrel Thomas, .230), or some more protection behind him. Colbert's 111 RBI were 22.75% of his team's runs scored, an all-time record. Only 10 men in baseball history have driven in more than 20% of their team's runs, and the only other hitter to do it in the 1970s was Frank Howard, who knocked in 126 of Washington's 626 runs (20.13%) in 1970.

1973

It was a banner year for the decade's biggest stars. NL MVP Pete Rose led the Reds to their third division title in four years with a major league leading 230 hits, an NL leading .338 average, plus 36 doubles and 115 runs scored. Cy Young winner Tom Seaver, whose Mets took a close NL East battle, had a 19-10 record and 2.08 ERA, tops in the majors. Jim Palmer won the award in the AL with a 22-9 mark and 2.40 ERA as Baltimore returned to claim the AL East. AL MVP Reggie Jackson's A's repeated in the West on the strength of his league leading 32 HR and 117 RBI. Pittsburgh's Willie Stargell moved back to the outfield from first base and terrorized pitchers, leading the majors with 44 HR and 119 RBI. Minnesota's Rod Carew won his 3rd batting crown with a .350 average, while also leading the AL in hits (203) and triples (11). Finally, California's Nolan Ryan threw 2 no-hitters, won 21 games, and set a new major league record with 383 strikeouts.

The Yankee's Ron Bloomberg became the American League's first designated hitter in the first game of the season, and hit .329 with 12 HR on the year. Other top DHs in 1973 were Minnesota's Tony Oliva (.289, 16 HR, 91 RBI), Baltimore's Tommy Davis (.306) and Boston's Orlando Cepeda (.289, 20 HR). With no need to pinch hit for pitchers, the league produced a record 12 20-game winners, including Chicago's Wilbur Wood, who lead the circuit in both wins (24) and losses (20).

Oakland won their division on the strength of a staff that featured 3 20 game winners - Hunter (21-5), Holtzman (21-13), and Blue (20-9), the continued bullpen excellence of Rollie Fingers (22 saves, 1.91 ERA), and the power of Jackson and Sal Bando (29 HR, 98 RBI, .287). Baltimore reclaimed the East behind their reliable pitching, but the difference between this year and last was the Bird's bats, which woke from a .229 slumber in '72 to a respectable .266, as rookie outfielders Rich Coggins (.319, 17 SB) and Rookie of the Year Al Bumbry (.337, 11 triples, 23 SB) emerged, while Bobby Grich shored up second base.

The Reds once again hold off the Dodgers in the NL West, this time by only 3 ½ games. Cincinnati rode strong seasons from Rose, Perez (27-101-.314), Morgan (26-82-.290), and Bench, who hit 25 HR and drove in 104 after a winter lung operation. Dave Concepcion provided an upgrade at shortstop, hitting .287 in 89 games before being lost to a season ending ankle injury in July. Jack Billingham (19-10), Don Gullett (18-8), and Fred Norman (12-6) bolstered the pitching. The Mets won an Eastern division where five teams finished within 5 games of first place with a surge of 29 wins in their final 43 games, led by strong defensive players like shortstop Bud Harrelson and catcher Jerry Grote helping the pitching of Seaver and left-handers Jerry Koosman, George Stone, Jon Matlack, and Tug McGraw (25 saves).

As expected, strong pitching dominated the ALCS. Palmer shut out Oakland 6-0 in the opener, then Hunter beat Baltimore's Dave McNally 6-3 in Game 2 to even the series. Oakland's Ken Holtzman outdueled Mike Cuellar 2-1 in Game 3. Game 4 saw the A's knock out Palmer in the 7th with a 4-0 lead, but Baltimore rallied against Vida Blue and Fingers for a 5-4 win. Finally, Hunter threw a 3-0 shutout to close out the Birds and send Oakland back to the Fall Classic.

The NLCS was equally thrilling, with the signature moment a brawl at second base between Harrelson and a frustrated Pete Rose during the Mets' 9-2 blowout win in Game 3. New York went on to shock heavily favored Cincinnati, overcoming Rose's clutch hitting (.381, Game 4 game winning HR) by taking the deciding game 7-2 behind a strong effort from Tom Seaver. Rusty Staub had all 3 Met home runs in the series.

The World Series opened in Oakland with the A's prevailing 2-1 in a pitcher's duel between lefties Matlack and Holtzman. Game 2 was a bizarre 12 inning, 6 error, 28 hit affair; Willie Mays' final game deciding hit was overshadowed by 2 subsequent Mike Andrews errors which allowed 3 more Met runs to score. Meddlesome owner Charlie Finley suspended Andrews after the game, only to have the decision reversed by commissioner Bowie Kuhn. It was not the last time the two would clash. The A's took a 3-2 11 inning battle in New York in Game 3, but Rusty Staub's 1st inning 3-run homer in Game 4 catapulted the Mets to a series tying 6-1 win, followed by Koosman outdueling Blue 2-0 in Game 5 to give the Mets a 3-2 series lead. On the brink of elimination, Oakland responded at home with a 3-1 win as Hunter bested Seaver on the strength of 2 Reggie Jackson RBI doubles. In the deciding game, Campaneris and Jackson each smacked 3rd inning 2-run HRs off Jon Matlack, and Oakland cruised to a 5-2 win and their second straight World Series championship. Jackson, with a .333 batting average, 5 extra base hits, and 6 RBI in the series, was named the MVP.

Who was the true 1973 National League MVP?

The National League MVP vote in 1973 was the closest of the decade, as Cincinnati's Pete Rose edged Pittsburgh's Willie Stargell, 274-250. Rose received 12 1st place votes to Stargell's 10. The finish was considered controversial by Pirate fans and Rose haters alike, so I thought a closer look was in order.

Stargell- Willie had a dominant year by any standards. He was only 2 years removed from another outstanding season, in 1971, when he had blasted 48 home runs with 125 RBI, only to finish second in MVP voting to St Louis' Joe Torre, who took the honors on the strength of a .363 batting average and 137 RBI. I think sometimes the 'shock effect' of a player performing so far above their career norms captures the writer's attention, and helped Torre's cause here. While Torre was certainly deserving, what was surprising was the voting landslide (318-222) in Torre's favor.

Stargell topped himself in 1973 with 90 extra base hits (43 doubles, 3 triples, and 44 homers), the most for any player during the decade, while slugging .646, the '70s second highest mark. He batted .299 with 80 walks, good for a .392 on base %, and drove in 119 runs. A far better outfielder than first baseman, Willie played the outfield exclusively in 1973, and contributed 14 outfield assists, 13 from left field.

Rose- The major league all-time hits leader notched his only MVP in 1973 by leading the majors with 230 hits, which tied Torre for most in the National League during the decade. The durable Rose also led baseball with 680 at-bats, 181 singles, and 301 times reaching base. He won the NL batting title with a .338 average to go with a .402 on-base %, 36 doubles, and 115 runs scored. Less talked about was Pete's defense – he led all left fielders in range factor, putouts (345) and assists (15), and finished second in fielding %. Batting leadoff, Rose was a catalyst for the NL West Champions, who had an MLB-best 99 wins. While the Reds were upset by the Mets in the NLCS, it was no fault of Charley Hustle, who went 8-21 (.381) with 2 home runs, one an 8th inning game-tying shot off Tom Seaver in Game 1, and the other a 12th inning game winner in Game 4.

Others- Some argue that the #3 finisher, San Francisco's Bobby Bonds, and the #4 finisher, Cincinnati second baseman Joe Morgan, were also more deserving than Rose. Bonds won a Gold Glove for his play in right field, and led the league with 341 total bases and 131 runs scored for the Giants, who finished in 3rd place with 88 wins. He hit .283 with 39 home runs, 43 stolen bases, and drove in 96 runs. Morgan led all position players with 9.2 WAR (wins above replacement), plus won a Gold Glove at second and had a .406 on base %, 67 steals, 26 home runs, 35 doubles, and 116 runs scored.

Conclusion- Rose's hard-nosed play and clutch performances transcended even his lofty statistics, and he gets my vote as the most deserving choice. A strong argument could be made that Stargell was only the fourth most valuable player in the league behind not only Rose, but also Bonds and Morgan. Those three players could beat you in a different way every day, while Willie's offensive game, while awe-inspiring, was much more one-dimensional, based almost exclusively on sheer power. And it was not nearly enough to prevent the Pirates from losing their grip on the NL East with a disappointing 80-82 3rd place finish. Morgan would go on to win the award twice, in 1975, and 1976, as Reds players won the award in 6 of the decade's first 8 seasons. Bonds, who had perhaps the most raw talent of all four players, and was one of the greatest power-speed men the game ever saw, was never an MVP. Stargell was a co-winner with St Louis first baseman Keith Hernandez, in 1979.

1974

Atlanta's Hank Aaron kicked off a season of milestones on April 8th when he launched home run # 715 into the left field bullpen off LA's Al Downing, breaking Babe Ruth's career record. Later in the year St. Louis' Bob Gibson joined Walter Johnson as the only pitchers with 3,000 strikeouts, and teammate Lou Brock broke a single season record with 118 stolen bases. In the AL, Detroit's Al Kaline closed out an outstanding career with his 3,000th hit, and California's Nolan Ryan tossed his 3rd no-hitter.

The Dodgers finally topped Cincinnati by 4 games in the NL West, on the strength of an MVP season by newcomer Steve Garvey, who hit .312 with 21 home runs and 111 RBI, and Cy Young winner Mike Marshall, who won 15, saved 21, and pitched in a record-setting 106 games. Cincinnati's Johnny Bench hit 33 HR and captured his 3rd RBI title with 129. Pittsburgh returned to the top of the East, edging the Cardinals by a mere 1 ½ games. In addition to Brock running wild on the base paths and batting .305 with 105 runs scored, St Louis received fine seasons from Reggie Smith (23-100-.309), Ted Simmons (20-103-.272), and Rookie of the Year Bake McBride (.309). Philadelphia's Mike Schmidt emerged as a rising star, leading the league with 36 HR while knocking in 116 runs.

The AL races were just as tight. In the West defending champ Oakland outlasted Texas by 5 games. Bert Campaneris (.290, 34 steals) and Bill North (54 steals) set the table for Reggie Jackson (29 HR, 93 RBI), Sal Bando (22 HR, 103 RBI), and Gold Glover Joe Rudi (22 HR, 99 RBI, 39 Doubles), while Catfish Hunter won 25 contests and the Cy Young Award. The upstart Rangers challenged all the way behind Fergie Jenkins' 25 wins and the MVP bat of Jeff Burroughs (25-118, .301). In the East, Baltimore edged New York by only 2 games. The Yankees continued to knock on the post-season door: Pat Dobson and Doc Medich won 19 games each and the foundation of their lineup solidified with 3B Graig Nettles, C Thurman Munson, 1B Chris Chambliss and OF Lou Piniella settling into starting roles.

The Dodgers entered the NLCS with more than just Garvey's power bat and Marshall's arm. 2B Dave Lopes (59 steals), 3B Ron Cey (97 RBI), along with outfielders Bill Buckner (.314, 31 steals) and Jimmy Wynn (32 HR, 108 RBI) formed an imposing lineup that provided plenty of run support for top starters Andy Messersmith (20-6, 2.59 ERA), Don Sutton (19-9, 3.23 ERA), and Tommy John (13-3, 2.59 ERA). In the series Sutton went 2-0, giving up only 1 run in 17 innings, and Garvey continued his dream season with a .389, 2 HR performance as the Dodgers closed out the Pirates in 4 games, ending the series with a 12-1 rout.

In the ALCS, Baltimore's 22 game winner Mike Cuellar topped Hunter 6-3 in the opener before Oakland's pitching took over the series, just as it had done one year earlier. Ken Holtzman tossed a 5-0 shutout in Game 2, then Vida Blue topped Jim Palmer 1-0 in Game 3, with Sal Bando's HR accounting for the game's only run. Hunter and Rollie Fingers combined for a 2-1 decision in Game 4, in a game that featured only 1 Oakland hit but 9 walks from Mike Cuellar.

The A's opened the World Series by topping hometown LA 3-2. The Dodgers would come right back to win Game 2 by the same score. In the 9th inning of that one-run game Joe Rudi hit a one-out single, and was promptly pinch-run for by Finley's latest novelty: Herb Washington, a track star with no baseball experience, signed exclusively to run the bases. Mike Marshall, who appeared in all 5 games, promptly picked Washington off first base. As was the case during most of their dynasty, Oakland's superior talent overcame their crazy antics; the A's went on to win the next three games, 3-2, 5-2, and 3-2 again, with Fingers closing out all three and winning MVP Honors. Garvey led both teams with 8 hits and a .381 batting average, but in the end his young Dodgers team was no match for battle-tested Oakland, who became the only team in baseball history other than the Yankees to win 3 straight World Championships.

1975

The Yankees made a huge off-season splash by signing Catfish Hunter away from Oakland with a then-lucrative 5 year $3.75 million dollar deal. They also traded fan favorite Bobby Murcer to the Giants for perennial 30/30 threat Bobby Bonds. While Hunter continued his claim as the decade's top pitcher with a 23-14 season, New York managed no better than third place in the AL East, 12 games behind surprising Boston. The Sox, with all-world rookies Jim Rice (22 HR, 102 RBI, .309) and AL Rookie of the Year/MVP Fred Lynn (21-105-.331) bested favorite Baltimore and Cy Young Award winner Jim Palmer (23-11, 2.09) by 4 ½ games.

Out west, Oakland, minus Hunter, held off Kansas City one last time on the strength of Reggie Jackson's 36 HR and 104 RBI, and the arms of Vida Blue (22-11), Ken Holtzman (18-14), and Rollie Fingers (10-6, 24 saves). The Royals were headed in the right direction with 3B George Brett (.308, 35 doubles, 13 triples), 1B John Mayberry (34 HR, 119 RBI, .291), OF Hal McRae (.306, 38 doubles) and young starters Dennis Leonard (15-7) and Steve Busby (18-12). Minnesota's Rod Carew quietly won his fourth straight batting title with a .359 average, and California's Nolan Ryan threw his 4th no-hitter.

Philadelphia boasted three league leaders; Mike Schmidt with 38 HR, Greg Luzinski with 120 RBI, and Dave Cash with 213 hits, but the Phils could not prevent Pittsburgh from taking their 4th NL East crown in 5 years. Veterans Willie Stargell (.295, 90 RBI), Manny Sanguillen (.328), and Richie Zisk (.290, 20 HR) continued to bash the ball, but the Bucs best all-around player was 24 year old Dave Parker, who showed a cannon arm in RF and hit .308 with 25 HR and 101 RBI. The Mets finished 10 ½ games behind the pack despite the consistency of Rusty Staub (.282, 105 RBI), the long ball heroics of newcomer Dave Kingman (36 HR), and Tom Seaver notching his 3rd Cy Young Award with a 22-9 record, 2.38 ERA, and league leading 243 strikeouts.

Cincinnati took back the NL West in convincing fashion, topping LA by 20 games with 108 wins. Pete Rose hit .317 with 47 doubles and was moved to 3B to make room in the outfield for George Foster, who responded with 23 HR and a .300 average. Foster joined Johnny Bench (28 HR, 110 RBI, .283) and Tony Perez (20-109-.282) in the middle of the lineup. Second baseman Joe Morgan took his first of two consecutive MVP awards, notching another Gold Glove while hitting .327 with 94 RBI, 67 stolen bases, 132 walks, and a .466 on-base %. Don Gullet led the staff with a 15-4 record and 2.42 ERA.

The LCS were one-sided affairs. Luis Tiant stifled Oakland on a three hitter in Game 1, beginning the upstart Red Sox dismantling of the A's in three straight, 7-1, 6-2, and 5-3, in the process outhitting Oakland .316 to .194. Despite the best efforts of Sal Bando and Reggie Jackson, who went a combined 11-24, the Oakland dynasty had ended. In the National League, Cincinnati bombed Pirate starters Jerry Reuss and Jim Rooker to take the first two games 8-3 and 6-1. Then in Game 3, Pete Rose spoiled 21 year old John Candelaria's 14 strikeout outing with an 8th inning 2-run HR, and the Reds went on to win in 10 innings to complete the sweep.

The Reds-Red Sox World Series has gone down in baseball folklore as one of the greatest of all time. The teams split the first four games, three of which were decided by 1 run. The Sox' 2 wins both came on complete game victories by Luis Tiant, the second a 163-pitch effort on 3 day's rest. Tony Perez hit 2 homeruns in Game 5 to bring Cincinnati within one game of the championship. Tiant went again in Game 6, a game that saw both clubs come back from 3-run deficits, and outfielders George Foster of the Reds and Dwight Evans of Boston making spectacular run saving plays to preserve the 6-6 tie. Carlton Fisk finally ended it with a dramatic walkoff homer in the top of the 12th. In Game 7 Boston took an early 3-0 lead, only to have Cincinnati tie it in the seventh, and go ahead for good in the 9th on a single by Joe Morgan. Pete Rose took MVP honors by hitting .370 (10-27) with 5 walks in the series.

1976

Cincinnati's 'Big Red Machine' was more powerful than ever in 1976, winning 102 games and outscoring anyone else in the NL West by 232 runs. They led the NL in hits, doubles, triples, home runs, runs, batting average, on-base %, and slugging. Joe Morgan took another MVP, hitting .320 with 27 HR, 111 RBI, 60 steals, and 113 runs. Pete Rose led the league with 130 runs, 215 hits, and 42 doubles, while George Foster (29 HR, 121 RBI, .306) established himself as one of the most dangerous run producers in the game. San Diego's soft-tossing Randy Jones captured Cy Young honors, leading the league with 22 wins and only 93 strikeouts.

In the NL East Philadelphia finally overtook the rival Pirates by 5 games, led by Gold Glover and homerun leader Mike Schmidt (38 HR, 107 RBI), repeat Gold Glove centerfielder Garry Maddox, who hit .330 with 37 doubles and 29 stolen bases, and ace Steve Carlton, who went 20-7. Chicago's Bill Madlock repeated as the NL batting champ with a .339 average after hitting .354 in 1975.

Detroit's Mark 'The Bird' Fidrych, exploded onto the national scene with quirky antics, including talking to the baseball and dropping on all fours to smooth the mound by hand. Fidrych stifled AL hitters, going 19-9 with a league leading 2.34 ERA. Despite Fidrych and reclamation project Ron LeFlore, who hit in 30 straight games and finished at .316 with 58 steals, the Tigers finished in 4th place, 24 games behind the Yankees. New York returned to a refurbished Yankee Stadium and played like the Yankees of old. Bobby Bonds had been traded to California for speedy outfielder Mickey Rivers, (.312, 43 steals), and pitcher Ed

Figueroa (19-10). 21 year old second baseman Willie Randolph (.267 with 37 steals) was also acquired along with pitcher Doc Ellis (17-8) from Pittsburgh. They joined Catfish Hunter (17 wins), MVP catcher Thurman Munson (.302, 105 RBI), third baseman Graig Nettles (AL leading 32 HR, plus 93 RBI), and relief ace Sparky Lyle (2.25 ERA, league leading 23 saves) to help New York pass perennial power Baltimore and defending AL Champ Boston in the AL East. Baltimore's Jim Palmer took a 3rd Cy Young Award with a 22-13 record and 2.51 ERA.

There was a changing of the guard in the AL West, where Kansas City overtook Oakland. The A's, now without Reggie Jackson and Ken Holtzman, who were shipped to Baltimore, still managed 87 wins and boasted 3 50+ base stealers in Bill North (75), Bert Campaneris (54) and Don Baylor (52). But KC's time had finally come, beginning a run of 4 AL West crowns in the 5 years. George Brett led the league with a .333 average and 14 triples, barely edging out teammate Hal McRae (.332) for the batting title. The Royals were a scrappy, spray hitting team with 7 players stealing 20 or more bases.

Once again the Reds took the NLCS quickly, winning the first two 6-3 and 6-2, and then overcoming a 6-4 deficit with a 3-run 9th inning rally in Game 3. The ALCS was a hard-fought battle that began a fierce rivalry between New York and Kansas City, who would meet in this venue 3 additional times in the next 4 years. Catfish Hunter built on his big-game resume with a complete-game 5 hitter in the opener for a 4-1 win. Then KC took advantage of 5 Yankee errors to take Game 2, 7-3. In Game 3 at Yankee Stadium, New York overcame a shaky 3-run 1st inning by Doc Ellis to take a 5-3 decision. The Royals again responded in Game 4, fueled by 5'4" shortstop Fred Patek's 3 hits, and beat up Hunter for a 7-4 win. In Game 5 both teams scored 2 in the first, then New York jumped out to a 6-3 lead, which was eventually erased on George Brett's 8th inning 3-run HR. Chris Chambliss, capping a fantastic 11 hit, .524, 8 RBI series, ended the tension with a leadoff 9th inning HR, as fans poured on the field to celebrate another pennant in the Bronx.

The World Series was one-sided, as Cincinnati swept New York in 4 straight, outscoring the Yankees, 22–8, and becoming the first N.L. team to repeat as World Champions since 1921. Johnny Bench would claim MVP honors for the series, hitting .533 with three home runs and six runs batted in. His counterpart Thurman Munson concluded his MVP regular season and .435 ALCS with 9 hits and a .529 World Series batting average in the losing cause.

1977

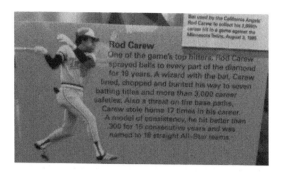

The American League expanded with two new teams, the Toronto Blue Jays and Seattle Mariners. The Jays finished dead last in the East at 54-107, 45 ½ games out of first, while Seattle fared ten games better and 'lost' last place in the West by ½ game to Charlie Finley's dismantled Oakland A's, only two years removed from a division title. Just as Finley's A's reached rock bottom, an equally ego-centric owner in New York was aiming for the ultimate prize. Never satisfied with second-best status, the Yankees, under free-spending owner George Steinbrenner, scored two big prizes in the free agent market, lefty starter Don Gullett and Finley's former long-time star right fielder, Reggie Jackson.

Clubhouse tensions and an early foot injury to Catfish Hunter led to a slow start, but New York found its stride and edged out hard slugging Boston and Baltimore by 2 ½ games each. Young Ron Guidry went 16-7 and led the starters with a 2.82 ERA, while Sparky Lyle (13-5, 26 saves, 2.17 ERA) turned in a Cy Young winning performance out of the bullpen. Table setter Mickey Rivers hit .326 behind bashers Munson (.308, 105 RBI), Jackson (32 HR, 110 RBI, .286), Nettles (37 HR, 107 RBI) and Chambliss (.287, 90 RBI). Jim Palmer led Baltimore again with another seemingly automatic 20 win season, while Boston had 5 players with 95 or more RBI, including Jim Rice with a 39 HR, 114 RBI, .320 breakout year.

Kansas City repeated in the AL West, holding off Texas by 8 games. George Brett hit .312, as did teammate Al Cowens, who led the team with 23 HR and 112 RBI. Dennis Leonard paced the staff with a 20-12 mark and 3.04 ERA. Minnesota's Rod Carew came as close to .400 as anyone since 1957 but fell short, capping off an MVP season with a major league leading .388 average, 239 hits, 128 runs, and 16 triples, along with 14 HR and 100 RBI.

The National League headliner was the Mets' mid-season trade of Tom Seaver to the Reds. Seaver won a combined 21 games, while New York sank to last place. The Dodgers made history as Steve Garvey, Ron Cey, Reggie Smith and Dusty Baker became the first 4 teammates to all eclipse 30 HR in the same season. LA took back the division handily, outpacing the Reds by 10 games despite Cincinnati's acquisition of Seaver and George Foster's monster MVP year - .320 batting average, 149 RBI, and 52 HR, which was the only 50 HR season of the decade and the first since Willie Mays in 1965.

In the NL East Pittsburgh's Dave Parker won the batting crown with a .338 mark, while teammate John Candelaria notched 20 wins and an NL-best 2.34 ERA. Rich Gossage was dominant out of the bullpen, with 26 saves and a 1.62 ERA. It still wasn't enough to keep Philadelphia from repeating as division champs on the strength of Mike Schmidt (38 HR, 101 RBI, .274) and Greg Luzinski (39-101-.309), plus starters Larry Christenson (19-6) and Cy Young award winner Steve Carlton (23-10, 2.64 ERA). St Louis' Lou Brock had 35 stolen bases, breaking Ty Cobb's all-time record along the way. Bruce Sutter of Chicago had a 1.34 ERA, 31 saves, 129 strikeouts and only 23 walks in 107 innings.

Two future Hall of Famers won Rookie of the Year awards: Montreal's Andre Dawson (19 HR, 65 RBI, .282, 21 steals) and Baltimore's Eddie Murray (27 HR, 88 RBI, .283).

The ALCS was another thriller, with New York again taking the series away from KC in the 9th inning of the deciding game. With the series split at two games each, George Brett and Graig Nettles kicked off Game 5 by trading punches in the 1st inning, and Kansas City opened a 3-1 lead, which the Yankees cut to 3-2 going into the 9th. The Bombers rallied for 3 in the 9th and Sparky Lyle closed it out in the bottom half. Philadelphia beat 20 game winner Tommy John in Game 1 of the NLCS, but Los Angeles took the next 3 straight, with John tossing a complete game 4-1 victory in Game 4.

Los Angeles and the Yankees split the first two World Series games in New York before the Yanks took control by winning the next two in LA, pushing the Dodgers to the brink. LA responded in Game 5 with a convincing 10-4 triumph. The Series moved back to Yankee Stadium, where Reggie Jackson took over with a game for the ages: 3 home runs on 3 consecutive swings as the Yankees prevailed 8-4. Jackson was an easy MVP choice by hitting .450 in the Series with 5 HR, 8 RBI, and 10 runs scored.

1978

By mid-season 1978, it looked like the Red Sox' year. They led their division by 10 games over Milwaukee, and Jim Rice was en route to a 46 HR, 139 RBI, .315 MVP season. The hated Yankees were 14 games back; other than Ron Guidry pitching lights out baseball, their pitching staff was unraveling with injuries, Reggie Jackson was suspended for 5 games by manager Billy Martin, and soon thereafter Martin was fired. Then the Red Sox began to flounder, New York stabilized under new manager Bob Lemon and Catfish Hunter's hot streak, and the Yankees went into a 4 game September series at Fenway Park down by only 4 games. What ensued was called the Boston Massacre – a Yankee 4 game sweep by scores of 15-3, 13-2, 7-0, and 7-4. New York soon went up by 1 ½ games, only to have Boston regroup and catch the Yankees, with the regular season ending in a tie. The Red Sox went up 2-0 in a one-game tie-breaker before Bucky Dent, a light hitting shortstop, slammed a 7th inning 3-run homer over the Green Monster to give the Yankees a lead they would not relinquish. The collapse was complete.

In the AL West Kansas City once again held off Texas and California, led by with George Brett's major league-best 45 doubles, and steady starters Dennis Leonard and Paul Splittorf earning 21 and 19 wins respectively. Lymon Bostock, California's promising young hitter who had been acquired from Minnesota, was murdered in September, the news shaking the baseball world. Minnesota's Rod Carew led the AL in batting average (.333) and OB% (.415) but the Twins could do no better than 4th place, 19 games back.

The Phillies, led by Greg Luzinski's 35 HR and 101 RBI, survived to win the NL East by 1 ½ games in a tough battle with Pittsburgh and their MVP/batting champ Dave Parker (30-117-.334). New York's Craig Swan won the NL ERA title with a 2.43 ERA, but the last place Mets' offensive attack was so weak that he still only managed 9 wins in 28 starts.

Los Angeles repeated as well; Steve Garvey led the NL with 202 hits, good for a .316 average and 113 RBI. The Dodgers strong staff boasted Burt Hooten (19-10), Tommy John (17-10), Doug Rau (15-9), and Don Sutton (15-11). Cincinnati finished 2 ½ games behind, despite George Foster's league-leading 40 HR and 120 RBI, and Tom Seaver's 16 wins, including the first no-hitter of his career. Pete Rose, in his last year as a Red, reached 3,000 hits and had a modern NL record 44 game hitting streak. Another veteran, 39 year-old Gaylord Perry, took Cy Young honors with a 21-6 record and 2.73 ERA, but the NL's most electrifying pitcher was 6'8" JR Richard, who led the majors with 303 strikeouts en route to 18 wins.

New York entered the ALCS with the major's best pitcher, Ron Guidry, who took the pitching triple crown with a 25-3 record, 1.74 ERA, and 248 strikeouts, plus Ed Figueroa (20-9) and veteran Catfish Hunter (12-6), backed by the unmatched bullpen combo of lefty Sparky Lyle and newly acquired flame thrower Goose Gossage (27 saves and 2.01 ERA). The third straight Yankees-Royals series seemed anti-climactic after the 163 game AL East battle. New York finished off KC in 4 games, even taking Game 3 despite Brett's 3 home run performance on an 8th inning 2-run blast by Thurman Munson. Reggie Jackson hit .462 in the series.

The Dodgers handed Philadelphia their third straight NLCS loss, taking the series in 4 behind Steve Garvey's .389, 4 HR, 7 RBI performance. LA won the clincher on a 2-out 10th inning Bill Russell single to drive home Ron Cey, moments after the Phillies' 8-time Gold Glove centerfielder Garry Maddox dropped a fly ball hit right at him.

In a rematch of the 1977 World Series, LA opened at home by bombing Ed Figueroa, 11-5, and then took Game 2 as well, 4-3, ended when hard-throwing rookie Bob Welch struck out Reggie Jackson with the tying run on second. Back in New York, ace Ron Guidry was aided by the spectacular defense of third baseman Graig Nettles, who saved several runs to preserve a 5-1 win. The Yankees came back from a 3-0 deficit in Game 4 for a controversial 4-3 win when Bill Russell's double play throw to first hit Reggie Jackson, who had stopped in the baseline halfway between first and second base. Dodger manager Tom Lasorda argued to no avail that Jackson had intentionally leaned into the throw. The Yankees rode Thurman Munson's 5 RBI to take Game 5 12-2, and Reggie Jackson got a measure of revenge off Welch in the clinching Game 6 when his 2-run homer capped the scoring of a 7-2 New York victory. Bucky Dent was named MVP, batting .417 with 10 hits, 7 RBI, and 3 runs scored.

1979

Veterans hogged the headlines, with big off-season news of Pete Rose moving from the Reds to the Phillies, who then slumped to 4th place. During the season St Louis' Lou Brock and Boston's Carl Yastrzemski reached 3,000 hits, with Yaz also notching his 400th homer. Atlanta's 40 year old Phil Neikro tied his brother, Houston's Joe Neikro, for the league lead with 21 wins. Willie 'Pops' Stargell stole the show, capturing a portion of the regular season MVP award and following that with NLCS and World Series MVP honors.

Pittsburgh edged up-and-coming Montreal by 2 games to reclaim the NL East crown after a three year Philadelphia run. Stargell's leadership, and clutch hits (including a team leading 32 HR), plus right fielder Dave Parker, who contributed a 25 HR, .310 season, paced the offense. John Candelaria led the team with 14 wins, and the bullpen was strong with Kent Tekulve (31 saves) and lefty Grant Jackson (14 saves).

The Expos showed great promise with the excellent young nucleus of catcher Gary Carter, 3B Larry Parrish, and outfielders Andre Dawson and rocket armed Ellis Valentine all exceeding 20 HR and 75 RBI. Left fielder Warren Cromartie added 46 doubles. St Louis' Keith Hernandez won the batting title with a .344 average and shared MVP honors with Stargell.

Chicago's Dave Kingman was the majors' top slugger (.613) during a career best 48 HR, 115 RBI campaign, and teammate Bruce Sutter took the Cy Young award with a 2.23 ERA and 37 saves.

Cincinnati took the NL West, setting up a rematch of the 1970, '72, and '75 NLCS. George Foster (30 HR, 98 RBI, .302 Avg) and Tom Seaver (16-6 record) led the way. Houston finished in second, only 1½ games back, as JR Richard finished second on the team to Neikro with 18 wins and led the majors with 313 strikeouts.

Baltimore won the AL East handily, riding strong seasons from Eddie Murray (25 HR, 99 RBI, .295), Ken Singleton (35 HR, 111 RBI, .295), and Cy Young award winner Mike Flanagan (23-9). Milwaukee finished second, as Gorman Thomas, despite striking out 175 times, still knocked in 123 runs and led the league with 45 home runs. Boston's Fred Lynn won the batting title at .333 with 39 HR and 122 RBI, while Jim Rice (39-130-.325) was just as dangerous. The Yankees slumped to 4th place and were left stunned by the death of captain Thurman Munson in August.

California won the first division title in their 19 year history on the power of Bobby Grich (30 HR, 101 RBI, .284), Dan Ford (21-101-.290), Brian Downing (12-75-.326), and MVP Don Baylor (36-139-.296). Kansas City's pitching slumped while George Brett led the league with 212 hits and 20 triples, plus 42 doubles, 119 runs, and 107 RBI. Teammate Darrell Porter drove in 112, and speedster Willie Wilson hit .315, stole 83 bases, and scored 113 runs.

Pittsburgh avenged their previous 3 NLCS losses to Cincinnati with a 3-0 sweep. Game 1 went 11 innings before Willie Stargell's 3-run homer decided it. Game 2 also went extra frames, with Dave Parker's 10th inning RBI single the difference. Bert Blyleven tossed a complete game in a 7-1 blowout to end the series. Stargell hit .455 with 2 HR and 6 RBI and Phil Garner hit .417 with a double and a triple.

In the ALCS opener Jim Palmer bested Nolan Ryan 6-3, while Game 2 saw the Birds jump out to a 9-1 3rd inning lead and survive a furious California late inning comeback for a 9-8 win. Down 3-2 in the 9th inning of Game 3, California extended the series with a 2-run 9th that was aided by Al Bumbry's error. Scott McGregor then threw a complete game 6-hit shutout in Game 4 for an 8-0 Orioles win.

The World Series was a re-match of 1971, with the same end result, a Pirates 7 game victory. The Orioles took back to back 1-run games in Baltimore and the teams split the next two in Pittsburgh, pushing the Pirates into a 3 games to 1 hole. From there it was all Pittsburgh, as a 1-0 Baltimore lead in Game 5 was quickly erased with 7 unanswered runs. Then back in Baltimore, John Candelaria and Kent Tekulve shut out the Birds' Jim Palmer 4-0. The Pirates capped their amazing comeback on the shoulders of Willie Stargell, who went 4 for 5 with a single, two doubles, and a long two-run homer in the sixth off loser Scott McGregor. Stargell was 12-30 (.400) in the series with a record 7 extra base hits (including 3 HR), 7 RBI, and 7 runs scored.

Player Rankings

Top 1st Basemen

There was no clear top player at this position throughout the 70s. While a lot of great players played first base in the 70s, few played the spot at a high level for the majority of the decade. Though Pete Rose closed his career as a first baseman, he did not move there until 1979, his first season with the Phillies. Dick Allen was an immense talent who was likely the best at his position from 1970-74, but his skills eroded quickly after that and he was out of the game by 1977. Willie McCovey had arguably the best career of anyone on the list, but his top seasons came in the 1960s, and after a dominating year in 1970, he was still productive but never again topped 30 HRs or 90 RBI. Willie Stargell played mostly left field until 1975, and Rod Carew moved from second to first in 1976. Neither played the spot defensively with any distinction. My pick for the top spot is Steve Garvey (he moved from 3B in 1972), who had a good glove at first and a steady bat. I could entertain valid arguments for Tony Perez (another former 3B), who was a great hitter often overshadowed by his Big Red Machine teammates, or Stargell.

1.   Steve Garvey - Dodgers : .304 Avg, 159 HR, 736 RBI

Garvey was a model of consistency after taking over as the Dodgers' regular first basemen and capturing NL MVP honors in 1974. He was the NL All-Star starter in each of the decade's final six years, and captured 4 Gold Gloves. In that stretch Garvey never played less than 156 games, and had 5 years of 200+ hits,.300+ batting average, 95+ RBI, and 30+ doubles.

2. Willie Stargell - Pirates : .287 Avg, 296 HR, 906 RBI

Stargell hit the baseball as hard and as far as anyone in the game's history. Willie made the transition from quiet, intimidating bomber in the early years of the decade to fun-loving, veteran team leader and league MVP as the Bucs captured World Series titles in 1971 and 1979. His 296 home runs and .555 Slugging % led all players in the 1970s.

3.   Tony Perez - Reds, Expos : .284 Avg, 226 HR, 954 RBI

Had 8 consecutive seasons of at least 90 RBI to begin the decade and was second to teammate Johnny Bench among all players for most RBI in the decade. The underrated Perez was named to 4 All-Star teams during the '70s, and 7 overall in his career.

4.   George Scott - Red Sox, Brewers, Royals, Yankees : .275 Avg, 206 HR, 802 RBI

'Boomer' had great hands at first base, capturing 6 Gold Gloves to go with 206 home runs and 802 RBI. He had 5 seasons of 20 or more HR and 3 years with 95 or more RBI. In 1975 Scott finished 8th in MVP voting, leading the American League with 109 RBI, and tying Reggie Jackson for the lead with 36 home runs.

5.   Lee May - Reds, Astros, Orioles : .263 Avg, 270 HR, 926 RBI

May was dealt to Houston for Joe Morgan partially because Cincinnati needed to move Tony Perez from third to first base. He couldn't run and was a shaky defender, but May was one of the decade's most feared run producers, tallying 98 or more RBI in 6 different seasons.

6.   Bob Watson – Astros : .301 Avg, 149 HR, 822 RBI

7.   Dick Allen – Cards, Dodgers, White Sox, Phillies, A's**: .284 Avg, 174 HR, 575 RBI**

8.   Willie McCovey – Giants, Padres : .256 Avg, 207 HR, 680 RBI

9.   Chris Chambliss – Indians, Yankees: .282 Avg, 105 HR, 606 RBI

10. Willie Montanez – Phils, Giants, Braves, Mets, Rangers**: .277 Avg, 132 HR, 730 RBI**

Just missed the cut: Bill Buckner, John Mayberry

Top 2ⁿᵈ Basemen

It is no stretch to say that in Carew and Morgan, two of the decade's best offensive players played primarily second base. Each started 8 All-Star games and they finished 1-2 among all players in OB%, and 7-3 respectively in runs scored. In addition they were both top base stealers and bunters throughout the decade.

Joe Morgan (9) forces the Pirates' Ronnie Stennett at second base to start a double play.

1. **Joe Morgan - Astros, Reds : .282 Avg, .404 OB%, 173 HR, 720 RBI, 488 SB, 1005 Runs**

Morgan led all players at his position in runs, doubles, home runs, RBI, stolen bases, and slugging %. Arguably the best all-around player in the decade, Morgan was a two-time MVP, an 8 time All-Star starter, and a 5 time Gold Glover at second for the National League. Joe scored 100 or more runs 7 times and led the league in on-base percentage 4 times, including an incredible .466 in 1975. He also stole 40 or more bases in the first 8 seasons of the decade before slowing down in 1978.

2. **Rod Carew - Twins, Angels : .343 Avg, .408 OB%, 253 SB, 837 Runs**

Carew was easily the best pure hitter of the 70s, capturing 6 batting titles, and topping .300 in all ten seasons, including *five* years of better than .350. He led all 70s players in batting average, on-base % (.408), and triples (80). Like Morgan, Rod did not have great hands or a strong arm at second. While Morgan developed good footwork and a quick first step to eventually become one of the game's top fielders, Carew was never considered better than average, so much so that he moved to first base in 1976.

3.   Bobby Grich - Orioles, Angels : .264 Avg, 113 HR, 473 RBI

Perhaps ahead of his time as a big-framed, power hitting middle infielder.   Despite not becoming a regular until 1972, Grich's 113 home runs ranked behind only Joe Morgan among second basemen.   He won 4 Gold Gloves and was a leader on strong early 70s Orioles teams and late 70s Angels squads.

4.   Davey Lopes - Dodgers : .267 Avg, 84 HR, 318 RBI, 375 SB

Lopes was an igniter on very successful mid-70s Dodgers teams.   He topped 30 steals in all of his 7 seasons as a regular, and scored 90 or more runs 4 times.   Lopes' 375 steals ranked #2 at his position, and 5th among all players.   For the majority of the decade he was widely regarded as the best National League second baseman not named Joe Morgan.

5.   Dave Cash - Pirates, Phillies, Expos : .287 Avg, 112 SB

Cash was a 3-time All-Star and one of the decade's best contact hitters, batting .280 or better in 8 seasons, and never striking out more than 36 times.   After being traded so the Pirates could make room for Rennie Stennett , Cash enjoyed his three finest seasons in Philadelphia, batting over .300 twice and averaging over 200 hits per season, including career highs of 213 hits, 111 runs, and 40 doubles in 1975.

6.   Dave Johnson – Orioles, Braves, Phillies, Cubs : .266 Avg, 103 HR, 375 RBI

7.   Frank White – Royals : .249 Avg, 101 SB, 3 Gold Gloves

8.   Rennie Stennett - Pirates: .278 Avg, 38 HR, 388 RBI

9.   Felix Milan – Braves, Mets: .281 Avg, 13 HR, 302 RBI

10. Phil Garner - A's, Pirates : .263 Avg, 52 HR, 331 RBI

Just missed the cut: Dick Green, Willie Randolph

Top Shortstops

It only seems to the modern day fantasy baseball fan that the shortstop position lacked star power in the 70s. The Oakland and Cincinnati dynasties, as well as perennial pennant contenders Philadelphia and Baltimore were led by great shortstops with slick gloves, accurate arms, good bat control and excellent speed. And who hit the most crushing blow of all in the decade? That came off the bat of Yankee shortstop Bucky Dent, who belted a three run homer to put the Yankees ahead of the Red Sox for good in their 1978 one-game playoff. The blast was an uppercut to the solar plexus of Red Sox nation which left the faithful doubled over and gasping before they finally straightened up to deliver a counter punch 26 years later. Two future offensive stars surfaced late in the 70s - Robin Yount played 5 ½ solid seasons in the 70s, but none at the level of productivity he reached in the 80s, while Gary Templeton became a regular in 1977 and over the next three seasons hit a combined .305 with 291 runs scored, 88 steals and 592 hits, including 50 triples.

1. **Bert Campaneris - A's, Rangers, Angels:** **.255 Avg, 52 HR, 406 RBI, 336 SB, 700 runs**

'Campy' was the leadoff hitter and sparkplug for the powerhouse Oakland teams that won 5 straight divisions and 3 straight World Series titles. A poor fielder and base runner when he came into the league in the 60s, he worked hard enough to eventually rank among the game's best defensive shortstops throughout the 70s, and was second at his position in runs and stolen bases. Campy was an excellent bunter (159 sacrifices) and wreaked havoc on the base paths, distracting pitchers dealing with Rudi, Jackson, Bando and Tenace behind him.

2. **Dave Concepcion - Reds:** **.270 Avg, 70 HR, 529 RBI**

A six-time All-Star and five time Gold Glove winner in the decade. Dave had great hands and the strongest shortstop arm in the game. Concepcion led all shortstops with 201 doubles, and his power numbers continued to improve through the decade, reaching a career high 16 home runs and 84 RBI in 1979.

3. **Larry Bowa - Phillies:** **.262 Avg, 11 HR, 351 RBI**

Bowa started 3 All-Star games, won 2 Gold Gloves, and led all shortstops in hits (1,552), triples (74), and runs scored (725).

4. **Toby Harrah – Senators/Rangers, Indians:** **.261 Avg, 128 HR, 560 RBI**

Harrah was the rare shortstop of his day known more for his bat than his glove. He led his position in home runs, RBI, slugging % (.397) and OB % (.355). By 1977 he was moved to third base.

5. **Mark Belanger - Orioles:** **.227 Avg, 14 HR, 272 RBI**

The anti-Harrah, Belanger hit only .227 during the 70s, but was generally acknowledged as the best defensive shortstop in the game, racking up 7 Gold Gloves.

6. **Rick Burleson - Red Sox:** **.273 Avg, 30 HR, 309 RBI**
7. **Chris Speier – Giants, Expos:** **.246 Avg, 73 HR, 465 RBI**
8. **Robin Yount - Brewers :** **.270 Avg, 34 HR, 303 RBI**
9. **Freddie Patek – Pirates, Royals :** **.241 Avg, 29 HR, 401 RBI, 344 SB**
10. **Bud Harrelson – Mets, Phillies:** **.234 Avg, 5 HR, 188 RBI**

Just missed the cut: Bill Russell, Gary Templeton, Don Kessinger

Top 3rd Basemen

There was an embarrassment of riches at the hot corner throughout the 70s. Mike Schmidt and George Brett won starting jobs in the early years of the decade and both went on to Hall of Fame careers as possibly the best two players ever at the position. Schmidt began the decade as a pure slugger; Brett as a slap singles/doubles hitter. Both vastly improved their defense and became more complete hitters over time. We can add in for good measure post-season human highlight film glove men Brooks Robinson and Graig Nettles, both good hitters in their own right, plus run producers Ron Cey and Sal Bando, and batting champs Joe Torre and Bill Madlock.

1. Mike Schmidt – Phillies: .255 Avg, 235 HR, 666 RBI

In Mike's 6 full seasons in the 70s he topped 35 home runs, 95 RBI, and 100 walks 5 times. He led the league in homers 3 times and won 4 Gold Gloves. Schmidt led all third basemen with a .511 slugging % and finished second with a .374 on-base %.

2. **Graig Nettles – Indians, Yankees: .254 Avg, 252 HR, 831 RBI**
Nettles led all third basemen in home runs and RBI. He was a top notch defensive player who was overshadowed by Brooks Robinson for much of the decade, but still won 2 Gold Gloves and was named to 5 All-Star teams.

3. **George Brett – Royals: .310 Avg, 74 HR, 461 RBI**
Brett was a fierce competitor who hit .375 in 3 ALCS. Despite only playing in 6 seasons of the decade, he led all third basemen with 73 triples, topped 30 doubles 5 times, and started 4 All-Star games.

4. **Sal Bando – A's, Brewers: .255 Avg, 195 HR, 812 RBI**
Highly respected team captain during the Oakland dynasty, Bando led all third basemen with 219 doubles. During the 70s he topped 20 home runs 5 times and 90 RBI 3 times, and played in 3 All-Star games.

5. **Ron Cey – Dodgers: .265 Avg, 163 HR, 636 RBI**
Cey was a six time All-Star who topped 15 home runs and 80 RBI in all of his 7 seasons during the decade, including 3 years where he topped 25 HR and 95 RBI.

6. **Brooks Robinson – Orioles: .255 Avg, 72 HR, 449 RBI, 6 Gold Gloves**
7. **Bill Madlock – Rangers, Cubs, Giants, Pirates: .320 Avg, 73 HR, 382 RBI**
8. **Darrell Evans – Braves, Giants: .248 Avg, 184 HR, 640 RBI**
9. **Joe Torre – Cardinals, Mets: .303 Avg, 92 HR, 532 RBI**
10. **(tie) Buddy Bell - Indians, Rangers : .277 Avg, 82 HR, 487 RBI,**
Doug Rader – Astros, Padres: .247 Avg, 136 HR, 570 RBI, 5 Gold Gloves

Just missed the cut: Rico Petrocelli, Richie Hebner, Bill Melton

Top Catchers

Johnny Bench is clearly the class of this (or any) era, but Fisk, Simmons, and Munson were all top players throughout the decade. In the first half of the decade Gene Tenace was a dangerous clutch hitter, albeit a shaky defender, and Bill Freehan was a defensive stalwart. Boone, Sundberg, and then later Carter emerged in the second half.

Johnny Lee Bench
Baseball's Greatest Catcher
Cincinnati Reds, 1967-1983
"I don't want to embarrass any other catcher by comparing him to Johnny Bench."
-Sparky Anderson

1. Johnny Bench – Reds: .267 Avg, 290 HR, 1013 RBI

Bench was the best offensive *and* best defensive catcher of the 1970s, and generally regarded as the top receiver of all-time. A two-time MVP in the 70s, he captured 8 Gold Gloves, exceeded 100 RBI 6 times, and 20 HR 9 times. The major league RBI leader in the decade, Bench led all catchers in runs, extra base hits, home runs, RBI, slugging %, and even stolen bases. In 45 post season games Bench belted 10 HR, and he won the 1976 World Series MVP award with a .533 batting average.

2. Thurman Munson – Yankees: .292 Avg, 112 HR, 692 RBI

Munson was the 1976 MVP when the Yankees won their first of three pennants in the decade. He was the best catcher in the game for the three year period 1975-77, when he hit over .300 and drove in 100 or more runs each season. Munson was a highly respected team leader who hit .357 over 30 post-season games. Thurman was also the 1970 Rookie of the Year, a 7 time All-Star, and an outstanding defender who won 3 Gold Gloves.

3. Ted Simmons – Cardinals: .297 Avg, 151 HR, 828 RBI

Simmons was a remarkably consistent hitter in the 70s, and though overshadowed by Bench, appeared in 6 All-Star games and led all catchers in hits (1,550), doubles (299), batting average, and on-base % (.365). He exceeded a .300 average and 90 RBI 5 times each in the decade.

4. Carlton Fisk - Red Sox: .284 Avg, 144 HR, 506 RBI

Known as a great competitor and leader of some excellent Red Sox teams, his 12th inning walk-off home run in Game 6 of the 1975 World Series put the Sox within one game of breaking their dreaded curse. Fisk was a six-time All-Star and won the AL Rookie of the Year Award and Gold Glove in 1972.

5. Bob Boone – Phillies: .268 Avg, 52 HR, 377 RBI

Boone was a solid defender whose bat improved as the decade progressed, and he led the Phillies to three straight division titles. He hit over .280 in all three years from 1977-79, played in 2 All-Star games, and won 2 Gold Gloves.

6. Gene Tenace - A's, Padres: .245 Avg, 171 HR, 576 RBI, .386 OBP

7. Manny Sanguillen - Pirates, A's: .297 Avg, 60 HR, 518 RBI

8. Bill Freehan – Tigers: .262 Avg, 90 HR, 342 RBI

9. Jim Sundberg – Rangers: .254 Avg, 29 HR, 293 RBI, 4 Gold Gloves

10. (tie) Darrell Porter – Brewers, Royals: .252 Avg, 108 HR, 476 RBI

   Gary Carter – Expos: .267 Avg, 97 HR, 343 RBI

<u>Just missed the cut</u>: Joe Ferguson, Earl Williams

Top Left Fielders

1. Pete Rose - Reds, Phillies: .314 Avg, 79 HR, 580 RBI

Rose played 5 70s seasons as an outfielder (3 in LF and 2 in RF), 4 at 3B, and 1 at first base, thus his classification here as a left fielder. Of all players in the decade classified as outfielders, Rose finished #1 in hits, runs, doubles, and triples. In the decade Rose won an MVP, a batting title, led the league in doubles and hits 4 times each, and led in runs scored 3 times. He hit over .300 9 times, and had 200+ hits 6 times, 30+ doubles 9 times, and scored 100+ runs 7 times.

2. Carl Yastrzemski - Red Sox: .283 Avg, 202 HR, 846 RBI

Though he enjoyed many of his best seasons in the 60s, Yaz continued to play at a consistently high level throughout the 70s and led all leftfielders with 846 RBI. He finished 5th among all players in runs scored (845), and 8th in both RBI and on base percentage (.384). Yaz was named to all 10 70s All-Star games and won 2 Gold Gloves for his play in LF, despite being moved between 1B and LF throughout his career.

3. Jim Rice - Red Sox: .310 Avg, 172 HR, 583 RBI

While it's strange ranking two players from the same team 2-3 at the same position, both men played here more than any other position. Rice broke in in 1975 and terrorized opposing pitchers for the decade's final 5 seasons. He finished in the Top 5 in MVP voting 4 times, winning the award in 1978. Rice topped 100 RBI and a .300 batting average 4 times and had 200 or more hits 3 times. He also led all leftfielders with a .551 slugging percentage. Though overshadowed by both George Foster and his Red Sox teammate Fred Lynn, the Hall of Famer had by far the best career of the three.

4. Lou Brock – Cardinals: .298 Avg, 47 HR, 481 RBI

One of the game's all-time greats, Brock stole 50 or more bases in each of the decade's first 7 seasons, and led all players with 551 70's steals. He also hit .300 or better 7 times, and had 190 or more hits 5 times.

5. George Foster – Reds: .287 Avg, 201 HR, 690 RBI

Though he didn't become a regular until 1975, Foster had some of the decade's most dominating seasons, including a 52 HR/149 RBI MVP year in 1977. Foster led the league in RBI 3 times, topping 120 or more in each of those seasons, and hit over .300 4 times.

6. Joe Rudi - A's, Angels: .277 Avg, 149 HR, 696 RBI

Rudi was the decade's best defensive left fielder and was a quiet team leader for the Swingin' A's powerhouse. In addition to winning 3 Gold Gloves, Rudi finished 3rd at his position with 251 doubles, and also ranked 3rd with 696 RBI.

7. Greg Luzinski – Phillies: .285 Avg, 204 HR, 755 RBI

The Bull was one of the game's best hitters in the second half of the decade, topping 30 home runs, 100 RBI, and a .300 batting average 3 times each. A four-time all-star, he finished 2nd at his position in both HR and RBI. He was a poor fielder and runner, but was without question one of the decade's most dangerous RBI men.

8. Billy Williams – Cubs, A's: .289 Avg, 177 HR, 620 RBI
9. Ralph Garr – Braves, White Sox, Angels: .307 Avg, 75 HR, 403 RBI, 170 SB
10. Hal McRae – Reds, Royals: .290 Avg, 106 HR, 603 RBI, 285 2B

Just missed the cut: Don Baylor, Gary Matthews, Rico Carty, Dave Kingman, Willie Horton

Top Center Fielders

1. Cesar Cedeno – Astros: **.289 Avg, 148 HR, 671 RBI**
Cedeno was a 5 time Gold Glover and 4 time All-Star who led all center fielders and ranked #3 overall with 427 stolen bases, including 6 seasons of 50 or more. He twice led the league in doubles, had 5 seasons with more than 30, and scored 90 or more runs 4 times. The versatile Cedeno was the second man in history (after Lou Brock) to hit 20 home runs and steal 50 bases in a season, doing it in three straight seasons (1972-74).

2. Bobby Murcer - Yankees, Giants, Cubs: **.282 Avg, 198 HR, 840 RBI**
While Murcer may have never had a season where he was considered the top CF in the game, he was arguably the most productive throughout the decade, topping all center fielders in home runs and RBI. And though he never lived up to his hype as the next Mickey Mantle, Murcer was a fan favorite and franchise player at Yankee Stadium until being traded for malcontent Bobby Bonds, who lasted in New York for only one season. Murcer was a 5-time All-Star and enjoyed his best seasons from 1971-73 when he batted .331, .294, .304 and averaged .308 with 27 homers and 95 RBI.

3. **Fred Lynn - Red Sox: .309 Avg, 112 HR, 460 RBI**
Lynn was easily the best centerfielder of the decade's second half, and his .526 slugging %, .383 on base %, and .309 batting average led all centerfielders with 2,500 or more at-bats. In his 5 full seasons in the decade Lynn played in 5 All-Star games, won 3 Gold Gloves, an MVP, Rookie of the Year, a batting title, and 2 slugging titles.

4. **Amos Otis – Royals: .284 Avg, 159 HR, 753 RBI**
Otis was a speedster with good power and great defensive range. He was a four-time All-Star, 3 time Gold Glover, and finished in the Top 10 in MVP voting four times in the 70s. He also led all 70's center fielders with 861 runs scored.

5. **Al Oliver – Pirates, Rangers: .303 Avg, 144 HR, 812 RBI**
Oliver hit third in front of Willie Stargell on many of the powerful Pirate teams in the decade. He was a steady gap hitter who averaged less than 48 strikeouts per season and never hit below .270, topping .300 and 30+ doubles six times each. Oliver did not have typical centerfielder speed or fielding ability, but he did lead all centerfielders in hits (1686), doubles (320), and triples (63), and finished in the Top 25 in MVP voting 6 times during the decade.

6. **Gary Maddox – Giants, Phillies: .293 Avg, 80 HR, 505 RBI, 5 Gold Gloves**

7. **Jim Wynn - Astros, Dodgers, Braves: .243 Avg, 146 HR, 523 RBI**

8. **Ron LeFlore – Tigers: .297 Avg, 51 HR, 265 RBI, 294 SB**

9. **Mickey Rivers - Angels, Yankees, Rangers: .291 Avg, 45 HR, 356 RBI, 226 SB**

10. **Bill North – Cubs, A's, Dodgers, Giants: .263 Avg, 18 HR, 199 RBI, 324 SB**

Just missed the cut: George Hendrick, Cesar Geronimo, Rick Monday, Paul Blair

Top Right Fielders

1. Reggie Jackson - A's, Orioles, Yankees: **.275 Avg, 292 HR, 922 RBI**
If it's possible to completely set aside Jackson's sterling post-season performances, he would still have to be considered the best of a loaded right field position. Reggie led his position in home runs, RBI, and doubles (270), and finished 2nd with 833 runs scored, and 3rd with 183 stolen bases. He was an All-Star and finished in the Top 25 in MVP voting in 9 70s seasons, winning the award in 1973, when in a league-wide season of low offensive numbers he led the AL in homers (32), RBI (117), runs (99), and slugging % (.531). Jackson was a good defensive outfielder, especially early in the decade when his still-healthy legs covered enough ground that Oakland also used him in center, and he had 5 seasons with at least 8 assists. In addition to those impressive regular season credentials, Jackson had a .305 batting average and 14 HR in 53 post-season games with 2 World Series MVP awards.

2. Bobby Bonds - Giants, Yankees, Angels, White Sox, Rangers, Indians: **.274 Avg, 280 HR, 856 RBI**
The much-traveled Bonds was a very productive offensive player everywhere he played, leading the position with 1,565 hits, 1,020 runs, 380 stolen bases, and 51 triples. He also finished 2nd in home runs, and 3rd in RBI and doubles (255). Bonds was a 3 time Gold Glove winner; in his prime he had excellent speed and great range, along with a powerful throwing arm, nailing 10 or more runners in 6 70s seasons. Bonds, who had 4 30-30 seasons in the 70s, made 3 All-Star appearances, and was named of MVP of the 1973 game.

3. Dave Parker – Pirates: **.317 Avg, 122 HR, 533 RBI**
Cobra was quite possibly the game's best all-around player in the second half of the 70s, hitting .308 or better in each of his 5 full seasons, while averaging 37 doubles and 95 runs scored. He won 3 Gold Gloves and 2 batting titles, and won the 1978 MVP award with a .334 batting average and 117 RBI. His 1977 season might have been his best – that year he led the league in batting (.338), doubles (44), hits (215), and outfield assists (26).

4. Dave Winfield – Padres: **.285 Avg, 134 HR, 539 RBI**
Though he had an even better decade in the 80s, Winfield was one of the 70s best young players after becoming a regular in 1974. Winfield finished the decade with three consecutive All-Star appearances and back to back .308 seasons, including his best season to date in 1979, when he won a Gold Glove and also hit 34 home runs with a league leading 118 RBI. By then Winfield had established himself as an intimidating presence in the batter's box, leading the league with 24 intentional walks.

5. Hank Aaron – Braves, Brewers: **.278 Avg, 201 HR, 573 RBI**
Hammerin' Hank was in the twilight of his career in the early 70s, passing the torch to the young great National League right fielders Parker and Winfield. He started the decade with two straight 118 RBI seasons and hit 34 or more home runs from 1970-73 before slowing down in 1974 and finishing his career as a DH with Milwaukee in '75-'76. Despite playing little more than half the decade Aaron finished 4th at his position with 201 HR and led all right fielders with a .527 slugging %.

6. Reggie Smith - Red Sox, Cardinals, Dodgers : **.292 Avg, 225 HR, 750 RBI**

7. Ken Singleton – Mets, Expos, Orioles: **.289 Avg, 171 HR, 715 RBI**

8. Rusty Staub - Expos, Mets, Tigers: **.280 Avg, 184 HR, 860 RBI**

9. Ken Griffey – Reds : **.310 Avg, 45 HR, 305 RBI**

10. Jeff Burroughs - Rangers, Braves: **.260 Avg, 183 HR, 650 RBI**

Just missed the cut: Richie Zisk, Dwight Evans

Top Starting Pitchers

1.   Jim Palmer – Orioles: 186-103, 2.58 ERA, 1559 SO, 175 CG, 44 SHO
Palmer led all 70s pitchers in wins, ERA, and shutouts, and was second in innings pitched. He also had the highest winning % of all pitchers with 150 or more wins. Palmer won 20 or more games and had an ERA lower than 3.00 in 8 of 10 70s seasons. He started 4 All-Star games for the American League, won 3 Cy Young Awards, and had a 5-2 record and 2.78 ERA in the post-season.

2. **Tom Seaver – Mets: 178-101, 2.61 ERA, 2304 SO, 147 CG, 40 SHO**
Seaver compiled stats very close to Palmer's while playing on much poorer teams through most of the decade. He finished second among all pitchers in strikeouts, shutouts, ERA, and strikeout-walk ratio. Seaver won 20 or more games 4 times, and had 200+ strikeouts and a sub-3.00 ERA 8 times. He pitched well in 5 post-season 70s starts, but had only 1 win.

3. **Steve Carlton – Phillies: 178-126, 3.18 ERA, 2097 SO, 165 CG, 32 SHO**
Carlton is best known for his monster 1972 season when he won 27 games with 310 strikeouts and a 1.97 ERA on a last place club. The best left handed starter of the decade, Carlton captured two Cy Young Awards, and won 20 or more games 4 times. Like Seaver, he did not distinguish himself in the post-season; going 1-2 with a 5.62 ERA in 4 starts during the Phil's 3 straight NLCS loses.

4. **Catfish Hunter - A's, Yankees: 169-102, 3.17 ERA, 1309 SO, 140 CG, 30 SHO**
Hunter had 5 straight 20 win seasons in the 70s, and was the ace of a pitching-oriented A's team that won 3 World Series championships. He went 7-2 for Oakland in the postseason. Overall in post-season play Catfish started 22 games and went 9-6 with a 3.26 ERA.

5. **Gaylord Perry – Giants, Indians, Rangers, Padres: 184-133, 2.92 ERA, 1907 SO, 197 CG, 36 SHO**
Perry pitched more innings (2,905) than any pitcher in the decade, and was second with 184 wins. He pitched for 4 different teams and won 2 Cy Young Awards, one in each league. In the 70s Perry topped 20 wins 4 times and had 5 seasons with 200 or more strikeouts.

6. **Ferguson Jenkins – Cubs, Rangers, Red Sox: 178-130, 3.38 ERA, 1841 SO, 184 CG, 33 SHO**

7. **Don Sutton – Dodgers: 166-110, 3.07 ERA, 1767 SO, 117 CG, 39 SHO**

8. **Nolan Ryan - Mets, Angels: 155-146, 3.14 ERA, 2678 SO, 164 CG, 42 SHO**

9. Vida Blue - A's, Giants: 155-109, 3.07 ERA, 1600 SO, 124 CG, 32 SHO

10. Don Gullett – Reds, Yankees: 109-50, 3.11 ERA, 921 SO, 44 CG, 14 SHO

11. Bert Blyleven – Twins, Rangers, Pirates: 148-128, 2.88 ERA, 2082 SO, 145 CG, 39 SHO

12. Luis Tiant – Twins, Red Sox, Yankees: 142-92, 3.42 ERA, 1229 SO, 120 CG, 28 SHO

13. Tommy John – White Sox, Dodgers, Yankees: 133-84, 3.09 ERA, 1029 SO, 74 CG, 20 SHO

14. Andy Messersmith - Angels, Dodgers, Braves, Yankees: 110-86, 2.93 ERA, 1340 SO, 86 CG, 24 SHO

15. Frank Tanana – Angels: 91-66, 2.93 ERA, 1120 SO, 85 CG, 24 SHO

Just missed the cut: Mike Torrez, Phil Niekro, Bob Gibson, Wilbur Wood, Ron Guidry, Mike Cuellar

Top Relief Pitchers

1. **Rollie Fingers - A's, Padres: 84-85, 2.89 ERA, 209 Saves, 973 SO, 353 BB**

Fingers was baseball's first 'star' relief pitcher, and led all 70s relievers in appearances (611), innings, strikeouts, and saves. He was selected to 5 All-Star games and became a household name in the middle of the decade, sporting his trademark handle bar mustache while playing a major role in nearly every big game Oakland played during their three-peat run. In the 1973 World Series he appeared in 6 games, yielding only 1 earned run in 13 2/3 innings, then took 1974 World Series MVP Honors with a win and 2 saves. In total, Fingers had a 1.35 ERA in 16 World Series appearances over 33 innings. He moved from Oakland to

San Diego after the 1976 season and led the National League in saves in both '77 and '78.

2. **Sparky Lyle - Red Sox, Yankees, Rangers: 69-59, 2.61 ERA, 190 Saves, 590 SO, 319 BB**

Lyle had the decade's lowest ERA among pitchers appearing in 300 or more games. He finished second to Fingers in saves, leading the league twice, and finished 3rd with 600 relief appearances. Sparky captured Cy Young Award Honors in New York's 1977 Championship season with a 13-5 record, 2.17 ERA, 26 saves, and a league leading 72 games and 60 game finishes.

3. **Mike Marshall – Astros, Expos, Dodgers, Braves, Rangers, Twins: 89-94, 2.98 ERA, 177 Saves, 771 SO, 439 BB**

Marshall was a rubber-armed workhorse who topped 100 innings 6 times and had 99 innings in 2 other seasons. He led the league in saves 3 times and games pitched 4 times, including a high of 106 in 1974. In that Cy Young Season, Marshall tossed 208 innings with 143 strikeouts, a 2.42 ERA, 15 wins and 21 saves. For the decade Mike finished 2nd among relievers in games pitched and innings, and 3rd in saves.

4. **Bruce Sutter – Cubs: 27-22, 2.33 ERA, 105 Saves, 418 SO, 115 BB**

Sutter brought the splitter into vogue, and was dominant in his 4 years in the majors during the decade. Sutter had the lowest ERA of any 70s pitcher with 200 or more appearances, including a 1.34 mark in 1977, when he struck out 129 batters with only 23 walks. In 1979 he won the NL Cy Young Award, tying a major league record with 37 saves. For the decade Sutter had 418 strikeouts with only 115 walks, and 281 hits allowed in 390 innings.

5. **Tug McGraw - Mets, Phillies: 69-58, 3.07 ERA, 132 Saves, 726 SO, 371 BB**

Though the order could be debated, my top 4 relief pitchers seemed pretty clear; all were the majors' best at some point during the decade. Below them are another 6-10 pitchers nearly indistinguishable, all good, none great. I went with McGraw as #5 due to his longevity (he appeared in at least 40 games every season in the decade), his two lights out seasons (in '71 and '72 he had identical 1.70 ERAs), and his brilliance in the post season of 1973. Hiller was dominant in 1973 when he set a record with 38 saves, and was very good in a strange 1974 where he went 17-14 with no starts. Arguments could be made for Carroll, Guisti, Tekulve, and Gossage, who all had between 83 and 140 saves, and all with strikeout-walk ratios between 1.5 and 1.8.

6. John Hiller – Tigers: 69-63, 2.74 ERA, 115 Saves, 812 SO, 414 BB
7. Clay Carroll - Reds, White Sox, Pirates: 61-39, 2.63 ERA, 106 Saves, 385 SO, 252 BB
8. Rich Gossage - White Sox, Pirates, Yankees: 55-59, 3.14 ERA, 101 Saves, 733 SO, 415 BB
9. Dave Guisti – Pirates: 50-33, 3.06 ERA, 140 Saves, 416 SO, 270 BB
10. Kent Tekulve – Pirates: 35-22, 2.65 ERA, 83 Saves, 313 SO, 190 BB

Just missed the cut: Gary Lavelle, Darold Knowles, Jim Brewer

Top Managers

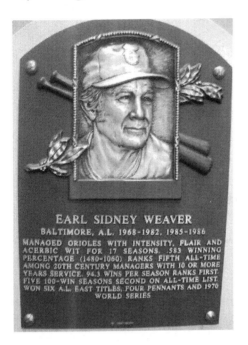

EARL SIDNEY WEAVER
BALTIMORE, A.L. 1968-1982, 1985-1986
MANAGED ORIOLES WITH INTENSITY, FLAIR AND
ACERBIC WIT FOR 17 SEASONS. .583 WINNING
PERCENTAGE (1480-1060) RANKS FIFTH ALL-TIME
AMONG 20TH CENTURY MANAGERS WITH 10 OR MORE
YEARS SERVICE. 94.3 WINS PER SEASON RANKS FIRST.
FIVE 100-WIN SEASONS SECOND ON ALL-TIME LIST.
WON SIX A.L. EAST TITLES, FOUR PENNANTS AND 1970
WORLD SERIES

1. Earl Weaver – Orioles '70-'79; 944-656

Fiery personality (91 career ejections) and credo of 'pitching, defense, and the 3-run homer' led to a decade of 3 100-win seasons, 8 90-win seasons, 3 pennants and a World Championship in 1970. Known as a great handler of pitching staffs, under Weaver Baltimore had at least one 20 game winner in all 10 years during the 70s, and a record 13 straight seasons overall.

2. Sparky Anderson – Reds '70-'78, Tigers '79; 919-636

Captain Hook was let go by Cincinnati in '78 after consecutive 2nd place finishes despite a 9 year run of 7 90-win seasons, 4 pennants, and 2 World Championships.

3. **Billy Martin – Tigers '71-'73, Rangers '73-'75, Yankees '75-'78,'79; 719-577**

What gets lost sometimes amid all the fights, tantrums, and controversies is that Martin won everywhere he went.

4. **Danny Murtaugh – Pirates '70-'71, '73-'76; 471-364**

Had 4 tenures as Pirate manager, 2 in the 70s, and won World Series with the Pirates in 1960 and 1971.

5. **Dick Williams – A's '71-'73, Angels '74-'76, Expos '77-'79; 681-622**

Walked away from Finley's A's after a 2nd straight Championship in 1973. Later in the decade won 95 games with Montreal.

6. **Walter Alston – Dodgers '70-'76; 636-485**

Wrapped up a 23 year managerial career with 7 straight winning seasons in the decade, never finishing below 3rd place or 85 wins.

7. **Chuck Tanner – White Sox '70-'75, A's '76, Pirates '77-'79; 770-691**

Tallied 4 second place finishes with 3 different clubs before winning a World Series with Pittsburgh in 1979.

8. **Tommy Lasorda – Dodgers '76-'79; 274-216**

Began a 21 year managerial career in the 70s with 2 pennants in his first 2 full seasons.

9. **Whitey Herzog – Rangers '73, Angels '74, Royals '75-'79; 459-397**

The 'White Rat' won 3 division titles in KC after a disastrous 1973 with Texas and 4 game interim role with the Angels.

10. **Ralph Houk – Yankees '70-'73, Tigers '74-'78; 697-750**

WWII Army Major won 2 World Championships with the Yankees in the 1960s but never came close during the '70s.

Top Defensive Players (by position)

Pitcher – Jim Kaat

Committed only 2 balks during his streak of 8 consecutive Gold Gloves with 3 different clubs from 1970-78, part of Kaat's run of 16 straight Gold Gloves dating back to 1962.

Other Standouts: Bob Gibson, Jim Palmer

Catcher – Johnny Bench

Bench is the standard bearer at his position and was the pioneer of the one-handed style of catching. His quick release and accurate arm helped nail 43% of total would be base-stealers, including a career best 56.4% in 1972. A great signal caller and an agile athlete in his prime, Bench won 10 Gold Gloves, 8 in the 70s.

Other Standouts: Jim Sundberg, Thurman Munson

1st Base – George Scott

Began his career as a third baseman, and displayed soft hands, good footwork, and surprising quickness in capturing 6 Gold Gloves. Other Standouts: Steve Garvey, Wes Parker, Jim Spencer, Keith Hernandez

2nd Base – Frank White

Earned 3 Gold Gloves in the late 70s, and 8 in his career, thanks to a powerful arm and great speed to cover the fast Royals Stadium carpet. Turned the double play effortlessly and had such a knack for running down fly balls to his left that John Mayberry would yell "Frank" instead of 'I got it' when pops came behind first base.

Others Standouts: Joe Morgan, Bobby Grich

Shortstop – Mark Belanger

'The Blade', who captured 7 Gold Gloves during the decade, was a confident, smooth ex-basketball star. With effortless transfers from his small black glove to throwing hand, he seemed to catch grounders and redirect them toward first base in one motion. Legend has it he never dove for a ball in his 18 year career.

Others Standouts: Dave Concepcion, Larry Bowa

3rd Base – Brooks Robinson

Robinson single-handedly took over the 1970 World Series with his glove, and in 1973 became the first player to start 2 triple plays in the same season. The Human Vacuum Cleaner won 10 Gold Gloves in the 60s and another 6 in the 70s.

Others Standouts: Mike Schmidt, Graig Nettles, Buddy Bell, Doug Rader

Left Field – Joe Rudi

Drafted as a third baseman, came up as a first baseman, and moved between left and first throughout the decade, Rudi still came away with 3 Gold Gloves for his work in left field. One was not deserved in '75 when he only played 44 games in the outfield, but no doubt that overall Rudi deserved at least 3 – he finished in the top 2 in fielding % among leftfielders 6 times and in the Top 5 among all outfielders 5 times.
Others Standouts: Carl Yastrzemski, Pete Rose, Roy White

Center Field – Paul Blair

Captured 6 Gold Gloves in the '70s; was able to take away routine hits because his great speed and range allowed him to play extremely shallow. Blair registered 300 or more putouts in 7 straight seasons to start the decade, including 447 in '74, and led the league with 14 assists in 1973.
Others Standouts: Cesar Cedeno, Amos Otis, Cesar Geronimo, Garry Maddox

Right Field – Roberto Clemente

The best defensive right fielder in baseball history. Clemente had centerfield range, but was more valuable to the Pirates as a right fielder so they could take advantage of the arm that produced 254 career assists. With his aggressive style, sliding catches were commonplace, and he earned Gold Gloves in all 3 seasons he played during the decade before his untimely death in '72.
Others Standouts: Dave Parker, Dwight Evans, Bobby Bonds

Top Clutch Players

1. Reggie Jackson

Quite possibly the greatest clutch hitter in the game's history, 'Mr.October' lived up to his nickname with outstanding heroics for Oakland and New York throughout the decade. From 1970-79, Jackson played in 7 ALCS and was a 5-time World Champion, taking home 2 World Series MVPs. Reggie played in 53 post-season games in the decade and hit .305 with 10 doubles, 14 home runs, and 38 RBI. He hit 9 homers and batted .360 in 24 World Series games. Most noted for his 3 HR game and 5 HR, .450 series to close out LA in 1977, Jackson had at least 2 other series equally impressive. In 1973 he made several fine catches in right field and filled in admirably in center for the injured Bill North. With Oakland down 3 games to 2, he walloped 2 RBI doubles in Game 6 and then a knockout blow 2-run homer in the Game 7 clincher. And in 1978, Jackson hit .391 with 2 HR and matched his 1977 total with 8 RBI.

2. Johnny Bench

With the Reds facing elimination in Game 5 of the 1972 NLCS, Bench hit a game-tying 9th inning home run off Pittsburgh's Dave Guisti, and Cincinnati won later in the inning. In 1976 Bench rebounded from an off-year in the regular season to hit .333 in a 3-game NLCS sweep of Philadelphia. In the 1976 World Series against the Yankees, Bench took MVP honors, leading the Reds to another sweep by hitting .533 on 8 hits including a double, triple and 2 home runs in 4 games. Bench hit an extremely productive .266 in 45 post-season games with 10 home runs, 8 doubles, 3 triples, 20 RBI and 27 runs scored.

3. Pete Rose

Charlie Hustle batted .318 with 10 doubles and 5 home runs in 43 post-season games in the 1970s. In 5 NLCS he hit a scorching .378, including 9-20 (.450) against Pittsburgh in 1972, and 6-14 (.429) vs Philadelphia in 1976. In 1973 against the Mets, Pete went 8-21 (.381) including home runs in both of Cincinnati's 2-1 wins; an 8th inning shot off Tom Seaver to tie Game 2 and a 12th-inning game winner in Game 4. While Rose hit a pedestrian .264 overall in 4 World Series in the decade, he captured MVP honors in the 1975 Fall Classic against Boston. In that series he went 10-27 (.370) and had a game-tying RBI single in the 7th inning of Cincinnati's Game 7 win.

4. George Brett

From 1976-78 Brett's Royals could not overtake the Yankees in 3 straight ALCS. What's amazing is that New York somehow managed to overcome *Brett,* who scored 13 runs and drove home 10 during the 14 contests in shellacking the Yankee staff for a .375 batting average, with 4 triples and 4 home runs. No game better epitomized Brett's plight than Game 3 of the 1978 ALCS, when George became the second player to hit 3 home runs in a single League Championship Series game. All 3 longballs either put KC ahead or tied the score, but the Yanks still prevailed 6-5. Brett's heroics continued in the 1980s, and he finished his career as one of the game's most outstanding post-season players, hitting .337 with 8 doubles, 5 triples, 10 home runs, 23 RBI, and 30 runs scored over 43 games.

5. Thurman Munson

How did the Yankee captain respond to his first post-season opportunity for the Yankees in 1976? The regular season MVP hit .435 in the ALCS against KC, going 10 for 23. He followed that up in the World Series in a losing cause against the Reds with 9 hits and a .529 average.

The following year Munson hit .320 in a 6 game World Series victory over Los Angeles, neutralizing LA's running game by throwing out 4 of 6 base stealers. Then in 1978, in Game 3 of the ALCS, with the Yankees trailing Kansas City 5-4, Thurman blasted a 460 foot 2-run home run in the 8th to give New York a game lead and series lead they would not relinquish. In 30 post season games, Munson hit .357 with 9 doubles, 3 home runs, and 22 RBI.

6. Rollie Fingers

Fingers was an iron man by modern day relief pitching standards. Pitching in an era immediately preceding the 1 inning save specialist, Fingers tossed over 52 innings for Oakland in 27 post-season games. That included 6 outings of 3 innings or more. In the 1973 World Series he appeared in 6 games, yielding only 1 run in 13 2/3 innings, and took World Series MVP Honors in 1974 with a win and 2 saves. In total, Fingers had a 2.24 post-season ERA with 3 wins and 8 saves over 27 games, with a 1.35 ERA in 16 appearances over 33 innings in 3 World Series during the 70s.

7. Steve Garvey

Like Munson did two years later, in 1974 Garvey lived up to an MVP season with a torrid League Championship Series and World Series. Steve led LA to the Fall Classic by hitting .389 with 2 home runs in a 4-game NLCS victory over Pittsburgh, and then hit .381 in a 5 game WS loss to Oakland. Garvey added 9 more hits and a .375 average in a 1977 World Series loss to New York. Steve took over the 1978 NLCS against Philadelphia with 2 homers and a triple in the opening game, en route to a 4 HR, 7 RBI, .389 series. While his Dodgers would not lock up a World Championship until 1981, in the 70s Garvey hit .339 in 29 post-season games with 40 hits, 7 HR, 20 runs scored and 16 RBI.

8. Catfish Hunter

A 5-time World Champion, Hunter pitched in 6 ALCS and 6 World Series for Oakland and New York during the 70s. He went 9-6 with a 3.26 ERA overall in 22 post-season games. Catfish enjoyed his best post-seasons with Oakland, going 7-2, including 4-0 in World Series contests. Hunter went 2-0 in the 1972 World Series, including a 3-2 victory in Game 7. In 1973 he notched a 5-hit shutout to close out Baltimore in the deciding Game 5 of the 1973 ALCS, and then outdueled Tom Seaver 3-1 in a potential elimination game against the Mets in Game 6 of the World Series. His top post-season performance as a Yankee was a complete game 5-hit 4-1 victory in the 1976 ALCS opener.

9. Jim Palmer

The decade's winningest pitcher had a 5-2 post season record in the 1970s, with 3 complete game victories and a 2.75 ERA in 12 starts. Palmer pitched Baltimore's pennant clinching game in 3 straight seasons from 1969-71. He went the distance in the 1970 ALCS clincher, allowing only 1 run while fanning 12. He then opened the 1970 World Series allowing only 5 hits to Cincinnati in 8 2/3 innings for a 4-3 win. In 1973 Palmer tossed a 5-hit complete game shutout with 12 strikeouts to open the ALCS against eventual World Champion Oakland.

10. Willie Stargell

Willie made his post-season debut in the 1970 NLCS, and turned in a 6-12 performance that was one of the Pirate's few bright spots in a 3-game sweep at the hands of the Reds. From there he was hot and cold in October, managing only 5-38 in the 1971 NLCS and World Series combined and 1-16 in the '72 NLCS before breaking out with a 6-15 (.400) 2 home run performance in the 1974 NLCS. Willie struggled again in the '75 NLCS, hitting .182 (2-11) in another loss to Cincinnati. In 1979, however, Stargell carried the Pirates on his shoulders, hitting .455 in the NLCS and .400 in the World Series, with a combined 5 homers, 6 doubles, and 13 RBI, and tying Reggie Jackson's World Series record with 25 total bases.

Top Power/Speed Men

Great power hitters are a rare breed, and they were in especially short supply during the 1970s. And while Lou Brock broke Maury Wills' stolen base record in 1974, the decade was not particularly well-known for its speedsters. Rarer still is the player who could both hit the ball out of the park and be a threat on the base paths. Going into the decade, a 30-30 season, where a player steals 30 or more bases and hits 30+ home runs in the same year, had been accomplished only 5 times in baseball history. It would happen 5 more times over the next 9 seasons.

Milwaukee's Tommy Harper was the first man in the 70s to join the 30-30 club. Harper swiped over 400 bases in his career, including 200 over his final 7 seasons from 1970-76, and led the league in steals twice. Harper's 38 thefts in 1970 were no surprise, but his 31 home runs that season were, as he never hit more than 18 in any of his 14 other years in the big leagues. 3 years later Bobby Bonds turned the feat, narrowly missing the first 40-40 season ever by wrapping out 39 home runs for the Giants with 43 stolen bases. It was Bonds' second time in the club; he had already done it in 1969, and would also reach 30-30 in 3 other 1970s seasons. Bonds became the first player with 5 30-30 seasons, and was later joined by his son Barry, who accomplished the feat for the 5th time in 1997.

The 1970s 30-30 Club				
Year	Name	Team	HR	SB
1970	Tommy Harper	Milwaukee Brewers	31	38
1973	Bobby Bonds	San Francisco Giants	39	43
1975	Bobby Bonds	New York Yankees	32	30
1977	Bobby Bonds	California Angels	37	41
1978	Bobby Bonds	Chicago (A)/Texas	31	43

Less rare is the 20-20 club. This was accomplished 47 times in the decade. It's worth noting that Philadelphia's Mike Schmidt just missed 30-30 in 1975 when he led the majors with 38 home runs and stole 29 bases. Schmidt was one of 7 men to reach 20-20 in multiple seasons during the 70s:

Most Seasons in the 20-20 club during the 1970s	
Bobby Bonds	9
Joe Morgan	4
Don Baylor	4
Reggie Jackson	4
Cesar Cedeno	3
Toby Harrah	3
Mike Schmidt	2

Bill James developed an actual statistic for these dual threats, called the Power-Speed #, which is the harmonic mean of a player's home runs and stolen bases. I used it to calculate the annual major league leaders and overall 10 best seasons during the decade. Bonds comes out on top here as well, registering the top 2 seasons in the '70s, and 4 of the Top 10. He was also led the majors 5 times; no other player led more than once.

Top 10 Power-Speed Seasons during the 1970s					
Name	Year	Team	HR	SB	P-S #
Bobby Bonds	1973	SF	39	43	40.90
Bobby Bonds	1977	Cal	37	41	38.90
Joe Morgan	1973	Cin	26	67	37.46
Joe Morgan	1976	Cin	27	60	37.24
Bobby Bonds	1978	ChW-Tex	31	43	36.03
Cesar Cedeno	1974	Hou	26	57	35.71
Cesar Cedeno	1973	Hou	25	56	34.57
Davey Lopes	1979	LA	28	44	34.22
Tommy Harper	1970	Mil	31	38	34.14
Bobby Bonds	1970	SF	26	48	33.73

1970s Year-by-Year Power-Speed ML Leaders					
Year	Name	Team	HR	SB	P-S #
1970	Tommy Harper	Mil	31	38	34.14
1971	Bobby Bonds	SF	33	26	29.08
1972	Bobby Bonds	SF	26	44	32.69
1973	Bobby Bonds	SF	39	43	40.90
1974	Cesar Cedeno	Hou	26	57	35.71
1975	Mike Schmidt	Phi	38	29	32.90
1976	Joe Morgan	Cin	27	60	37.24
1977	Bobby Bonds	Cal	37	41	38.90
1978	Bobby Bonds	ChW-Tex	31	43	36.03
1979	Davey Lopes	LA	28	44	34.22

The final table below lists all players with 100 home runs and 100 steals in the decade, along with their major league rank in each category; the 100-100 club if you will. Note that Bobby Bonds ranked #4 in both home runs and steals, while no other player even finished in the Top 20 in both, and only two, Morgan and Jackson, finished in the Top 30. By any measure, the much travelled Bonds was consistently the top power-speed threat of the decade, and one of the best all-time.

100 HR, 100 SB in the 1970s					
Name	HR	Rk	SB	Rk	P-S #
Bobby Bonds	280	4th	380	4th	322.42
Joe Morgan	173	26th	488	3rd	255.44
Reggie Jackson	292	2nd	183	21st	224.99
Cesar Cedeno	148	41st	427	3rd	219.81
Amos Otis	159	33rd	294	9th	206.38
Don Baylor	167	31st	240	14th	196.95
Mike Schmidt	225	8th	117	36th	153.95
Roy White	127	58th	169	28th	145.02
Bobby Murcer	198	17th	114	40th	144.69
Toby Harrah	128	57th	160	28th	142.22
Jimmy Wynn	146	42nd	110	44th	125.47
Dave Winfield	134	52nd	110	44th	120.82
Larry Hisle	134	53rd	109	47th	120.21
Gary Matthews	126	59th	101	52nd	112.12

Top 5:

1. **Bobby Bonds** - Amazingly, Bonds never led the league in home runs or stolen bases. But he was remarkably proficient in both, ranking in the Top 4 in each and enjoying 4 30-30 seasons and 9 20-20 years in the decade.

2. **Joe Morgan** – The 5'7", 160 pound Morgan had the frame of a base stealer, but added surprising pop. In his second straight MVP year (1976) he led the majors in slugging (.576) and on-base% (.466) while stealing 60 bases.

3. **Reggie Jackson** - Everyone knows about Mr. October's power, but the former Arizona State football star was a consistent base stealing threat early in his career. He stole home on Detroit in the deciding game of the ALCS in 1972, injuring himself on the play and spending the '72 World Series out of action on crutches.

4. <u>Cesar Cedeno</u> - His manager Leo Durocher once compared Cedeno to a young Willie Mays, and for a brief period it did not seem so crazy. In the 7 years from '71-'77 Cedeno had 6 seasons of 50+ steals, averaged 18.3 home runs a year, led the league in doubles twice, and captured 5 Gold Gloves.

5. <u>Amos Otis</u> - Like Cedeno, Otis was a centerfielder who seemed like he could do anything on the baseball diamond effortlessly. Otis had 4 seasons where he finished in the Top 10 in MVP voting, topped 15 home runs 6 times, won 3 Gold Gloves, and led the league with 52 stolen bases in 1971, once swiping 5 in a single game.

Top Designated Hitters

Though discussed around baseball for most of the 20th century, the Designated Hitter rule did not became official until 1973. Owners and managers weary of watching hapless pitchers struggle through at-bats spawned thoughts of implementing a 10th starting player, and the idea of a DH was proposed in the National League as early as 1929, but went nowhere. In spring training of 1969, following what had been known as the 'Year of the Pitcher', both leagues experimented with the idea during some Grapefruit League contests. Oakland owner Charlie Finley led the cause, and by 1973 convinced his fellow American League owners to vote in favor of implementing the DH rule on a three year trial basis.

On April 6, 1973 at Fenway Park, the Yankees' Ron Blomberg became the Major League's first designated hitter, walking with the bases loaded against Luis Tiant of the Red Sox. Not exactly the explosive start the league had in mind, but an RBI nonetheless! On that same day, Tony Oliva of Minnesota hit the first home run as a DH, a two-run shot off the A's Catfish Hunter at the Oakland Coliseum. Oliva, who had some serious knee issues, was able to extend his career until 1976 as Minnesota's DH, the position he played in his final 406 games.

With the introduction of the Designated Hitter rule, several veterans returned to stardom in 1973. Oliva hit .289 with 16 home runs, and his 91 RBI were tops among all DHs. Future Hall of Famer Frank Robinson of California topped the position with 26 home runs to go with 83 RBI. After playing only 41 games in 1972,

Baltimore's veteran Tommy Davis hit .293 with 83 RBI in 127 games. Carlos May of Chicago overcame a thumb injury to hit .307 with 14 homers, and Boston signed future Hall of Famer Orlando Cepeda, who battled back from knee problems in '72 to smash 20 HRs with 86 RBI and a .289 average in 142 games in 1973.

There was no DH rule in place for the 1973 World Series, but maybe the Mets wish there had been. Oakland pitcher Ken Holtzman hit one double each in Games 1 and 7, both times eventually scoring crucial runs in Oakland victories. By 1976 it was decided the DH rule would be utilized in the World Series in even numbered years. Undeterred, the National League Champion Reds swept the Yankees anyway, and Cincinnati DH Dan Driessen went 5-14 (.357) with a home run. Since 1986 the DH rule during the Fall Classic is in effect only in American League parks.

In 1974, Tommy Davis rapped out 180 hits as Baltimore's DH, tied for the most for the position in the decade with Willie Horton of Seattle in 1979. Horton DH'd in all 162 games that year for the Mariners, belting 29 home runs and 106 RBI. The only other player to appear as a DH in all 162 games during the 70s was Detroit's Rusty Staub in 1978. Rusty did not disappoint with 24 homers and 121 RBI (the 70s' most by a DH in a season), finishing 5th in MVP voting.

The year before Staub had also been the major's most productive designated hitter with 22 home runs and 101 RBI.

Another player who added years to the end of his career was Rico Carty, who had won a batting title with a .366 mark in 1970 as Atlanta's leftfielder, and then did not exceed 400 at bats again until 1976 when he hit .317 as Cleveland's DH. In 1978, the 38 year old Carty split his season between Toronto and Oakland and tallied a career high 31 home runs (tied with Boston's Jim Rice in 1977 for tops at the position in the 70s) while driving in 99 runs, all as a DH.

My pick as the decade's finest designated hitter is Kansas City's Hal McRae. McRae topped all 70s DHs in Hits (707), Batting Average (.297), Runs (361), Doubles (173), and Stolen Bases (56). Willie Horton (89 HR, 376RBI, .271) and Rico Carty (83-372-.284) also deserve strong consideration.

More than 40 years later, the National League has still not picked up the rule, while the AL has thrived under it, with players such as Frank Thomas, Edgar Martinez, David Ortiz, and Harold Baines playing the majority of their games as Designated Hitters. Purists still insist the rule takes away strategic situations such as sacrifice bunts and pinch hitting decisions, and should be eliminated. Like it or not, the rule has added excitement to the game, and is probably here to stay.

Longest Tape Measure Home Runs

1. Reggie Jackson – A's, July 13, 1971, All-Star game @ Tiger Stadium (RCF) – 540 feet

1. Dave Kingman – Mets, April 14, 1976, vs Cubs @ Wrigley Field (LF) – 540 feet

3. Dick Allen – White Sox, July 6, 1974, vs Tigers @ Tiger Stadium (LCF) – 535 feet

4. Frank Howard – Senators, April 24, 1970, vs Angels @ RFK Stadium (LF) – 525 feet

5. Greg Luzinski – Phillies, May 21, 1977, vs Astros @ Houston Astrodome (LF) – 515 feet

5. Willie Stargell- Pirates, May 20, 1978 @, vs Expos @ Olympic Stadium (RF) – 515 feet

7. Willie Stargell- Pirates, August 9, 1970, @ vs Mets @ Three Rivers Stadium (RF) – 510 feet

7. Willie Stargell- Pirates, July 4, 1979, vs Cardinals @ Busch Memorial Stadium (RF) – 510 feet

9. George Foster – Reds, July 29, 1978, vs Phillies @ Riverfront Stadium (LF) – 509 feet

10. Frank Howard – Senators, August25, 1971, vs Angels @ Angels Stadium (CF) – 506 feet

Courtesy of Baseball's Ultimate Power, Bill Jenkinson

Team Rankings

1. <u>Cincinnati Reds</u> – Decade Record: 953-657, 6 Divisional Titles, 4 Pennants, 2 World Championships

The Big Red Machine won more Pennants (4) in the decade than any other team and tied with the Pittsburgh Pirates for the most division titles with 6. They led the majors with 953 regular season wins, one more than Baltimore and 37 more than anyone else in the National League.

Cincinnati boasted the game's best all-around catcher, Johnny Bench (8 Gold Gloves, 290 HRs and an MLB high 1013 RBI), and MLBs' all-time (and 1970s) hit leader in Pete Rose, who was also the decade leader in doubles and runs scored. From '70-'78 while in Cincinnati, Rose scored 978 runs, hit .312, and notched 1,853 hits, including 354 doubles and 59 triples.

The move that cemented the club's dominance was the 1971 blockbuster trade of 2-time Gold Glove second baseman Tommy Helms and first baseman Lee May (who had bashed 73 HR and 192 RBI from '70-'71) to Houston for 2B Joe Morgan, P Jack Billingham, and CF Cesar Geronimo, who would win 4 Gold Gloves. Morgan emerged as the decade's best second baseman, winning 5 Gold Gloves with 488 stolen bases and an on-base% of .404.

That trade allowed third baseman Tony Perez, the decade's #2 RBI man behind Bench, to move over to first base in 1972. Two years later Rose moved to third, replacing the mostly ineffective Denis Menke, and when OF Bobby Tolan (.273 from 1970-73) was traded, room in the outfield opened for the second half of the decade's most feared run producer, George Foster, who topped the 1970s single season marks with 52 home runs and 149 RBI in 1977, and Ken Griffey, who hit .310 with over 900 hits in the decade.

Bench ('70,'72) and Morgan ('75,'76) took home two MVP trophies each in the 1970s, and Rose ('73) and Foster ('77) one each, giving the Reds 6 MVPs within 8 seasons.

Surprisingly, no Reds pitcher won 100 games for the club during the 1970s. Until Tom Seaver (46-23, 2.83 E.R.A. as a Red) was acquired in 1977, the club lacked star power in their starting rotation, but Billingham (87-63), Don Gullett (91-44), Gary Nolan (79-47) and Fred Norman (85-64) were all among the league's best. Manager Sparky Anderson earned the nickname 'Captain Hook' for his quick calls to the bullpen, but he had that luxury with reliable big game pitchers such as Clay Carroll (95 saves, 2.62 E.R.A), Pedro Borbon (76 saves, 3.32), Rawly Eastwick (57 saves, 2.40), Wayne Granger (46 saves, 3.02), and Doug Bair (44 saves, 3.10).

The Reds fell short in the 1970 and 1972 World Series, and were upset by the Mets in the 1973 NLCS. Anderson's club shed their reputation for not being able to win the big one with a 108 win season in 1975, where they outdistanced defending NL Champ Los Angeles by 20 games. Then came a 3 game NLCS sweep of rival Pittsburgh, followed by a gutty 7 game win over Boston in a classic World Series battle. Cincinnati was even more convincing in 1976, becoming the NL's first repeat World Champs in 54 years, with 102 regular season wins, a 3 game sweep of Philadelphia in the NLCS, and a 4 game dismantling of the Yankees in the Fall Classic.

Offensive Leaders

Batting Avg		On Base %		Slugging %	
Pete Rose	.312	Joe Morgan	.415	George Foster	.519
Ken Griffey	.310	Pete Rose	.386	Johnny Bench	.491
George Foster	.288	Ken Griffey	.377	Tony Perez	.490

Hits		Runs		Stolen Bases	
Pete Rose	1837	Pete Rose	978	Joe Morgan	406
Johnny Bench	1396	Joe Morgan	816	Dave Concepcion	220
Dave Concepcion	1268	Johnny Bench	792	Ken Griffey	115

HR		RBI		Doubles		Triples	
Johnny Bench	290	Johnny Bench	1013	Pete Rose	354	Pete Rose	59
George Foster	197	Tony Perez	712	Johnny Bench	264	Ken Griffey	44
Tony Perez	180	George Foster	678	Joe Morgan	220	Cesar Geronimo	43

Pitching Leaders

Wins		Earned Run Average	
Don Gullett	91	Clay Carroll	2.62
Jack Billingham	87	Tom Seaver	2.83
Fred Norman	85	Don Gullett	3.03

Strikeouts		Shutouts	
Fred Norman	864	Jack Billingham	18
Don Gullett	777	Don Gullett	13
Gary Nolan	635	Tom Seaver	10

Saves	
Clay Carroll	105
Pedro Borbon	29
Rawly Eastwick	24

2. Oakland A's – Decade Record: 838-772, 5 Divisional Titles, 3 Pennants, 3 World Championships

During the decade Oakland became the only franchise other than the Yankees to win 3 straight World Series, and the first since New York in 1949-53. They also won 5 consecutive AL West division titles, and wrapped around that streak were two second place finishes. That 7 year run of 652-473 was one of the best in modern history, but Oakland closed the decade with only a .520 winning percentage after 3 rough seasons from '77-'79.

The A's were built on the pitching threesome of ace Catfish Hunter (106-49, 2.89 E.R.A.) and lefties Vida Blue (123-85 2.87) and two-time All-Star Ken Holtzman (77-55, 2.92). Hunter won 20+ games in 4 straight years, capped with a 25-12, 2.49 Cy Young Award season in 1974. Vida Blue had 3 20+ win seasons, including one of the best individual performances of the decade in 1971, when he took the Cy Young and the American League MVP on a 24-8 record with a 1.82 ERA and 301 strikeouts.

The bullpen was led by Rollie Fingers (2.76, 124 saves) and Darold Knowles (2.99, 30 saves). The 1974 World Series MVP, Fingers pitched 52 innings in 27 total post-season games for the A's, including 6 outings of 3 innings or more. He had a 2.24 post season ERA with 8 saves and 3 wins, and a 1.35 ERA over 3 World Series.

Oakland's lineup featured speed at the top with centerfielder Bill North (.275, 232 stolen bases, including a league leading 54 in '74 and 75 in '76), and shortstop Bert Campaneris (.261 with a team leading 564 runs, 1036 hits, 274 steals and 84 sacrifices). The corner outfielders were 1973 MVP Reggie Jackson (who led the league that year with 32 HR, 117 RBI, 99 runs, and a .531 slugging %, and had a team leading 177 home runs during the decade) and 3-time Gold Glover Joe Rudi, who paced the AL with 181 hits and 9 triples in 1972, and with 39 doubles in '74. Captain Sal Bando finished in the Top 5 in MVP voting 3 times and led the 70s A's with 609 RBI. 1972 World Series MVP Gene Tenace (.348, 8-25, 4 HR, 9 RBI), who split his time between first base and catcher, had good power and led the team during the 70s with a .377 OBP. Dave Duncan and Ray Fosse both filled in behind the dish as well, and Dick Green was the mainstay at second base.

By 1977 all of the above players except North had left the club, most through free agency, and the young talent such as leftfielder Mitchell Page (21-75-.307) and third baseman Wayne Gross (22 home runs) was not enough to continue the winning tradition. The A's finished dead last, behind even the expansion Seattle Mariners, and 38 ½ games out of first. They finished 6th in 1978, and last again in 1979 with a 54-108 record.

Despite their success though most of the 70s, the franchise went through 7 different managers, most of whom found owner Charlie Finley too meddlesome and controlling to work for. In June 1976 Finley attempted to sell Vida Blue to the Yankees and Joe Rudi and Rollie Fingers to Boston before commissioner Bowie Kuhn 'disallowed the assignments', stating they were not in the best interest of baseball. The circus-like atmosphere Finley brought to Oakland was nothing new; in a prior infamous move he 'fired' second baseman Mike Andrews after two errors in the 1973 World Series, only to have Kuhn step in and reinstate him. Gimmicks were commonplace, such as orange baseballs, and hiring track star Herb Washington as a 'Designated Runner'.

Through it all the 'Swingin' A's' enjoyed the greatest championship streak of the decade.

	Offensive Leaders						
Batting Avg		On Base %		Slugging %			
Joe Rudi	.285	Gene Tenace	.377	Reggie Jackson	.501		
Bill North	.271	Bill North	.364	Joe Rudi	.453		
Reggie Jackson	.270	Sal Bando	.361	Gene Tenace	.438		
Hits		Runs		Stolen Bases			
Bert Campaneris	1036	Bert Campaneris	564	Bert Campaneris	274		
Joe Rudi	983	Sal Bando	552	Bill North	232		
Sal Bando	956	Reggie Jackson	496	Reggie Jackson	115		
HR		RBI		Doubles		Triples	
Reggie Jackson	177	Sal Bando	609	Joe Rudi	200	Joe Rudi	29
Sal Bando	152	Reggie Jackson	535	Reggie Jackson	167	Bert Campaneris	28
Gene Tenace	120	Joe Rudi	503	Sal Bando	158	Bill North	23

Pitching Leaders			
Wins		Earned Run Average	
Vida Blue	123	Rollie Fingers	2.76
Catfish Hunter	106	Vida Blue	2.87
Ken Holtzman	77	Catfish Hunter	2.89
Strikeouts		Shutouts	
Vida Blue	1291	Vida Blue	28
Catfish Hunter	817	Catfish Hunter	19
Rollie Fingers	723	Ken Holtzman	13
Saves			
Rollie Fingers	124		
Darold Knowles	30		
Mudcat Grant	27		

Designated Runner

One of the most interesting players of the 1970s never batted, fielded, or threw a pitch. Yet he appeared in 105 games and scored 33 runs during a brief 2 year 'career'.

Herb Washington was a 4 time All-American sprinter at Michigan State University who had broken world records in the 50 and 60 yard dash. In mid-spring training 1974, owner Charlie Finley signed Washington on to his defending two-time champion Oakland A's despite Herb not having played baseball since his high school junior year. The A's sent out a press release that "Finley and (manager) Alvin Dark feel that Washington will be directly responsible for winning 10 games this year".

The move infuriated the rebellious A's players, and this would be far from the last time Finley and his players would clash. Veterans Gene Tenace, Joe Rudi and Sal Bando were among the more outspoken A's who felt the move would be taking a roster spot away from a 'real' player, and resented being pinch run for by a man clearly lacking in baseball experience and instincts. As the season moved on, it was obvious the indulgent new manager Dark was going to great lengths to utilize Finley's new toy as often as possible. Washington did steal 29 bases in 45 attempts and scored 29 runs during the 1974 regular season as the A's rolled to a 4th consecutive AL West title.

But Mr. October he was not - Washington appeared in two AL Playoff games against Baltimore and was thrown out stealing in both games. Oakland moved on to the World Series against the Los Angeles Dodgers nonetheless, and Herb made his World Series debut in the 9th inning of Game 2. Oakland had trailed 3-0 before Joe Rudi's 2-run single just made it a one-run game. With one out, the slow footed Rudi was replaced by Washington. Fellow MSU alumnus Steve Garvey held Washington on at first, while another former MSU student and professor, pitcher Mike Marshall, stepped off the rubber twice as Washington scrambled back each time. He stepped off a third time and Washington walked back and then took a lead again. Finally Marshall whirled and side armed a throw to first before Washington had set himself, and Garvey, partially blocking off the base with his foot and knee, slapped down a hard tag well ahead of Washington's desperate dive back, his arm aiming for the middle of the bag rather than the outside edge that base runners are taught to reach for. The Dodger Stadium crowd erupted and Garvey began whipping the ball around the infield as Washington punched at the dirt in disgust. Marshall finally turned his attention to pinch hitter Angel Mangual, and struck him out to end the game.

Washington did have two additional and uneventful pinch running appearances during the series, and the A's went on to win the Series for their third straight title despite the Game 2 blunder.

Washington returned to the team in 1975, and stole 2 bases and scored 4 runs before being released a month into the season. The 'Designated Runner' experiment was over.

3. Pittsburgh Pirates – Decade Record: 916-695, 6 Divisional Titles, 2
    Pennants, 2 World Championships

The Pirates had the majors' third best regular season record during the
70s, and only Cincinnati won as many division titles. Pittsburgh was built
on offense – they finished in the league's Top 5 in runs scored for 9
consecutive years, and ranked 1st in 1971 and 1979, their World
Championship seasons. In the early part of the decade the 'Lumber
Company', as they were known, flat out bludgeoned teams with a fearful
attack throughout the lineup. By the end of the 70s Pittsburgh could still
mash the baseball but had improved their team speed significantly, as
Frank Tavares led the league with 70 steals in 1977, and outfielder Omar
Moreno paced the NL in '78 and '79 (71 and 77 steals respectively). The
underrated pitching did not get a lot of credit, but was strong
throughout, particularly in the bullpen.

Roberto Clemente was the Pirates' leader and most complete player
from 1970-72, winning three Gold Gloves with 28 assists, while batting
.336 with a .378 on base %, and taking MVP honors in the 1971 World
Series (12-29, .414). Following Clemente's untimely death after the
1972 season, the Pirates had their worst season of the decade in 1973,
finishing at 80-82, in 3rd place. Pittsburgh resumed their winning ways in

1974 and '75, making it 5 division titles in 6 years, but were turned away by the Dodgers and then the Reds in the NLCS. They did not make it back to the NLCS until 1979, and this time they knocked off the Reds and then, like in 1971, took care of Baltimore in a 7 game World Series.

Willie Stargell was the 1979 World Series MVP, going 12-30 (.400) with 3 home runs, 4 doubles, and 7 RBI. The 39-year-old was also named National League co-MVP along with St Louis first baseman Keith Hernandez. It was a long overdue honor for the decade's top power hitter, who led the majors with 296 home runs and a .555 slugging %, and finished 5th with 906 RBI, topping 90 6 times. Stargell had been MVP runner-up in 1971 & '73, finished 3rd in '74, and had 3 other Top 10 finishes.

There may have not been a better all-around talent in the decade's second half than right fielder Dave Parker, a 3 time Gold Glove winner who led the league in hitting (.338), hits (215), and doubles (44) in 1977, and followed that up in 1978 with another batting title (.334), plus 30 HR, 117 RBI, and the National League MVP award.

The Pirates' best pure hitter during the 70s was not Stargell or Parker, but another lefty, center fielder Al Oliver. Oliver hit .298 during 8 years in Pittsburgh, and led the club for the decade in hits (1357), doubles (257), and triples (54). Other standouts included 3-time All-Star catcher Manny Sanguillen (.300), third baseman Richie Hebner, left fielder Richie Zisk, and speedster Omar Moreno (217 steals in 521 games).

The pitching, while never dominant, was in fine hands with mainstay starters Jim Rooker (80-63), Bruce Kison (81-63), Doc Ellis (79-58), and Jerry Reuss (61-46). In the 1971 World Series against the powerful Orioles, Steve Blass, who had went 15-8 in the regular season, tossed a complete game 3 hitter in Game 3, then a complete game 4 hitter in the deciding game 7, winning 5-1 and 2-1. He went 19-8 with a 2.49 ERA in 1972, then inexplicably lost the strike zone in 1973, going 3-9 with a 9.85 ERA, walking 84 batters and hitting 12 in 88 innings. He was out of the game by 1974.

The best of all the Pirate starters was likely 6'7" lefthander John 'Candy Man' Candelaria, who went 70-38 with a team best 2.94 ERA, including a 20-5 1977 when he led the National League with a 2.34 ERA. The bullpen was anchored in the early years by Dave Guisti (47-28, 2.94, 133 saves), and then later by submariner Kent Tekulve (35-22, 2.65, 83 saves).

Offensive Leaders

Batting Avg		On Base %		Slugging %	
Dave Parker	.317	Willie Stargell	.374	Willie Stargell	.555
Manny Sanguillen	.300	Dave Parker	.370	Dave Parker	.521
Richie Zisk	.299	Richie Zisk	.366	Bill Robinson	.487

Hits		Runs		Stolen Bases	
Al Oliver	1357	Willie Stargell	719	Omar Moreno	217
Willie Stargell	1261	Al Oliver	633	Frank Taveras	206
Manny Sanguillen	1166	Dave Parker	519	Dave Parker	88

HR		RBI		Doubles		Triples	
Willie Stargell	296	Willie Stargell	906	Al Oliver	257	Al Oliver	54
Dave Parker	122	Al Oliver	647	Willie Stargell	253	Dave Parker	51
Al Oliver	118	Dave Parker	533	Dave Parker	203	Manny Sanguillen	46

Pitching Leaders

Wins		Earned Run Average	
Bruce Kison	81	Kent Tekulve	2.65
Jim Rooker	80	John Candelaria	2.94
Dock Ellis	79	Dave Giusti	2.94

Strikeouts		Shutouts	
Bruce Kison	735	Jerry Reuss	13
Jim Rooker	664	Dock Ellis	10
Dock Ellis	644	Bob Moose	9

Saves	
Dave Giusti	133
Kent Tekulve	83
Ramon Hernandez	39

Hero For the Ages

On New Year's Eve 1972, the world lost a quiet gentleman, the Pittsburgh Pirates' Roberto Clemente. The Puerto Rican-born Clemente was a four-time batting champion and a career .317 hitter. He hit a combined .336 in his only three seasons during the 1970s.

Clemente made his major league debut in 1955, and by 1960 came into his own, earning his first All-Star selection and hitting .310 in the 1960 World Series as the Pirates defeated the Yankees in 7 games. The following year Clemente batted .352 and won his first batting title. In the 13 seasons from 1960-1972, Clemente was a model of consistency, hitting over .300 12 times, earning 12 Gold Gloves and 12 All-Star appearances. He finished in the Top 10 in Most Valuable Player voting 8 times, winning the award in 1966 with a .357 average, 210 hits, and 110 RBI. Clemente was a fantastic defensive right fielder with a powerful throwing arm - he had 266 career outfield assists and led the league in that category 5 times.

In 1970 Clemente began the new decade much as he had left off in the 60s – he hit .352 with 10 triples, the ninth and final time in his career he eclipsed double figures in three baggers. The Pirates won the National League's Eastern division but came up short against Cincinnati in the NLCS. 1971 was even better - Clemente batted .341 with 86 RBI and the Pirates won 97 games. They captured another NL East flag and overtook the Giants to win the NL pennant behind a .333 effort from Clemente in the NLCS. In the 1971 World Series, Pittsburgh fell behind 2 games to 0 to the defending World Champion Baltimore Orioles before storming back to take the series in 7 games. Clemente led all players in hits (12), extra base hits (5), and batting average (.414). He hit 2 home runs, including one in the Pirates 2-1 win in the decisive 7th game. He was an easy choice for Most Valuable Player.

In 1972, the 38 year old Clemente struggled through the season with an ankle injury and played in a career-low 102 games, though he still managed to hit .312. In his final regular season at-bat, he doubled off New York's Jon Matlack for his 3,000th hit, becoming the first Hispanic player to reach that milestone, and only the 11th all-time.

A father of three boys, and a United States Marine Core reserve veteran, Clemente was proud of his Puerto Rican heritage and spent much of his time off the field involved in charitable causes. In the fall of 1972 Roberto was the leader of Puerto Rican efforts to aid victims of an earthquake in Nicaragua. His organization had raised more than $150,000 in cash, food, and clothing, and had already made three deliveries to Nicaragua. Hearing rumors that not all the proceeds had reached the victims in the previous trips, Clemente insisted he make the next plane trip to personally see to it that the supplies got into the hands of those that needed them. On December 31, Clemente drove to San Juan International Airport with his wife Vera, his friend Cristobal Colon, and teammate Tom Walker, who helped him load the plane. Walker wanted to accompany Clemente on the plane trip, but Clemente convinced the single Walker to stay back and enjoy a New Year's Eve party instead. Vera was worried that the plane seemed old and overloaded, but Roberto assured her he was fine as he said goodbye to her and his friends.

The DC-7 plane, carrying a crew of three, plus Clemente and the supplies, crashed minutes after take-off into seas a mile and a half from shore. The underwater wreckage was not found until two day later, and Clemente's body was never recovered. He left behind Vera, three young sons - Roberto Jr., Luis, and Enrique, and a world of heartbroken fans.

"He did not just lend his name to the fund-raising activities the way some famous personalities do," said Luis Vigoraux, a TV producer who had asked Clemente to take part in the collection. "He took over the entire thing, arranging for collection points, publicity, and the transportation to Nicaragua."

In 1973, the standard five year waiting period was waived for only the second time in baseball history, and Roberto Clemente was elected to the National Baseball Hall of Fame.

4. New York Yankees – Decade Record: 892-715, 3 Divisional Titles, 3 Pennants, 2 World Championships

Lasting images of the Yankees during the decade include Reggie's 3 homer World Series game against the Dodgers, and Chris Chambliss' walk-off shot in Game 5 of the 1976 ALCS vs Kansas City. The Yankees enjoyed a special three year run of pennants from 1976-78, winning 297 regular season games and 2 World Series. Much less noted is the fact that the Yankees started the decade with a 2nd place 93 win season, finished in 2nd again only 2 games out of first in 1974, and won 89 games in 1979. In all 3 of those seasons Baltimore took the division crown.

The Yankees were built around home-grown catcher Thurman Munson, a three time Gold Glove winner, the 1970 Rookie of the Year and 1976 MVP who enjoyed three straight 100 RBI seasons, and the underrated Roy White, who played an excellent defensive left field, and paced the American League with 104 runs scored in 1976 and led the Yanks with

752 runs, 169 steals, and 37 triples. The farm system also produced center fielder Bobby Murcer, one of the game's best players from 1970-74, but New York traded him away for Bobby Bonds before the '75 season, and then a year later swapped Bonds to California for Mickey Rivers and Ed Figueroa.

Additional smart trades rounded out the club – Nettles was acquired from Cleveland (before the 1973 season), as was Chris Chambliss (before the 1974 campaign), giving New York strength on the corners of the infield for the rest of the decade. Sparky Lyle was stolen from Boston for Danny Cater and saved 141 games in 7 years, leading the league in saves twice ('72 and '76), and capturing the Cy Young Award in 1977. Lou Piniella came over from Kansas City for Lindy McDaniel. Willie Randolph was acquired from the Pirates for Doc Medich. Free Agency brought in Reggie Jackson, Catfish Hunter (23 wins in 1975), and Don Gullett. Then, right before opening day in 1977, shortstop Bucky Dent came over from the White Sox. After winning their first pennant in 1976 but getting swept by the Reds in the World Series, all the pieces now seemed to be in place.

In 1977, the Yanks beat Kansas City in 5 games again, then won their first World Series since 1962. During the winter they added Goose Gossage to the bullpen for the 1978 season. But by August the Yanks were 14 games behind Boston. Other than Ron Guidry enjoying a career year (25-3, 1.74 ERA), the pitching staff was injury prone and ineffective, and Billy Martin was fired. Under the calm Bob Lemon, the Yankees heated up while Boston wilted. They eventually caught Boston, went ahead, then fell back. After 162 games the teams were tied, but in a one-game playoff at Fenway, Bucky Dent crushed the Sox hopes with a game-breaking 3-run homer. The Yanks proceeded to knock off the Royals in 4 games and the Dodgers once more in a 6 game World Series behind MVP Dent and the defensive heroics of two time Gold Glover ('77,'78) Graig Nettles. Goose led the league with 27 saves, while Jackson (110) and Nettles (107) became the only 70s Yankees other than Munson to drive in over 100 runs.

In 1979 New York slipped to 4th place despite Ron Guidry taking his second straight ERA title (2.78), and 21 wins from fellow lefty Tommy John. In 116 games during the decade, Guidry posted a 59-19 record with a 2.49 ERA and 652 strikeouts. Ed Figueroa was nearly as good, with a 59-36 mark from 1976-79. Hunter, though not quite the ace he was in Oakland after his initial season in the Bronx (23-14, 2.48), went 63-53 in pinstripes.

Offensive Leaders							
Batting Avg		**On Base %**		**Slugging %**			
Mickey Rivers	.299	Reggie Jackson	.371	Reggie Jackson	.524		
Lou Piniella	.296	Willie Randolph	.365	Bobby Murcer	.461		
Thurman Munson	.292	Roy White	.364	Graig Nettles	.437		
Hits		**Runs**		**Stolen Bases**			
Thurman Munson	1536	Roy White	752	Roy White	169		
Roy White	1386	Thurman Munson	690	Willie Randolph	119		
Graig Nettles	1015	Graig Nettles	549	Mickey Rivers	93		
HR		**RBI**		**Doubles**		**Triples**	
Graig Nettles	181	Thurman Munson	692	Thurman Munson	228	Roy White	37
Roy White	127	Graig Nettles	613	Roy White	227	Willie Randolph	34
Bobby Murcer	121	Roy White	581	Chris Chambliss	171	Thurman Munson	30

Pitching Leaders			
Wins		**Earned Run Average**	
Mel Stottlemyre	67	Sparky Lyle	2.41
Catfish Hunter	63	Ron Guidry	2.49
Fritz Peterson	60	Steve Kline	2.96
Strikeouts		**Shutouts**	
Ron Guidry	652	Mel Stottlemyre	18
Mel Stottlemyre	503	Ron Guidry	16
Catfish Hunter	492	Catfish Hunter	11
Saves			
Sparky Lyle	141		
Rich Gossage	45		
Lindy McDaniel	43		

The End of Loyalty?

An article from early 2014 speculated that it could eventually cost the Angels $400 million to keep Mike Trout in Anaheim his entire career.

$400 Million? Modern day players and owners are ruining our game! Whatever happened to loyalty, to franchise players wearing the same uniform for life? Like in my favorite decade, the 70s, for instance? Here's a look at how that went for 5 prominent stars (and eventual Hall of Famers) from the decade:

- Catfish Hunter was the Oakland A's ace during their 1972-74 three-peat World Championship run and won 161 games from 1965-1974, including a 1974 Cy Young Award and 4 consecutive 20-win seasons. He then became baseball's first major free agent, signing with the Yankees on a 5 year, $3.7 Million deal.
- In a little more than 8 seasons from 1967-1975, Reggie Jackson hit 254 home runs and was Oakland's biggest star during their 1972-74 World Championships. In 1973, Jackson was the World Series and American League Most Valuable Player. Right before the 1976 season, with only a year left on his contract, he was traded along with Ken Holtzman to Baltimore for Don Baylor and Mike Torrez. In 1977 Reggie was signed by the Yankees as a free agent, and along with Hunter helped New York win the 1977 and 1978 World Series.

- Beginning in 1967, Tom Seaver won 175 games, a World Championship, and 3 Cy Young Awards for the New York Mets in 10+ years, but a contract renegotiation dispute led to Chairman of the Board M Donald Grant trading his ace to Cincinnati midway through the 1977 season in exchange for Steve Henderson, Pat Zachry, Doug Flynn, and Dan Norman.
- Rod Carew led the Major Leagues with a .343 batting average in the 1970s, and hit .334 with 7 batting titles in 12 straight All-Star seasons with Minnesota from 1967-1978. Frustrated with the Twins inability to build a winning team around him, Carew asked to be traded and was swapped to California before the 1979 season in exchange for Ken Landreaux, Dave Engle, Paul Hartzell and Brad Havens.
- In that same off-season, Pete Rose, the 1973 MVP, a two-time World Champion, and an 11-time All-Star who had already collected over 3,000 hits for the Cincinnati Reds, signed on with the Philadelphia Phillies for 4 years and $3.2 Million dollars. He helped Philadelphia win their first World Series in 1980.

These were by no means isolated cases: the Braves traded home run king Hank Aaron to Milwaukee after the 1974 season, and in 1977 Tony Perez was traded from Cincinnati to Montreal, while Rollie Fingers left Oakland for San Diego. Steve Garvey, Dave Parker, and Dave Winfield eventually changed clubs as well. And legends Joe Morgan, Steve Carlton, Nolan Ryan, and Gaylord Perry all played for multiple organizations.

Of course there were actually several true 'franchise players' in the 1970s. Johnny Bench, quite possibly baseball's greatest catcher ever, played his whole career in Cincinnati. Jim Palmer, the American League's best pitcher in the decade, played his entire career with Baltimore, as did his teammate Brooks Robinson. Willie Stargell of Pittsburgh, Carl Yastrzemski and Jim Rice of Boston, Mike Schmidt of Philadelphia, George Brett of Kansas City, Robin Yount of Milwaukee, and Lou Brock of St Louis are other notable true franchise players who starred during the decade. More modern examples include Kirby Puckett of

Minnesota, Cal Ripken of Baltimore, Mariano Rivera and Derek Jeter of the Yankees.

So while the one-team franchise player is a rarity, this is by no means a recent development. It's basically been the norm for more than 40 years.

5. Baltimore Orioles – Decade Record: 944-656, 5 Divisional Titles, 3 Pennants, 1 World Championship

Baltimore opened the decade in dominating fashion, winning 108 games during the regular season. Slugging first baseman Boog Powell was the AL MVP with 35 HR and 114 RBI. They swept Minnesota 3 straight in the ALCS and dispatched Cincinnati 4 games to 1 in the 1970 World Series. The series MVP, third baseman Brooks Robinson, turned in one spectacular defensive play after another and went 9-21 (.429) with 2 home runs and a record 17 total bases.

The Birds took the pennant again in 1971 with another 3 game ALCS sweep, this time against Oakland, but were turned away by Pittsburgh in the World Series in 7 games.

While they did not return to the Fall Classic until 1979, the Orioles were a model of consistency throughout the 70s, never finishing below .500 with 8 90+ win seasons, 3 100+ wins seasons, and the 2nd best winning percentage in the majors. The Birds won 5 AL East flags and had an additional 3 2nd place finishes. Pitching and defense was the O's recipe for success. Baltimore had 4 Cy Young Award winners, 17 20- game winners (including 3 in 1970 and 4 in 1971), and 29 Gold Glove awards: P Palmer (4), 2B Dave Johnson (2), 2B Bobby Grich (4), SS Mark Belanger (7), 3B Brooks Robinson (6), and CF Paul Blair (6).

Jim Palmer led all major league starting pitchers with a 2.58 ERA, 186 wins (including 8 years of 20 or more), 44 shutouts, and 3 Cy Young Awards. Cuban born Mike Cuellar won 20+ games 3 times and contributed an overall record of 120-77 and 3.31 ERA. Dave NcNally was 91-58 with a 3.18 ERA.

Al Bumbry won 1973 Rookie of the Year honors, hitting .337 with a league-leading 11 triples. Eddie Murray began his Hall Of Fame career by winning the award in 1977 with a .283 average and 27 HR. Lee May became the only Oriole of the decade to lead the league in any major offensive category when he drove in 109 runs in 1976.

Mike Flanagan was the 1979 Cy Young winner with a 23-9 record, and finished the 70s at 60-40 overall. Baltimore advanced to another World Series in '79, but the Birds fell just short in a 7 game rematch against the Pirates.

Offensive Leaders

Batting Avg		On Base %		Slugging %	
Ken Singleton	.299	Ken Singleton	.407	Eddie Murray	.475
Tommy Davis	.291	Boog Powell	.381	Ken Singleton	.472
Eddie Murray	.288	Bobby Grich	.372	Boog Powell	.457

Hits		Runs		Stolen Bases	
Mark Belanger	934	Mark Belanger	486	Al Bumbry	155
Brooks Robinson	917	Bobby Grich	432	Mark Belanger	128
Paul Blair	828	Paul Blair	431	Paul Blair	122

HR		RBI		Doubles		Triples	
Lee May	116	Lee May	456	Paul Blair	149	Al Bumbry	32
Ken Singleton	107	Brooks Robinson	449	Brooks Robinson	144	Paul Blair	29
Boog Powell	101	Ken Singleton	416	Bobby Grich	137	Bobby Grich	27

Pitching Leaders

Wins		Earned Run Average	
Jim Palmer	186	Jim Palmer	2.58
Mike Cuellar	120	Pat Dobson	2.78
Dave McNally	91	Dave McNally	3.18

Strikeouts		Shutouts	
Jim Palmer	1559	Jim Palmer	44
Mike Cuellar	829	Mike Cuellar	25
Dave McNally	594	Dave McNally	16

Saves	
Don Stanhouse	45
Grant Jackson	39
Eddie Watt	35

Your Grandfather's Rotation

In 1970, the World Champion Baltimore Orioles had 3 20-game winners, a feat that had not been accomplished since 1956.

Left-handed screwball specialist Mike Cuellar went 24-8, Dave McNally, another lefty who was once credited by Mickey Mantle as having the league's best curveball, was 24-9, and future Hall of Famer Jim Palmer went 20-10. It would be the first of 8 20-win seasons for Palmer in the decade. The trio were the only starting pitchers the Orioles in the post-season that year, leading a 3 game sweep of Minnesota in the ALCS, and a 5 game World Series win over Cincinnati, holding the Reds to a .213 batting average.

The following year, in 1971, 6'3" righty Pat Dobson, acquired from San Diego, put together a 12 game winning streak during the season and ended with a 20-8 record. Dobson joined McNally (who went 21-5), Cuellar, and Palmer (both 20-9) in the rotation as Baltimore became only the second team in baseball history with 4 20-game winners, and the first since the 1920 Chicago White Sox. The Orioles again used the three man rotation of Cuellar, McNally, and Palmer in the post-season, with Dobson working out of the bullpen. They swept Oakland in the ALCS before being turned away in 7 games by Roberto Clemente and the Pittsburgh Pirates.

Those same Oakland A's won the World Series in 1972, and in 1973, in the middle of their 3 year World Championship run, became the next team in the majors with 3 20-game winners. Catfish Hunter went 21-5, and was joined by left handers Ken Holtzman (21-13) and Vida Blue (20-9). The trio bested Baltimore's

Palmer, Cuellar, and McNally in the ALCS, with Hunter outdueling Palmer 3-0 in the decisive 5th game.

In some ways that series was the end of an era. Oakland went on to outlast the New York Mets in a 7-game World Series. Notable was the fact that Rollie Fingers, the game's first true star relief pitcher, pitched in 6 games and actually led the Oakland staff with 13 2/3 innings. The following year, Oakland again reached the World Series, this time against Los Angeles and their Cy Young Award winner Mike Marshall, a relief pitcher with 106 appearances during the 1974 regular season. Marshall pitched in all 5 games, allowing 1 run and striking out 10 in 9 innings, while his counterpart Fingers had 4 appearances and was the Series MVP with a win and 3 saves as Oakland prevailed 3 games to 1.

Now, 40+ seasons later, no team since the 1973 Oakland A's has ever boasted 3 20-game winners, much less 4. It may never happen again, as 4 man rotations and complete games continue to fade from our memories. The foundation for this transformation, perhaps a long time in coming, was clearly cemented during the two Octobers in 1973 and 1974.

6. Los Angeles Dodgers – Decade Record: 910-701, 3 Divisional Titles, 3 Pennants

During the 1970s the Dodgers were a perennial contender, finishing lower than 2nd place or under .500 only once, in 1979. They ranked 4th in the majors with 910 wins, good for 3rd in the National League, and 98 more than Philadelphia. There was a clear changing of the guard that took place as the holdovers from the '65-'66 World Series teams – Wes Parker, Maury Wills, Willie Davis, Claude Osteen, and Jim Brewer – aged, and by mid decade were replaced by a new core, especially the infield that would play together as starters from mid-1973 through 1981- Steve Garvey at first, Davey Lopes at second, Bill Russell at shortstop, and Ron Cey at third.

Garvey was the team's leader. In the final 6 years of the decade after becoming a full-timer in 1974, Steve finished in the Top 20 in MVP voting each year and the Top 10 4 times. He won 4 Gold Gloves and had 5 seasons of 200+ hits and 4 seasons of 110 or more RBI. The speedy Lopes was an excellent table-setter who stole a team-high 375 bases and tied with Garvey for the team lead in runs (645). Russell led the team with 46 triples and 74 sacrifices, while Cey had 2 100+ RBI seasons and led the Dodgers with 163 home runs.

The common thread from the two eras was Don Sutton, who went 12-12 as a rookie on the 1966 pennant winner and was the 1970s staff ace, leading the team with 166 wins, 117 complete games, 39 shutouts, and 1,767 strikeouts. He won a career-best 21 games in 1976 and fanned 200 or more batters 3 times. Lefty Tommy John went 87-42 as a Dodger with a 2.97 ERA, and most of those wins came after he missed all of 1975 recovering from the innovative new elbow surgery that now bears his name.

The Dodgers finished one game out of first in 1971, and 3½ out in 1973 (despite winning 95 games). They traded Davis to Montreal for relief ace Mike Marshall, and dealt Osteen to Houston for center fielder Jimmy Wynn. In '74 Los Angeles won 102 games and captured their first pennant of the decade. Garvey was a write-in All-Star starter and won National League MVP honors, while Marshall finished 3rd in the MVP balloting and captured the Cy Young Award, going 15-12 with 21 saves and a 2.42 ERA in 106 appearances. Wynn was #5 in the MVP vote, adding 32 home runs and 108 RBI. Right hander Andy Messersmith won 20 games and struck out 221 batters. The Dodgers fell short in the World Series, losing 4 games to 1 as Oakland captured their third straight World Championship.

Following two consecutive second place finishes, the legendary Walter Alston stepped down as manager after 23 seasons at the helm and was replaced by Tom Lasorda, who would lead the Dodgers for the next 21 years. L.A. won another pennant in 1977, with their signature infield, Tommy John's 20 wins, and the additions of outfielders Dusty Baker (acquired from Atlanta for Wynn), Rick Monday (acquired as part of the Bill Buckner trade), and Reggie Smith (acquired from St Louis for Joe Ferguson), who led the league with a .427 OB% and finished 4th in MVP balloting in both '77 and '78. Though not normally known for their power, LA had 4 hitters with 30+ home runs in 1977 (and 5 for all of the decade!) – Garvey, Cey, Smith, and Baker. However in 1977, and again in 1978, the Dodgers were turned away in 6 games by the Reggie Jackson-led Yankees.

Offensive Leaders

Batting Avg		On Base %		Slugging %			
Manny Mota	.313	Manny Mota	.374	Steve Garvey	.468		
Steve Garvey	.304	Wes Parker	.370	Ron Cey	.444		
Willie Davis	.297	Ron Cey	.366	Willie Davis	.440		
Hits		Runs		Stolen Bases			
Steve Garvey	1469	Steve Garvey	645	Davey Lopes	375		
Bill Russell	1279	Davey Lopes	645	Bill Russell	110		
Davey Lopes	1021	Ron Cey	530	Willie Davis	95		
HR		RBI		Doubles		Triples	
Ron Cey	163	Steve Garvey	736	Steve Garvey	248	Bill Russell	46
Steve Garvey	159	Ron Cey	636	Bill Russell	193	Willie Davis	42
Davey Lopes	84	Bill Russell	430	Ron Cey	160	Davey Lopes	36

Pitching Leaders

Wins		Earned Run Average	
Don Sutton	166	Andy Messersmith	2.67
Tommy John	87	Burt Hooton	2.87
Doug Rau	80	Tommy John	2.97
Strikeouts		Shutouts	
Don Sutton	1767	Don Sutton	39
Doug Rau	694	Claude Osteen	15
Burt Hooton	650	Burt Hooton	14
Saves			
Jim Brewer	85		
Charlie Hough	59		
Mike Marshall	42		

Toy Cannon

Pound for pound, there have been few sluggers in Major League history more impressive than Jimmy Wynn. Generously listed in his playing days at 5'9", 170 pounds, Wynn smashed 291 career home runs, with half of them (146) coming in the 1970s. In 1967 he was credited with hitting the longest shot ever at Crosley Field in Cincinnati: a bomb sailing over a 58 foot high scoreboard in left center field and onto Interstate 75, an estimated 507 feet from home plate. And in 1970 he became the first player to hit a ball into the upper deck of the Astrodome.

A high school shortstop, Wynn was signed by his hometown Cincinnati Reds in 1962. After his first year in pro ball he was left unprotected and drafted by the expansion Houston Colt .45s. Wynn started his first game in the majors at shortstop in 1963, but was converted to the outfield for good in 1964. In 1965 Houston changed its name to the Astros and moved into the indoor Astrodome. The 23 year old was the team's starting center fielder and led his club in homeruns (22), RBI (73), stolen bases (43 – a career high), and outfield assists (13). His surprising pop at the plate and rocket arm earned him the nickname "Toy Cannon".

Over the next 7 years Wynn established himself as one of the greatest Astros of all time, and one of the game's top offensive stars. In 1967 he was an All-Star selection, driving in 107 runs and scoring 102 runs while belting a career high 37 HRs despite playing his home games in the spacious Astrodome. Atlanta's Hank Aaron, whose home park was cozy Fulton County Stadium and led the league with 39 home runs, commented that he considered Wynn the season's true home run champion. In 1969 Wynn hit 33 home runs and scored 113, but most notable were his phenomenal 148 walks and .436 on-base percentage. In 1972 Wynn set another career high with 117 runs scored, to go with 29 doubles, 24 home runs and 103 walks. In all, the patient Wynn exceeded 100 walks in a season 6 times.

After the 1973 season Wynn was traded to the Los Angeles Dodgers for pitcher Claude Osteen. Wynn's veteran presence was a key for the young 1974 Dodgers, as LA won their first National League pennant in 8 years. Hitting in the 3 spot all year in front of eventual MVP Steve Garvey, Wynn drove in 108 runs and led the club in home runs (32), runs scored (104), walks (108), slugging (.497), and on base % (.387). He was honored as Comeback Player of the Year, finished #5 in MVP voting, and was named to his second All-Star team.

By 1975 Wynn developed shoulder issues, and though he was selected to his third All-Star team, he missed 32 games and was never again the same player. Wynn was traded to Atlanta in 1976, and managed 17 home runs with a league leading 127 walks. He signed with the Yankees that off-season, and in his first at-bat on Opening Day of 1977 at Yankee Stadium, Wynn hit the last home run of his career. Fittingly, it was a tape measure shot, traveling an estimated 435 feet to straight away centerfield. The Toy Cannon went out as he had come in, with a blast.

7. <u>Boston Red Sox</u> – Decade Record: 895-714, 1 Division Title, 1 Pennant

Boston had baseball's 5th best regular season 1970s record, ahead of New York, Kansas City, and Oakland. The Red Sox, along with the Orioles, were the only teams to finish above .500 in every season during the decade. But they came away with only a single division title, winning the pennant in 1975, and staging a classic World Series against Cincinnati. Most memorable was Carlton Fisk's 12th inning game-winning home run in Game 6 before the Sox fell short in the decisive seventh game.

Boston finished third in the AL East 5 times, and second four times, including a back-breaking collapse in 1978 when they blew a 14 game lead against the Yankees. Nearly as gut-wrenching for hardcore Sox fans was the surprising 1972 season. Buoyed by Rookie of the Year Carlton Fisk and the unexpected excellence of pitcher Luis Tiant, Boston took Detroit to the season's final weekend but finished a half game behind.

No individual performance stands out more than the 1975 season of center fielder Fred Lynn, who hit .331 and notched Rookie of the Year, Gold Glove, and MVP honors. Lynn might have been even better in 1979, when he slugged .637 with 42 doubles and 39 HR. Left fielder Jim Rice was the 1978 MVP on the strength of 46 HR and 139 RBI. Carl Yastrzemski was the only other Boston hitter to top 40 homers, hitting

40 in 1970 with a .329 batting average that fell percentage points short of the batting title, and a .452 on-base % that was the AL's best single season mark in the decade.

Outfielders Lynn and Dwight Evans won three Gold Gloves each, with Yastrzemski taking two. Fisk (C), George Scott (1B), and Rick Burleson (SS) all earned one.

Luis Tiant was the franchise's best pitcher, with a 122-81 record, 3.36 E.R.A. and 26 shutouts from 1971-78. In addition, he was a post-season workhorse; his 3-0 mark included 25 gritty innings pitched in the 1975 World Series. Tiant had 3 20-win seasons, but his best year was in 1972. He began that season in the bullpen, but wound up starting 19 games, going the distance in 9 of his last 10 starts. Tiant finished 1972 with an overall record of 15-6, with 6 shutouts and a 1.91 E.R.A.

Offensive Leaders

Batting Avg		On Base %		Slugging %	
Jim Rice	.310	Carl Yastrzemski	.384	Jim Rice	.552
Fred Lynn	.309	Fred Lynn	.383	Fred Lynn	.526
Reggie Smith	.290	Reggie Smith	.367	Reggie Smith	.493

Hits		Runs		Stolen Bases	
Carl Yastrzemski	1492	Carl Yastrzemski	845	Tommy Harper	107
Jim Rice	976	Carlton Fisk	554	Carl Yastrzemski	88
Carlton Fisk	959	Jim Rice	515	Rick Burleson	55

HR		RBI		Doubles		Triples	
Carl Yastrzemski	202	Carl Yastrzemski	846	Carl Yastrzemski	247	Jim Rice	49
Jim Rice	172	Jim Rice	583	Fred Lynn	185	Carlton Fisk	30
Carlton Fisk	144	Carlton Fisk	506	Carlton Fisk	182	Fred Lynn	26

Pitching Leaders

Wins		Earned Run Average	
Luis Tiant	122	Dennis Eckersley	2.99
Bill Lee	93	Luis Tiant	3.36
Rick Wise	47	Sonny Siebert	3.37

Strikeouts		Shutouts	
Luis Tiant	1075	Luis Tiant	26
Bill Lee	533	Sonny Siebert	9
Ray Culp	432	Bill Lee	7
		John Curtis	7
Saves		Rick Wise	7
Bill Campbell	44		
Dick Drago	38		
Sparky Lyle	36		

8. <u>Kansas City Royals</u> – Decade Record: 851-760, 3 Division Titles, 0 Pennants

A 1969 expansion team, the Royals spent little time as a second division club before making their mark as one of the finest organizations in baseball. Kansas City had three losing seasons during the 1970s, and finished in either 1st or 2nd place in the other seven. Not coincidentally, the team's good year/bad year pattern from '70-'74 came to an end when third baseman George Brett became a regular in 1975. The Royals won a franchise-high 91 games that year, finishing 7 games behind their nemesis Oakland. By 1976 KC passed the A's for good, winning their first of three straight AL West titles.

Brett emerged as one of the decade's greatest players, leading the club with a .310 average and .475 slugging %. In the years '75-'79 he was the game's most complete hitter, finishing in the Top 20 in MVP voting each year, winning a batting title in 1976, and pacing the league in hits 3 times ('75 – 195, '76 – 215, '79 – 212), triples twice ('75 – 13, '76 – 14, '79 -20), and doubles once ('78 – 45). The Royals built the foundation of a strong lineup with one-sided trades that brought in outfielder Hal McRae from Cincinnati, centerfielder Amos Otis from the Mets, and first baseman John Mayberry from Houston. Otis played the entire decade in KC and led the team in games, hits, runs scored, doubles, home runs, and RBI. He won 3 Gold Gloves and led the American League in doubles twice and stolen bases once. McRae became the league's best designated hitter, hitting .294 with 251 doubles in 7 seasons with the Royals, including 54 two-baggers in 1977, the best single season mark all decade.

Mayberry was the Royals top power threat, eclipsing 100 RBI three times and banging 143 home runs and 552 RBI in 6 seasons. John's tenure in Kansas City ended badly, however. After a late night outing, he showed up late for Game 4 of the 1977 ALCS against the Yankees, and proceeded to strike out twice and drop a popup and a routine infield throw. He was benched for the remainder of the game and for the deciding Game 5. Manager Whitey Herzog blamed Mayberry for the Royals' ALCS loss and had him traded in the off-season.

Other key players were shortstop Fred Patek, who stole 336 bases, second baseman Frank White, a three-time Gold Glover, catcher Darrel Porter, and outfielders Al Cowens and speedster Willie Wilson.

The Kansas City pitching was solid, if not spectacular. Paul Splittorff (123-106) and Dennis Leonard (87-62) were the co-aces of the decade. Larry Gura pitched well in relief in 1976 and '77, before moving into the starting rotation in '78 and turning in a 16-4 season. Gura went 41-21 with a 3.40 ERA from 1976-79. Steve Busby won 56 games and threw 2 no hitters within his first 3 full seasons from 1973-75, but then suffered a rotator cuff tear and finished his career with only 70 wins. The main bullpen contributors were Ted Abernathy, Doug Bird, and Al Hrabosky.

The Royals could not get past the Yankees in 3 straight ALCS, losing in 5 games in '76 and '77, and in 4 in 1978. This despite the efforts of Brett, who hit a torrid .375 (21-56) over the 14 games with 4 HR, 4 triples, 10 RBI, 13 runs scored, and a .768 slugging percentage. Kansas City finally broke the spell and won their first pennant in 1980, and a World Series Championship in 1985.

Offensive Leaders							
Batting Avg		On Base %		Slugging %			
George Brett	.310	John Mayberry	.374	George Brett	.475		
Hal McRae	.294	Paul Schaal	.361	Hal McRae	.458		
Lou Piniella	.286	Hal McRae	.360	John Mayberry	.448		
Hits		Runs		Stolen Bases			
Amos Otis	1549	Amos Otis	861	Freddie Patek	336		
George Brett	1082	Freddie Patek	571	Amos Otis	294		
Hal McRae	1042	George Brett	532	Willie Wilson	137		
HR		RBI		Doubles		Triples	
Amos Otis	159	Amos Otis	753	Amos Otis	286	George Brett	73
John Mayberry	143	John Mayberry	552	Hal McRae	251	Amos Otis	53
Hal McRae	84	Hal McRae	520	George Brett	211	Al Cowens	44

Pitching Leaders			
Wins		Earned Run Average	
Paul Splittorff	123	Larry Gura	3.40
Dennis Leonard	87	Al Fitzmorris	3.45
Al Fitzmorris	69	Marty Pattin	3.46
Strikeouts		Shutouts	
Dennis Leonard	857	Paul Splittorff	17
Paul Splittorff	817	Dennis Leonard	16
Steve Busby	647	Al Fitzmorris	11
Saves			
Doug Bird	58		
Ted Abernathy	40		
Al Hrabosky	31		

George Brett: Ceaseless Intensity

George Brett's Hall of Fame plaque begins, "Played each game with ceaseless intensity and unbridled passion". This is the highest compliment any athlete can receive, and one that can be said of few modern-day players. Nothing demonstrates this more than Brett's ALCS performances against the Yankees from 1976-78, and in particular, on October 6, 1978, when he crushed 3 home runs. Brett was the ultimate gamer – in the post season he played even better than his normal superstar level.

Brett entered the 1978 ALCS a lifetime .305 hitter who had won the 1976 batting title and had averaged 8 home runs a year, including 9 during the 1978 regular season. With the Series tied 1-1, the Royals faced the Yankee's big-game pitcher Catfish Hunter, and Brett led off Game 3 by taking a high fastball into Yankee Stadium's upper deck in straight away right field. In the 3rd inning Catfish stayed off the fat part of the plate, but Brett crushed his low and away offering for a 400 foot bomb to right center, breaking a 1-1 tie.

He came up in the 4th with 2 out, the same 2-1 score, and team-leading base stealer Freddie Patek on first base. Patek was nailed trying to swipe second, taking the bat out of the red-hot Brett's hands. After the Yankees took a 3-2 lead in their half of the 4th, he led off the 5th. Hunter gave him a big curve on the outside corner at the knees, but Brett reached out and to pulled it over the right field fence to tie the score; he was in that kind of zone. Brett flew out in his last two at bats against Goose Gossage, and the Yankees rallied to win the game, 6-5. They wrapped up the Series and another pennant the next day.

By 1978 Brett was no stranger to the Yankees in the ALCS – but he was becoming their recurring nightmare. He had averaged .444 in the 1976 ALCS, including a game tying 3-run homer in the 8th inning of Game 5 before the Yank's Chris Chambliss hit the famous walk-off game winner in the 9th. In 1977 Brett hit .300 against New York, with his biggest blow a Game 5 first inning RBI triple that touched off a bench clearing brawl between Brett and Graig Nettles. The Royals went ahead 2-0 and then 3-2 before losing the lead on a 3-run Yankee 9th inning.

In the three series from 1976-78 Brett finished a combined 21-56 (.375) over 14 games with 4 HR, 4 triples, 10 RBI, and 13 runs scored. His slugging % was .768. Yet in all 3 years New York captured the pennant. KC finally turned the tables in 1980; behind season MVP Brett they swept New York in 3 games to advance to their first World Series – George's go-ahead 3-run homer in the 7th locked up the final game. In 1985 Kansas City returned to the World Series and captured their first World Championship, and as expected, Brett led all hitters with a .370 batting average. Overall in 43 career post-season games Brett hit .337 with 10 HR, 23 RBI, 30 runs, and a .627 slugging %.

The last sentence on Brett's plaque says it all – "A clutch hitter whose profound respect for the game led to universal reverence". Just ask the Yankees.

9. <u>Philadelphia Phillies</u> – Decade Record: 812-801, 3 Division Titles, 0 Pennants

Imagine a team with a Cy Young Award winning pitcher who sweeps the 'triple crown' of pitching with 27 wins, 310 strikeouts, and a 1.97 ERA. You also have a Gold Glove shortstop leading the league in triples (13), and your centerfielder leads the league with 39 doubles. Not bad right? Wrong. The 1972 Phillies went 59-97, 37 ½ games behind the first place Pirates. Steve Carlton had the most dominant pitching year of the decade, winning 45.8% of his team's games, a record that still stands. The Phils' second leading pitcher registered 7 wins. And the accomplishments of Larry Bowa and Willie Montanez were not nearly enough to prevent the offense from sputtering; the club had only 99 home runs and 42 stolen bases, and ranked last in runs scored.

'72 was just one year of seven straight where the Phils had a losing record, but hope was on the way. Mike Schmidt had been drafted a year earlier in 1971 out of Ohio University, while left fielder Greg Luzinski, a 1968 1st round pick, and catcher Bob Boone, drafted in 1969, moved into the starting lineup. In mid-1975 centerfielder Garry Maddox was acquired from the Giants for Montanez, and the Phillies closed out the decade with 5 straight winning seasons, including two 101 win years and three straight division championships. Maddox won five consecutive Gold Gloves, earning the nickname "The Minister of Defense". Announcer Harry Kalas said "2/3 of the earth is covered by water and the other third is covered by Garry Maddox". For the decade Maddox also stole 134 bases and hit .296 as a Phillie, with a career best .330 in 1976. Bowa played the entire decade in Philadelphia, winning two Gold Gloves and leading the team in hits (1552), runs (725), triples (74), steals (251), and sacrifices (116). His double play partner for three years at second was Dave Cash, who batted .296 with 608 hits and 292 runs from '74-'76 before leaving for Montreal via free agency. The middle of the order was manned by Luzinski (204 HR and team-high 755 RBI, including a league leading 120 in 1975 and 130 in 1977), who enjoyed four straight All-Star appearances and Top 10 MVP finishes, and Mike Schmidt. After struggling initially, Schmidt came into his own in the latter part of the decade, capturing 4 Gold Gloves and 3 straight home run titles. He was the decade's top third baseman and eventually established himself as the best ever at his position by the time he retired in 1987. Bake McBride became the starting left fielder in 1977, and hit .303 from '77-79 with 33 homers (which he liked to call 'Bake Taters'). Boone, a Stanford graduate and second generation major leaguer, was a steady presence behind the dish who made 3 All-Star appearances and won 2 Gold Gloves during the 70s (he won 5 more Gold Gloves during the 80s).

Carlton was the Phil's undisputed ace, taking the 1977 Cy Young Award to go with his 1972 trophy, and went 148-98 overall with a 3.07 ERA. When the Phils traded Don Money to Milwaukee to make room for Schmidt at third, they acquired Jim Lonborg, who became Philly's second winningest pitcher at 75-60. The bullpen, a weakness in the first half the 70's, was manned capably once Tug McGraw (3.26, 59 saves) was acquired after the 1974 season from the Mets for John Stearns. Other key bullpen contributors were Ron Reed (2.86, 51 saves), and side-armer Gene Garber (2.68, 51 saves).

Despite Philadelphia's turn-around in fortunes in the second half of the decade, which coincided with Danny Ozark's hiring in 1974, the club did not capture a pennant during the 70s. They were swept by the powerhouse Reds in '76, then lost consecutive NLCS in 4 games to the Dodgers in '77 and '78. The 1978 series was especially hard to swallow, as Maddox made two errors in the 10th inning of Game 4. In '79 Pete Rose was acquired as a free agent, and did not disappoint, hitting .331 with 208 hits, including 40 doubles. But the team slumped to 4th place and Ozark was replaced by Dallas Green. Philly would finally get a pennant, and a World Series title, in 1980.

Offensive Leaders								
Batting Avg		On Base %		Slugging %				
Dave Cash	.296	Mike Schmidt	.374	Mike Schmidt	.511			
Garry Maddox	.296	Greg Luzinski	.365	Greg Luzinski	.493			
Greg Luzinski	.285	Dave Cash	.348	Garry Maddox	.434			
Hits		Runs		Stolen Bases				
Larry Bowa	1552	Larry Bowa	725	Larry Bowa	251			
Greg Luzinski	1215	Mike Schmidt	674	Garry Maddox	134			
Mike Schmidt	947	Greg Luzinski	574	Mike Schmidt	117			
HR		RBI		Doubles		Triples		
Mike Schmidt	235	Greg Luzinski	755	Greg Luzinski	234	Larry Bowa	74	
Greg Luzinski	204	Mike Schmidt	666	Mike Schmidt	183	Garry Maddox	33	
Deron Johnson	71	Bob Boone	377	Larry Bowa	176	Mike Schmidt	31	

Pitching Leaders			
Wins		Earned Run Average	
Steve Carlton	148	Steve Carlton	3.07
Jim Lonborg	75	Wayne Twitchell	3.57
Larry Christenson	63	Barry Lersch	3.62
Strikeouts		Shutouts	
Steve Carlton	1732	Steve Carlton	26
Wayne Twitchell	573	Jim Lonborg	7
Jim Lonborg	548	Woodie Fryman	7
Saves			
Tug McGraw	59		
Ron Reed	51		
Gene Garber	51		

Greatest Game Performances of the 1970s

Back on April 17, 1976, the Phillies' Mike Schmidt clubbed 4 home runs with 8 RBI in a wild 18-16 win over the Cubs at Wrigley Field, the only 4 HR game of the decade. Schmidt also had a single in the game, going 5 for 6 in all, for a decade-best 17 total bases. An interesting side note: Philly trailed in the game 12-1 and 13-2. There were 57 3 HR games in the 70s; Schmidt had one and Dave Kingman had the most with 4, 3 as a Cub and 1 for the Mets.

As part of his magical 1975 rookie season, Boston's Fred Lynn had a 3 HR game, and also added a triple and single, going 5-6 with a decade-best 10 RBI in a 15-1 drubbing over Detroit. Other decade bests in a single game include 5 runs scored (done 20 times), 4 doubles (done by Dave Duncan of Baltimore, Jim Mason of the Yankees, and Boston's Orlando Cepeda), and 5 Stolen Bases (Bert Campaneris for Oakland, Dave Lopes for the Dodgers, and Amos Otis for Kansas City). The Dodgers' Steve Garvey and Pittsburgh's Willie Stargell were the only players with 5 extra-base hits in a game, each registering 2 HR and 3 doubles.

In 1975, the Pirates' Rennie Stennett set a 9-inning game record (also against the Cubs at Wrigley) with 7 hits – 4 singles, 2 doubles and a triple in a 22-0 blowout. In 1970 Cesar Gutierrez, a shortstop for Detroit, also had 7 hits, in a 12-inning 9-8 win over Cleveland. The only other 2 players to ever record as many hits in a game were Detroit's Rocky Colavito, who had 7 in a 1962 22-inning loss to the Yankees, and Johnny Burnett of Cleveland, who registered 9 hits in an 18 inning game back in 1932.

Finally, what about the best post-season offensive performances in the decade? George Brett of Kansas City hit 3 home runs in a 1978 ALCS loss to the Yankees, and in 1971 Bob Robertson of Pittsburgh had 3 HR, a double and 5 RBI in a 9-4 NLCS win over San

Francisco. In the 1977 World Series Reggie Jackson went 3-3 with a walk and 5 RBI, hitting 3 HR on consecutive pitches thrown to him as the Yankees closed out the Los Angeles Dodgers 8-4 in Game 6. And in the decade's final game, the Pirates' Willie Stargell went 4-5 with a double and a home run in Game 7 of the 1979 World Series, a 4-1 victory over Baltimore.

10. <u>Minnesota Twins</u> – Decade Record: 812-794, 1 Division Title, 0 Pennants

The Twins began the 70s with a second straight American League Western Division title, winning 98 games. Harmon Killebrew, the defending American League Most Valuable Player, crushed 41 home runs and drove in 113, and finished 3rd in the MVP voting. His teammate Tony Oliva finished 2nd, hitting .325 with 107 RBI while leading the league with 204 hits and tying for the league lead in doubles (36) with outfield mate Cesar Tovar. Tovar also led the AL with 13 triples. On the mound Jim Perry enjoyed his second straight 20-win season, going a career best 24-12 and capturing Cy Young Award honors. Reliever Ron Perranoski was Fireman of the Year with an American League record 34 saves. Unfortunately the Twins were swept 3 straight for the second consecutive year in the ALCS by the Baltimore Orioles, who had won 108 games during the regular season and would go on to the World Championship.

In 1971, despite Tony Oliva's batting (.337) and slugging (.546) titles, Tovar's league leading 204 hits, and Killebrew's league leading 119 RBI, the Twins slumped to fifth place at 74-86, 26 ½ games out of first. They did not win another division title or finish higher than third place again during the decade, with 8 straight 3rd or 4th place finishes. The AL West belonged to Oakland and then Kansas City from '71-'78 until California took the title in 1979.

Minnesota's mediocrity was certainly no fault of Hall of Famer Rod Carew, one of the game's top players. Carew took 6 batting titles and 4 on base % titles during the decade, leading all players with an overall .343 batting average, .408 on-base %, and 80 triples. In 1977 he was the league's Most Valuable Player, leading the majors in hitting (.388-the highest average in the baseball since Ted Williams hit .406 in 1941), OB% (.449), hits (239), and runs scored (128), while also pacing the AL with 16 triples. Other notable performers for the Twins included Killebrew, who led the franchise with 113 home runs despite only playing 5 70s seasons in Minnesota, Larry Hisle, who took the RBI crown in 1977 with 119, Roy Smalley, who emerged as one of the game's best hitting shortstops, and catcher Butch Wynegar, an All-Star in his first two seasons in 1976-'77.

Bert Blyleven (99-90, 2.80 ERA) and Dave Goltz (96-79, 3.48) were the staff's aces, and the only pitchers besides Perry and Jerry Koosman (20-13 in 1979) to win 20 games in a season during the decade. Minnesota had strong relief pitching throughout the 1970s - in addition to Perranoski, Bill Campbell saved 51 games from 1973-76 and went 17-5 with 20 saves in 167 innings out of the pen in 1976 before signing with Boston as a free agent. In 1978 Minnesota signed veteran Mike Marshall, who saved 53 games for the Twins with a 2.57 ERA from 1978-79.

Offensive Leaders

Batting Avg		On Base %		Slugging %	
Rod Carew	.345	Rod Carew	.407	Rod Carew	.460
Tony Oliva	.299	Steve Braun	.376	Larry Hisle	.457
Cesar Tovar	.293	Harmon Killebrew	.373	Harmon Killebrew	.451

Hits		Runs		Stolen Bases	
Rod Carew	1657	Rod Carew	759	Rod Carew	235
Tony Oliva	823	Larry Hisle	369	Larry Hisle	92
Larry Hisle	697	Steve Braun	333	Cesar Tovar	69

HR		RBI		Doubles		Triples	
Harmon Killebrew	113	Rod Carew	584	Rod Carew	226	Rod Carew	77
Tony Oliva	88	Tony Oliva	412	Tony Oliva	116	Lyman Bostock	26
Larry Hisle	87	Larry Hisle	409	Larry Hisle	109	Dan Ford	25

Pitching Leaders

Wins		Earned Run Average	
Bert Blyleven	99	Bert Blyleven	2.80
Dave Goltz	96	Jim Kaat	3.46
Jim Perry	54	Dave Goltz	3.48

Strikeouts		Shutouts	
Bert Blyleven	1402	Bert Blyleven	24
Dave Goltz	887	Dave Goltz	11
Jim Kaat	414	Jim Kaat	7

Saves	
Mike Marshall	53
Bill Campbell	51
Ron Perranoski	39

11. <u>San Francisco Giants</u> – Decade Record: 794-818, 1 Division Title, 0 Pennants

The Giants of the 1970s started with an aging core of all-time greats who were never sufficiently replaced. Willie Mays hit .291 with 28 home runs and 91 runs scored in 1970, led the league with a .425 on-base % as a 40-year-old in 1971, then declined quickly and was traded to the Mets in mid-'72. Willie McCovey wrapped up a three year period from '68-'70 where he was the best hitter on the planet (.300, 120HR, 357 RBI while leading the league in slugging and OPS all three seasons) – with a great 1970: 39 HR, 39 doubles, 126 RBI, 137 walks, and a major league leading .612 slugging% that was somehow only good enough for 9th in MVP voting. Stretch was just 32 at the time, and though he remained a solid pro for the remainder of the decade, he never came close to those numbers again. Willie was traded away in 1973 and re-acquired in 1977.

Juan Marichal had a similar career trajectory, winning 20 games 6 times during the 60s, but he never did it again after 1969 at age 31, and had only one more solid season, in 1971, when he went 18-11 with a 2.94 ERA. Gaylord Perry notched a 23-13 mark with 214 strikeouts in 1970, but was traded in 1971 for Sam McDowell, who won 19 games in total the rest of his career, 11 with the Giants. Meanwhile Perry won 180 more games, including 3 20 win seasons and 2 Cy Young Awards.

Ah, the trades. San Francisco's farm system produced an almost endless supply of outfield talent like George Foster, Garry Maddox, Dave Kingman, and 1973 Rookie of the Year Gary Matthews, and lost or traded them all away, receiving little or nothing in return. They even swapped Bobby Bonds to the Yankees, but they did get Bobby Murcer in return, and heck, *everyone* traded Bobby Bonds. Bonds played for 8 different clubs during his career, but had his longest stint in San Francisco. There he established himself as one of the game's most talented stars, and in only 5 seasons as a Giant during the decade tallied 590 runs, 867 hits, 153 doubles, 31 triples, and 202 stolen bases, all '70s Giants bests. His 145 HR and 427 RBI ranked second only to McCovey. Overall in the 1970s Bonds enjoyed 4 30-30 seasons, won 3 Gold Gloves, ranked 4th in the majors in both home runs (280) and steals (380), and tied Reggie Jackson for the most extra base hits (586).

San Francisco opened the decade with two winning seasons, including a division title in 1971. The Giants took Game 1 of the NLCS against Pittsburgh, but then dropped three straight. After a down 1972 they rebounded well with 88 wins and third place in 1973, mostly on the strength of a monster year from Bonds (131 runs, 39 home runs, 34 doubles, 43 steals), plus solid contributions from McCovey (29 homers) and Matthews (12 HR, 51 RBI, .300), and the pitching of Ron Bryant (24-12). The franchise faltered after that, enjoying their only other winning season of the decade in 1978 (89-73, 3rd place).

That '78 club was led by second year man Jack (The Ripper) Clark (.306, 25 HR, 46 2B, 98 RBI), former A's lefty Vida Blue (NL All-Star starter, 18-10), Bob Knepper (17-11), and Bill Madlock (.309). Madlock won 2 batting titles with the Cubs before the Giants acquired him in a good trade for an over-the-hill Bobby Murcer. Mad Dog hit .296 in 3 years with San Francisco before being traded away to the Pirates, where he won two more batting titles. Other notables in the decade included catcher Dick Dietz' career year in 1970, (23-107-.300), John Montefusco's Rookie of the Year award in 1975 (15-9, 2.88, 215K), 3 – time All-Star Shortstop Chris Speier, and closer Gary Lavelle (43-38, 74 saves, 2.66 ERA).

This was a franchise with enough talent passing through its doors to accomplish more, but the judgment and timing of their transactions prevented them from making consistent challenges to the Reds and Dodgers in the NL West.

Offensive Leaders							
Batting Avg		**On Base %**		**Slugging %**			
Gary Matthews	.287	Willie McCovey	.375	Willie McCovey	.489		
Garry Maddox	.287	Gary Matthews	.367	Bobby Bonds	.487		
Bobby Bonds	.278	Bobby Bonds	.358	Jack Clark	.472		
Hits		**Runs**		**Stolen Bases**			
Bobby Bonds	867	Bobby Bonds	590	Bobby Bonds	202		
Chris Speier	799	Chris Speier	373	Garry Maddox	59		
Tito Fuentes	718	Willie McCovey	345	Bill North	58		
HR		**RBI**		**Doubles**		**Triples**	
Willie McCovey	155	Willie McCovey	513	Bobby Bonds	153	Bobby Bonds	31
Bobby Bonds	145	Bobby Bonds	427	Chris Speier	127	Chris Speier	26
Dave Kingman	77	Chris Speier	350	Willie McCovey	123	Tito Fuentes	26

Pitching Leaders			
Wins		**Earned Run Average**	
Jim Barr	81	Gary Lavelle	2.66
John Montefusco	55	Gaylord Perry	3.00
Ron Bryant	53	John Montefusco	3.38
Strikeouts		**Shutouts**	
John Montefusco	784	Jim Barr	19
Ed Halicki	677	Ed Halicki	13
Jim Barr	567	John Montefusco	11
Saves			
Randy Moffitt	83		
Gary Lavelle	74		
Don McMahon	34		

12. <u>Detroit Tigers</u> – Decade Record: 789-820, 1 Division Title, 0 Pennants

Flanked somewhere between the aging nucleus of the dominant World Champion 1968 Tiger team that won 103 games, and the building of a young nucleus for a team that would win 104 games and the 1984 World Championship, were the Detroit Tigers of the 1970s. Detroit had the misfortune of playing in perhaps the decade's strongest division, the American League East, where in 5 of 10 seasons at least one team won 100 games.

The old guard was led by Hall of Famer Al Kaline (399 lifetime home runs and 3,007 hits), sluggers Willie Horton and Jim Northrup, fellow outfielder Mickey Stanley ('70 and '73 Gold Glove), plus first baseman Norm Cash (377 lifetime home runs), All-Star catcher Bill Freehan, and longtime left-handed ace Mickey Lolich.

After a disappointing 1970, the club traded Denny McClain, a former 31 win pitcher who had been suspended for gambling and drug use, to Washington for third baseman Aurelio Rodriguez (1976 Gold Glove) shortstop Ed Brinkman (1972 Gold Glove), and pitcher Joe Coleman.

They hired fiery Billy Martin as their manager and the club won 91 games in 1971, only to finish 12 behind the powerful Baltimore Orioles. Lolich enjoyed his best season, going 25-12 with 308 strikeouts, while Coleman went 20-9 with 236 Ks. They formed one of the game's best 1-2 tandems in the early 1970s. Lolich reeled off 200+ strikeouts 6 straight years from 1969-74 and Coleman did it 3 straight times from '71-'73; they also reached 20 wins twice apiece.

In 1972 the club went 86-71 and won the division by 1/2 game over Boston, but they were upended by Oakland in the ALCS in 5 games. That bizarre playoff series saw the normally mild mannered Oakland shortstop Bert Campaneris, who had been running wild on Detroit, take a pitch off his kneecap and then hurl his bat at pitcher Lerrin LaGrow. The A's felt certain that Billy Martin had ordered LaGrow to throw at Campy. Oakland won the series with a 2-1 victory in Game 5, tying the game on a Reggie Jackson steal of home.

The '73 Detroit club was nearly as strong, winning 85 games, but Martin wore out his welcome and was fired in September; from there the veteran squad was broken up for good. The rebuilding began with two consecutive last place finishes, including a disastrous 57-102 1975.

Detroit enjoyed a revival of sorts in 1976 as flakey rookie pitcher Mark 'The Bird' Fidrych became a national phenomenon, starting the All-Star game and capturing Rookie of the Year honors with 19 wins and a 2.34 ERA. Fidrych was joined in the starting All-Star lineup by outfielders Ron Leflore (a former heroin addict discovered in a prison baseball league) and Rusty Staub, who was acquired from the Mets in exchange for Mickey Lolich, and drove in 318 runs for Detroit from '76-'78.

It took until 1978 for the Tigers to return to their winning ways behind Leflore's league-leading 68 stolen bases and 126 runs, Staub's 121 RBI, and the freshman double play tandem of shortstop Alex Trammell and Rookie of the Year second baseman Lou Whitaker. Detroit's 86 wins were only good for 5th place in a crowded AL East that saw four teams win over 90 games. But another championship nucleus was being built with Trammell and Whitaker, who played together for 1,918 games, plus 23 year old battery mates Lance Parrish and Jack Morris. All four would rank among the very top players at their positions for the next 10-15 years.

Offensive Leaders

Batting Avg		On Base %		Slugging %	
Ron LeFlore	.297	Steve Kemp	.373	Norm Cash	.469
Steve Kemp	.283	Al Kaline	.366	Willie Horton	.458
Willie Horton	.282	Norm Cash	.359	Steve Kemp	.450

Hits		Runs		Stolen Bases	
Aurelio Rodriguez	1040	Ron LeFlore	532	Ron LeFlore	294
Ron LeFlore	970	Aurelio Rodriguez	417	Ben Oglivie	41
Willie Horton	796	Mickey Stanley	397	Lou Whitaker	29

HR		RBI		Doubles		Triples	
Willie Horton	121	Willie Horton	425	Aurelio Rodriguez	193	Ron LeFlore	38
Norm Cash	95	Aurelio Rodriguez	423	Mickey Stanley	129	Mickey Stanley	34
Jason Thompson	94	Rusty Staub	358	Ron LeFlore	126	Aurelio Rodriguez	31

Pitching Leaders

Wins		Earned Run Average	
Mickey Lolich	105	John Hiller	2.74
Joe Coleman	88	Dave Rozema	3.19
John Hiller	69	Mickey Lolich	3.45

Strikeouts		Shutouts	
Mickey Lolich	1343	Mickey Lolich	18
Joe Coleman	1000	Joe Coleman	11
John Hiller	812	Mark Fidrych	5

Saves	
John Hiller	115
Fred Scherman	34
Tom Timmermann	32

13. <u>New York Mets</u> – Decade Record: 763-850, 1 Division Title, 1
    Pennant

The Mets entered the decade as defending World Champions, but there
would be no miracles in Queens to speak of during the 1970s. The Mets
did manage a pennant in 1973, when they took the division no one
seemed to want to take, with an 82-79 mark. '73 was actually the Mets'
worst record of the decade up to that point – from 1970-72 New York
won 83 games each year. A disappointing 5th place finish in 1974 was
followed by two more 3rd place finishes, including a high of 86 wins in
1976. Then the bottom fell out on the franchise, as key players were
traded away, and the club suffered through three straight last place
finishes.

The Mets were continually plagued by an anemic lineup – when 1970
Gold Glove outfielder Tommy Agee scored 107 runs, it turned out to be
the only time a Met would reach 100 runs in a season all decade. During
those years only Cleon Jones (.319 in 1971), Len Randle (.304 in 1977),
and Lee Mazzilli (.303 in 1979) hit over .300 in a full season. Power was
in short supply as well; first baseman John Milner led the club during the
decade with 94 home runs and 338 RBI, while all-or-nothing slugger
Dave Kingman was the only Met to reach 30 home runs (36 in 1975 and
37 in 1976). Rusty Staub was the only Met to reach the century mark
with 105 RBI in 1975.

The trademark pitching staff carried the club, particularly ace Tom
Seaver, the 1973 and 1975 Cy Young Award winner. In Seaver's 7 full
seasons during the decade in New York he went 132-78 with a 2.54 ERA,

and led the National League in strikeouts 5 times and ERA 3 times. Other mainstays were lefty starters Jerry Koosman (104 wins, 3.29 ERA), and 1972 Rookie of the Year Jon Matlack (82 wins, 3.03 ERA, 26 shutouts). Tug McGraw (73 saves, 2.90 ERA) and Skip Lockwood (65 saves, 2.80) paced the bullpen.

1973 was by far the Mets most (only?) entertaining season of the 70s; in all other years they were either middle of the road or flat-out terrible. In last place in late August, the Mets went 24-11 the rest of the way, capturing the division while riding the 'Ya Gotta Believe' slogan of McGraw (0.88 ERA with 12 saves and 5 wins in his final 19 appearances). They then surprised the defending National League champion Big Red Machine, winners of 99 games during the regular season, in a 5 game NLCS. The series was overshadowed by the Game 3 brawl between Mets shortstop Bud Harrelson and Cincinnati left fielder Pete Rose, the NL MVP who hit crucial late-inning home runs in both Reds wins.

In the World Series against the Oakland A's, New York fell just short despite Rusty Staub hitting .423 with a bad shoulder. After the Mets took a 3-2 Series lead, Oakland captured the last two games on the heroics of American League regular season and World Series MVP Reggie Jackson.

If 1973 was the decade's high point, the low came on June 15, 1977 when 'The Franchise', Tom Seaver, was traded to the Reds for Steve Henderson, Pat Zachry, Doug Flynn and Dan Norman. While Henderson and Flynn became serviceable players, the team's icon and winning identity was lost. A year earlier Staub had been dealt away for Mickey Lolich. Dave Kingman, New York's only remaining power threat, was traded the same night as Seaver for Paul Siebert and a washed-up Bobby Valentine. By the end of the year Matlack was also dealt, and a year later Koosman was swapped to Minnesota in a trade that did net eventual 1980s relief ace Jesse Orosco.

The Mets lost 95+ games in the final three seasons of the decade, but did feature a couple of solid young players such as Henderson (.285 average), Mazzilli (team-high .362 OB% and 81 stolen bases), and catcher John Stearns, who made 2 70s All-Star teams and 4 overall. Pitcher Craig Swan led the league with a 2.43 ERA in 1978, and won a career high 14 games in '79.

Offensive Leaders

Batting Avg		On Base %		Slugging %	
Cleon Jones	.279	Lee Mazzilli	.362	Rusty Staub	.428
Felix Millan	.278	Rusty Staub	.361	John Milner	.415
Ed Kranepool	.276	Wayne Garrett	.357	Cleon Jones	.409

Hits		Runs		Stolen Bases	
Felix Millan	743	Wayne Garrett	351	Bud Harrelson	91
Ed Kranepool	705	Bud Harrelson	328	Lee Mazzilli	81
Bud Harrelson	680	John Milner	315	Tommie Agee	67

HR		RBI		Doubles		Triples	
John Milner	94	John Milner	338	Ed Kranepool	115	Bud Harrelson	27
Dave Kingman	82	Ed Kranepool	322	Felix Millan	111	Steve Henderson	23
Rusty Staub	62	Rusty Staub	297	Cleon Jones	101	Wayne Garrett	17

Pitching Leaders

Wins		Earned Run Average	
Tom Seaver	132	Tom Seaver	2.54
Jerry Koosman	104	Tug McGraw	2.90
Jon Matlack	82	Jon Matlack	3.03

Strikeouts		Shutouts	
Tom Seaver	1823	Tom Seaver	30
Jerry Koosman	1430	Jon Matlack	26
Jon Matlack	1023	Jerry Koosman	13

Saves	
Tug McGraw	73
Skip Lockwood	65
Bob Apodaca	26

'Le Grand Orange'

One would have to look far and wide to find a player who was more popular in more baseball cities than Rusty Staub. The sweet-swinging outfielder played 23 seasons in the majors for 5 different organizations, and made quite a mark wherever he went. Daniel Joseph Staub was known as 'Rusty' for his red hair, and broke into the big leagues in 1963 with the Houston Colt .45s as a 19-year-old. Staub struggled his first two seasons before hitting .256 with 14 home runs in 1965 for the re-named Astros, then improved to .280 with 13 home runs and 81 RBI in 1966. 1967 was Staub's breakout year; he hit a career high .333 with a league-leading 44 doubles, and made his first All-Star team.

In 1969 Rusty was traded to the expansion Montreal Expos and hit an impressive .302 with 29 homers, while setting career highs in slugging % (.526) and on-base % (.426). Staub followed that up in 1970 with a career-best 30 home runs along with 112 walks. He drove in 94 runs and even stole 12 bases. In 1971 Staub hit .311 and knocked in 97 while playing in all 162 games, but at season's end the Expos dealt Staub, coming off his 5th straight All-Star selection, to the New York Mets for Mike Jorgensen, Tim Foli, and Ken Singleton. In his time with Montreal Rusty learned French and became a fan favorite as French-Canadian fans nicknamed him 'Le Grand Orange'.

New York embraced Staub quickly and in 1973 Rusty got his first (and only) taste of the post-season as the Mets (82-79) captured an unlikely National League East title by winning 20 of their last 28 games. Playing in a pitcher's park at Shea Stadium, Staub hit a solid .279 with 36 doubles and 15 home runs during the regular season. In the NLCS, heavily favored Cincinnati took the first game at Riverfront Stadium. In Game 2, Staub, batting 3rd and playing right field, broke a scoreless tie with a home run as the Mets rolled to a 5-0 victory. Then, in Game 3, Staub homered in his first two at-bats as the Mets coasted to a 9-2 win in a contest that became famous for the 5th inning fight between the Reds' left fielder Pete Rose and Mets' shortstop Bud Harrelson. In Game 4 Staub made the defensive play of the game in a losing cause, robbing Dan Driessen of a double in the right center field gap in the 11th inning. Staub hit the fence hard on the play, injuring his left shoulder. As a result he missed the Mets clincher in Game 5 and most of Game 1 of the World Series against Oakland.

Staub's injured shoulder forced him to throw almost completely underhanded, and made it difficult for him to pull the ball with any authority. Undaunted, he led all players in the 1973 World Series with 11 hits and a .423 batting average, including a 4-hit performance at Shea Stadium in Game 4 that featured an opposite field 3-run 1st inning homer. The Mets took the defending champs to 7 games before falling just short.

Rusty set a Mets record with 105 RBI in 1975, then was traded to Detroit before the 1976 season. There Staub enjoyed the best run-producing span of his career, driving in 318 runs in his first three seasons for the Tigers, and appeared in his final All-Star game as the starting right fielder for the American League in 1976. Staub registered a personal best 121 RBI in 1978 as primarily a Designated Hitter. It would be his last season as a regular. After holding out to start the 1979 season, Staub was traded back to Montreal in mid-season, then played for Texas in 1980 before returning to New York. For the next four seasons he played some outfield and first base, but carved out a niche as the club's top pinch-hitter. In 1983 Rusty tied an NL record with 8 straight pinch-hits and set the MLB record with 25 RBI as a pinch-hitter.

Staub retired in 1985 at age 41, and is one of only 3 players in major league history to homer as a teenager and as a 40-year old.

Rusty was undoubtedly one of the 1970's most consistent players, hitting .280 and ranking in the decade's Top 20 with 860 RBI (6th), 1,487 hits (15th), 475 extra-base hits (16th), 732 runs (15th), 263 doubles (12th), and 184 home runs (20th). He was a 6-time All-Star, including 3 selections during the 70s.

Staub was inducted into the Texas Baseball Hall of Fame in 2006 and the Canadian Baseball Hall of Fame in 2012. New York considers him one of their own; Staub has owned 2 restaurants in Manhattan, had a TV broadcasting stint for the Mets, and established a foundation to benefit the families of NYC police officers and fire fighters killed in the line of duty.

14. <u>California Angels</u> – Decade Record: 781-831, 1 Division Title, 0
   Pennants

The Angels were a middle-of-the-pack baseball team during the 1970s.
They never won more than 88 games and only lost more than 90 once,
when they dropped 94 contests in 1975.

In 1970 the team showed promise, finishing at 86-76. But for the second
straight year, they finished in third place in the American League West
behind the powerful Minnesota Twins and the youthful Oakland A's.
Clyde Wright enjoyed a 22-12, 2.83 career year, first baseman Jim
Spencer won a Gold Glove, and left fielder Alex Johnson won the batting
crown with a .329 mark. The bottom fell out the next season; by mid-
year Johnson had been suspended for poor hustle and never played
another game in an Angels uniform. Wright slumped to 16-17. Andy
Messersmith enjoyed a fine year at 20-12, but overall the club won only
76 games, 25½ out of first. Despite trading for Nolan Ryan in the off-
season, and bringing up 19 year-old lefty flamethrower Frank Tanana in
1973, the Angels would struggle through 7 straight losing years. After
1970, the AL West was dominated first by Oakland, who won
consecutive crowns from '71-'75, and then by Kansas City, who took the
division from '76-'78.

Even in the losing seasons, California enjoyed notable individual
achievements, such as center fielder Ken Berry's Gold Glove Award in
1973, one of only three Angels to win the honor all decade. Ryan

improved from 10-14 with 137 strikeouts as a Met in 1971 to 19-16 and 329 Ks for California in '72, and he fanned over 300 batters in 4 of his first 5 seasons as an Angel, including a record 383 in 1973. Ryan led the American League in strikeouts in 7 of 8 years, and during the one season in that span when he did not, 1975, teammate Frank Tanana led the circuit with 269. '73 and '74 were the only times in Ryan's storied career that he topped 20 wins; in '73 Bill Singer also won 20. For the decade, Ryan was the team's ace with a 138-121 record, 3.07 ERA, 2,416 strikeouts, 4 no-hitters, 40 shutouts, and 156 complete games in 288 starts over 8 seasons. Tanana was #1B, going 91-66 with a 2.93 ERA, 1,120 strikeouts, 24 shutouts, and 85 complete games in 187 starts over 7 seasons.

The Angels were offensively challenged for much of the decade; from 1970-78, the only Angel to lead the league in any major offensive category was outfielder Mickey Rivers, who led the AL in triples in 1974 (11) and 1975 (13), and with 70 stolen bases in 1975.

By 1978 Brian Downing had emerged as an All-Star caliber catcher, and California acquired veteran position players who knew how to win: second baseman Bobby Grich from Baltimore, outfielders Don Baylor and Joe Rudi from Oakland, and center fielder Rick Miller from Boston, who immediately won his first Gold Glove award. The club responded with an 87-75 record, only 2 games back of Kansas City, in a season marred by the senseless and tragic shooting death of outfielder Lymon Bostock, a promising young player with a career .311 batting average. Bostock had been signed away from Minnesota in November 1977 as a free agent.

Prior to the 1979 season California acquired two more ex-Twins: 7-time batting champ Rod Carew to play first base, and outfielder 'Disco' Dan Ford. California finished the decade with its first AL West title, and the club turned out the first 3 100 RBI men in franchise history – Ford (.290-21-101), Grich (.294, 30-101), and league MVP Don Baylor (.295, 36 home runs plus a league leading 139 RBI and 120 runs scored). In the ALCS, California was stopped in 4 games by Baltimore. But as the decade closed, Angels' fans finally had a team they could cheer about.

Offensive Leaders

Batting Avg		On Base %		Slugging %	
Mickey Rivers	.280	Don Baylor	.347	Don Baylor	.480
Don Baylor	.269	Mickey Rivers	.330	Leroy Stanton	.381
Jerry Remy	.258	Dave Chalk	.327	Mickey Rivers	.365

Hits		Runs		Stolen Bases	
Dave Chalk	631	Don Baylor	310	Mickey Rivers	126
Sandy Alomar	618	Sandy Alomar	281	Sandy Alomar	121
Don Baylor	478	Dave Chalk	256	Jerry Remy	110

HR		RBI		Doubles		Triples	
Don Baylor	95	Don Baylor	313	Dave Chalk	88	Mickey Rivers	32
Frank Robinson	50	Leroy Stanton	242	Don Baylor	86	Jerry Remy	18
Bobby Bonds	47	Bob Oliver	214	Leroy Stanton	78	Bobby Bonds	12
Leroy Stanton	47						

Pitching Leaders

Wins		Earned Run Average	
Nolan Ryan	138	Frank Tanana	2.93
Frank Tanana	91	Andy Messersmith	2.95
Clyde Wright	67	Nolan Ryan	3.07

Strikeouts		Shutouts	
Nolan Ryan	2416	Nolan Ryan	40
Frank Tanana	1120	Frank Tanana	24
Rudy May	635	Rudy May	11

Saves	
Dave LaRoche	61
Lloyd Allen	21
Ken Tatum	17

Strikeout King

Like a .300 batting average, 30 home runs, and 100 RBI for hitters, 200 strikeouts in a season has always been a benchmark of excellence for pitchers. In turn, a 2,000 strikeout decade is truly a measure of sustained excellence, perhaps even greatness.

In baseball's modern era, since 1900, pitchers have topped 2000 strikeouts within a decade only 13 times. In the 1970s four players achieved this feat - Tom Seaver (Mets-Reds, 2304), Steve Carlton (Cardinals-Phillies, 2097), Bert Blyleven (Twins-Rangers-Pirates, 2082), and Nolan Ryan, who had the most ever in a decade while pitching for the Mets and Angels (2678). No other decade has ever had more than two pitchers exceed 2000 strikeouts. In the 1980s only one pitcher topped 2000: Ryan again, this time with 2167. Randy Johnson eventually joined Ryan as the only other pitcher in baseball history to exceed the 2K mark in strikeouts twice; Johnson did it in the 1990s (2538- second most in a decade all-time), followed by 2182 strikeouts in the 2000s.

2000+ Strikeouts in a Decade

1900s	Rube Waddell	2251
1910s	Walter Johnson	2219
1960s	Bob Gibson	2071
1960s	Jim Bunning	2019
1970s	Nolan Ryan	2678
1970s	Tom Seaver	2304
1970s	Steve Carlton	2097
1970s	Bert Blyleven	2082
1980s	Nolan Ryan	2167
1990s	Randy Johnson	2538
1990s	Roger Clemens	2101
2000s	Randy Johnson	2182
2000s	Javier Vasquez	2001

Johnson and Ryan share another notable decade strikeout achievement - they are the only pitchers to ever lead two different decades in strikeouts. Only 5 other pitchers even finished in the Top 10 twice - Walter Johnson ('10s and '20s), Lefty Grove ('20s and '30s), plus Bert Blyleven and Steve Carlton (like Ryan also '70s and '80s), and Pedro Martinez, who joined Johnson in the Top 10 of the 1990s and 2000s.

Ryan, who holds the career strikeout record of 5714 (839 more than second place Randy Johnson), is clearly the most prolific strikeout artist in baseball history. He holds the single season record with 383 strikeouts in 1973, and exceeded 300 strikeouts in a season 6 times (tied with Johnson for the most ever). Nolan also holds records for most 200+ strikeout seasons (15) and the most games with 10 or more strikeouts (215). Ryan had 15 or more strikeouts in a game 26 times (second to Johnson's 28). He led the league in strikeouts 11 times (second all-time to Walter Johnson's 12) - with his first strikeout title coming as a 25-year-old in 1972, and his last four crowns at the ages of 40, 41, 42, and 43.

15. St.Louis Cardinals – Decade Record: 800-813, 0 Division Titles

The 1970s Cardinals were a talented bunch that never quite put it all together to overtake the Pirates or Phillies in the National League East. In 1973, the only season a team other than Pittsburgh or Philadelphia took the division flag, St Louis finished 1½ games behind the Mets, marking their 3rd second place finish in 4 years. It was the closest they came to first place in the decade.

Lou Brock was the Cardinals' marquee player – he had two 200 hit seasons and led the majors with 126 runs scored in 1971. Overall he batted .298, led the club in runs (843), hits (1617), and triples (43), and was the major league's top base stealer with 551 thefts. The mark of a Hall of Fame player is continued excellence past the traditional peak years of 28-31 years of age; Brock stole a record 118 bases at 35 and continued his streak of 12 straight 50+ steal seasons until he was 37. In his final season, at age 40, he reached 3,000 career hits and batted .304. The only other Cardinal to spend the full decade with the team was catcher Ted Simmons. A six time All-Star during the 1970s, Simmons batted .297, with 5 seasons over .300, and led the team in doubles (299), home runs (151), and RBI (828).

Joe Torre had St Louis' best individual single season in his 1971 MVP year, hitting .363 with 137 RBI and 230 hits, including 24 homers. Keith

Hernandez was a co-MVP in 1979, leading the league in batting average (.344), doubles (48), and runs (116). His 210 hits were second to teammate Gary Templeton, who had 211 and became the first switch hitter to collect 100 hits from each side of the plate. Templeton, a shortstop with great range, had 2 200 hit years, 654 total hits, 52 triples, and 99 stolen bases in his first 3½ seasons from '76-'79. Oddly, he seemed to peak at 23, never again registering more than 161 hits in a season, and had only one more .300+ season for the remainder of his 16 year career. Templeton is best known as the man dealt for Ozzie Smith in 1982.

By the time the 1970s came around, Hall of Famer Bob Gibson had one more great year left in the tank, and several good ones. In 1970 Gibby took National League Cy Young honors with a 23-7 record and 274 strikeouts. Overall Gibson led the team with an 84-64 record, 998 strikeouts, 14 shutouts, and 3.20 ERA. Bob Forsch (72-59, 3.50 and 20 wins in 1977) was the team's only other consistent starter, though John Denny did enjoy strong seasons in 1976 (11-9, league leading 2.52 ERA) and 1978 (14-11, 2.96).

The Cardinals had one other 20 win pitcher in the decade: Steve Carlton, who went 20-9 in 1971 before being dealt to the Phillies for Rick Wise. Wise enjoyed two solid seasons for the Cardinals, but Carlton won 2 Cy Young Awards and established himself as the decade's best left-handed starter while in Philadelphia. Then Wise was traded away for Reggie Smith, who in turn had 2 very good seasons. Smith, thought to be reinforcing his reputation as an injury-feigner, was shipped to the Dodgers for a washed-up Joe Ferguson in 1976. After off-season shoulder surgery Smith contributed consecutive MVP caliber years for the pennant winning Dodgers. Likewise, outfielder Jose Cruz, who had shown little with the Cardinals, was shipped to Houston in a cash deal and eventually developed into a consistent .300 hitter with the Astros. 1974 Rookie of the Year Bake McBride, who hit .307 in 5 years as a Cardinal, was swapped to Philadelphia, and a young Larry Hisle had been traded away in the 1972 off-season as a minor leaguer to Minnesota, with neither deal returning anything of value. In all fairness, St. Louis was on the right side of a mid-season deal in 1978 when they acquired slugger George Hendrick from San Diego for Eric Rasmussen.

It's interesting to wonder what the Cardinals could have achieved in the 70s by retaining Carlton and even 1 or 2 of their young outfielders, but as it was, the franchise would have to wait until the 80s to taste real success.

Offensive Leaders

Batting Avg		On Base %		Slugging %			
Joe Torre	.312	Joe Torre	.386	Joe Torre	.460		
Garry Templeton	.304	Keith Hernandez	.377	Ted Simmons	.455		
Lou Brock	.298	Ted Simmons	.365	Keith Hernandez	.444		
Hits		Runs		Stolen Bases			
Lou Brock	1617	Lou Brock	843	Lou Brock	551		
Ted Simmons	1550	Ted Simmons	652	Garry Templeton	99		
Ken Reitz	892	Joe Torre	383	Bake McBride	75		
HR		RBI		Doubles		Triples	
Ted Simmons	151	Ted Simmons	828	Ted Simmons	299	Lou Brock	56
Joe Torre	80	Lou Brock	481	Lou Brock	243	Garry Templeton	52
Ken Reitz	53	Joe Torre	457	Ken Reitz	180	Ted Simmons	34

Pitching Leaders

Wins		Earned Run Average	
Bob Gibson	84	Bob Gibson	3.20
Bob Forsch	72	Rick Wise	3.24
John Denny	51	Lynn McGlothen	3.49
Strikeouts		Shutouts	
Bob Gibson	998	Bob Gibson	14
Bob Forsch	524	Bob Forsch	12
Reggie Cleveland	445	John Denny	10
Saves			
Al Hrabosky	59		
Diego Segui	26		
Mark Littell	24		

16. Houston Astros – Decade Record: 793-817, 0 Division Titles

As their decade record suggests, Houston spent the vast majority of the 1970s hovering right around .500. The low water mark was in 1975 when the Astros lost 97 games and finished dead last, 43½ games behind the Big Red Machine. The high was a very good 1979 with 89 wins, 1½ games behind those same Reds. Taken a step further, Houston had one 5th place finish in 1978 and one other 2nd place year, in 1972. In the six other seasons you could find the Astros neatly placed in 3rd or 4th place, within a range of 79-82 wins.

Despite the overall mediocrity, the '70 Astros were an entertaining bunch cursed to be in the same division as the Reds and Dodgers, who took the National League West a combined 9 times in 10 years. Few players were more talented than centerfielder Cesar Cedeno. When Leo Durocher took over the helm with Houston late in 1972, he compared Cedeno to a young Willie Mays. In the six years from 1972-77 Cesar could make a case for being baseball's best all-around player, winning 5 Gold Gloves and stealing over 50 bases each year; he led the league in doubles twice, hit .320 in back to back seasons, and averaged .295 with 33 doubles and 20 home runs. For the decade Cedeno led Houston with 1,422 hits, 427 steals, 292 doubles, 777 runs, and 148 home runs.

While no Astro reached 30 home runs, 200 hits, or 100 runs in a season during the 70s, the club included solid position players such as first baseman Bob Watson (136 HRs, 2 100+ RBI seasons, and a team leading .299 average and 769 RBI) and leftfielder Jose Cruz (.296, and a team high .377 on base %). Shortstop Roger Metzger was a triples specialist – he led the league in '71 and '72 and had a total of 62 triples with just 5 home runs, and won a Gold Glove in 1973. Third baseman Doug Rader won 5 straight Gold Gloves from 1970-74, and hit 109 home runs in his 6 '70s seasons in Houston.

The intimidating 6'8" JR Richard was the club's ace with a fastball and slider each approaching 100 miles an hour. After experiencing some wildness early in his career, he won 20 games in 1976 and 18 in each of the next four seasons, leading the club overall with 97 wins and 1,374 strikeouts. JR topped 200 strikeouts 4 times and fanned a league-leading 303 batters in 1978, and 313 in '79. Richard also led the NL with a 2.71 ERA in 1979. The pitching rich Astros staff also included flamethrower Don Wilson, who won 64 games from 1970-75 and tragically died in 1975 at age 29. Other notables included Larry Dierker, who went 82-67 and threw a no-hitter for Houston's 1,000[th] win at the Astrodome, swingman Ken Forsch, who won 66 games while making 121 starts (including a 1979 no-hitter) and notching a team leading 50 saves, and knuckleballer Joe Neikro, who won 21 games in 1979. Tragedy struck the Astros again in 1980, as Richard suffered a career-ending stroke originating from a blood clot in his pitching arm.

Moving forward, after years of being an up and down franchise with no apparent direction, Houston's strong 1979 core, even minus Richard, moved the franchise in the right direction, and the Astros made the playoffs in 1980, '81, and '86.

Offensive Leaders

Batting Avg		On Base %		Slugging %	
Bob Watson	.299	Greg Gross	.379	Lee May	.471
Greg Gross	.298	Jose Cruz	.370	Cesar Cedeno	.457
Jose Cruz	.296	Bob Watson	.366	Bob Watson	.448

Hits		Runs		Stolen Bases	
Cesar Cedeno	1422	Cesar Cedeno	777	Cesar Cedeno	427
Bob Watson	1402	Bob Watson	623	Enos Cabell	159
Roger Metzger	844	Roger Metzger	407	Jose Cruz	151

HR		RBI		Doubles		Triples	
Cesar Cedeno	148	Bob Watson	769	Cesar Cedeno	292	Roger Metzger	62
Bob Watson	136	Cesar Cedeno	671	Bob Watson	231	Cesar Cedeno	47
Doug Rader	109	Doug Rader	448	Doug Rader	146	Jose Cruz	33

Pitching Leaders

Wins		Earned Run Average	
J.R. Richard	97	Don Wilson	3.01
Larry Dierker	82	Ken Forsch	3.18
Ken Forsch	66	J.R. Richard	3.24

Strikeouts		Shutouts	
J.R. Richard	1374	Larry Dierker	18
Larry Dierker	804	J.R. Richard	15
Ken Forsch	731	Don Wilson	13

Saves	
Ken Forsch	50
Fred Gladding	45
Joe Sambito	41

17. <u>Chicago Cubs</u> – Decade Record: 785-827, 0 Division Titles

The Cubs began the decade as serious contenders, boasting 4 future Hall of Famers – Ferguson Jenkins, Billy Williams, Ron Santo, and Ernie Banks. They won 84 games in 1970, finishing in 2nd place, only 5 games behind Pittsburgh. They placed 3rd in 1971, and then 2nd again in 1972, winning 83 and 85 games respectively. But as their superstars aged, the club failed to replenish the talent pool. In addition, lefty pitcher Ken Holtzman and outfielder Bill North were traded to Oakland, where they developed into key contributors for the A's 3-time World Championship teams. Meanwhile, 1970-1972 became the only 3 seasons of the decade that the Cubs finished above .500. Few organizations in history could boast of so much individual talent with so little winning to show for it.

Left fielder Williams enjoyed his two finest seasons in 1970 and 1972, finishing as the National League MVP runner-up both times. In 1970 Williams led the league with 205 hits and scored 137 runs, the most by any player all decade. In addition, he hit 42 home runs and drove in 129. He was joined in the powerful Cub lineup by third baseman Ron Santo (26-114-.267), first baseman Jim Hickman (32-115-.315), and shortstop Don Kessinger (168 hits, 100 runs, 14 triples, and Chicago's only Gold Glove of the decade).

In 1971, the Cubs enjoyed a career year from second baseman Glenn Beckert, who hit .342, his career's only full season above .300. Then, in 1972, Williams took the batting crown with a .333 mark to go along with 37 home runs, 122 RBI, and a .606 slugging percentage (one of only 10 .600+ seasons in the decade).

Offense was never the problem for the Cubs – third baseman Bill Madlock won consecutive batting titles in 1975 (.354) and 1976 (.339) before being traded to San Francisco for Bobby Murcer. In 1978, shortstop Ivan Dejesus stole 42 bases and led the National League with 104 runs scored. And in 1979, Dave Kingman took to the friendly confines of Wrigley Field with the best season of his major league career. 'Kong' launched 48 home runs (tied for the second most in the 1970s) with 115 RBI, hit .288, 52 points above his 16 career average, and slugged .613.

While Chicago's pitching was far from stellar, the club did enjoy some fine single-season efforts. Ferguson Jenkins, often lost in the shadows of Bob Gibson and Tom Seaver, won 22 games in 1970 with 274 strikeouts. In 1971, he took Cy Young Award honors on a 24-13 record, 263 strikeouts and a 2.77 ERA, then won 20 more games in 1972. Jenkins was the Cub's best starter with a 4 year record of 80-57 and 3.29 ERA. Chicago's winningest pitcher was Rick Reuschel, who went 114-101 with a team-high 17 shutouts from 1972-79, including a 20-10 campaign in 1977. The Cubs developed and then subsequently traded away another Hall of Famer, relief ace Bruce Sutter. Sutter's 2.33 ERA was the lowest for any 1970s pitcher making 200 or more appearances. In 1977 he had a 1.34 ERA, and became the first Cub to save 30 games while striking out 129 batters with only 23 walks. In 1979 Sutter won the Cy Young Award with a record-tying 37 saves and 2.22 ERA.

Offensive Leaders

Batting Avg		On Base %		Slugging %	
Billy Williams	.307	Billy Williams	.385	Billy Williams	.523
Jose Cardenal	.296	Rick Monday	.366	Rick Monday	.460
Glenn Beckert	.292	Ron Santo	.365	Ron Santo	.455

Hits		Runs		Stolen Bases	
Don Kessinger	937	Don Kessinger	466	Jose Cardenal	129
Jose Cardenal	864	Billy Williams	445	Ivan de Jesus	89
Billy Williams	854	Rick Monday	441	Don Kessinger	52

HR		RBI		Doubles		Triples	
Billy Williams	143	Billy Williams	498	Jose Cardenal	159	Don Kessinger	46
Rick Monday	106	Ron Santo	353	Billy Williams	139	Rick Monday	26
Ron Santo	84	Jose Cardenal	343	Don Kessinger	127	Ivan de Jesus	24

Pitching Leaders

Wins		Earned Run Average	
Rick Reuschel	114	Fergie Jenkins	3.29
Fergie Jenkins	80	Milt Pappas	3.33
Ray Burris	55	Bill Hands	3.41

Strikeouts		Shutouts	
Rick Reuschel	1122	Rick Reuschel	17
Fergie Jenkins	891	Fergie Jenkins	13
Bill Bonham	811	Milt Pappas	11

Saves	
Bruce Sutter	105
Jack Aker	29
Darold Knowles	24

18. Chicago White Sox – Decade Record: 752-853, 0 Division Titles

Like their cross-town rivals, the Cubs, the White Sox failed to reach the post-season in the 1970s. The low point came early, in 1970, when the club finished dead last with a 56-106 mark, 42 games behind AL West champion Minnesota. Late in that season Chicago brought in Chuck Tanner to manage the team, and in 1971 the Sox turned things around a bit with a 79-83 record, good for third place. Tanner converted lefty knuckleballer Wilbur Wood from the bullpen to the starting rotation and Wood responded with his first of 4 consecutive 20 win seasons, going 22-13 with a 1.91 ERA. Third baseman Bill Melton led the league with 33 home runs.

In 1972 Chicago surged to 87 wins (their only 2nd place finish of the 1970s) on the strength of an MVP season from first baseman Dick Allen, who had been acquired in the offseason from the Dodgers for pitcher Tommy John. Allen enjoyed one of the best seasons of any player all decade, hitting .308 while leading the American League in RBI (113), home runs (a team record 37, including two inside-the-park homers in one game), on base % (.420), and slugging (.603). Wilbur Wood led the league with 24 wins while Stan Bahnsen won 21.

Allen was injured in 1973, and despite another 24 wins from Wood, the club slumped to 5th place. The White Sox rebounded somewhat in '74 with an 80-80 3rd place campaign as Allen again led the AL in home runs (32) and slugging (.563). The year ended on an extremely sour note when Dick left the club with two weeks remaining in the season – he blamed it on an injury, then later on a feud with Ron Santo. More to the point, the much-travelled Dick Allen eventually found himself in the midst of controversy with just about every team he played for. His legacy is unquestionably one of immense, Hall of Fame-caliber talent offset by a poor attitude, perhaps fuelled by alcoholism.

Chicago slipped back into 5th place in 1975 before the team was bought again by showman owner Bill Veeck. 1976 was even worse; another last place finish at 64-97. What followed was one of most exciting seasons in club history – in 1977 the White Sox set team records in attendance (1,657,135) and home runs (192), led by 'rent-a-player' acquisitions right fielder Richie Zisk (30 HR-101 RBI-.290 Avg), DH Oscar Gamble (31-83-.297), third baseman Eric Soderholm (25 HR, .280), plus home-grown rookie center fielder Chet Lemon (19 HR, 38 doubles). The Sox had a 5½ game lead on July 31, but their lack of pitching depth and poor defense up the middle (2B Jorge Orta ranked last at his position with a .970 fielding %, SS Alan Bannister registered a league high 40 errors) caught up to them and they finished in 3rd place at 90-72, 12 games back. The last two seasons of the decade were forgettable on the field with consecutive 5th place finishes, though Lemon continued to emerge as one of the league's best young players, leading the league with 44 doubles in 1979.

Overall in the 1970s, the franchise finished 101 games below .500 and gained more attention for Veeck's publicity stunts than for on-field excellence. The lasting images of those White Sox includes players sporting shorts in three 1976 contests, and a disastrous 1979 'Disco Demolition Night' promotion that led to a riot on the field and forfeit of a game.

Chet Lemon and Dick Allen were the team's best position players during the decade, though they only spent 4 and 3 years respectively with the team. Also notable is second baseman-outfielder Jorge Orta, who was never the team's best player in any single season and was no better than average defensively, but he did hit .281 and led the team in games (990), runs (442), hits (1,002), doubles (162), triples (44), and RBI (456) during 8 years with the club.

Wilbur Wood is an easy choice as the team's ace – he led the club with 21 saves in 1970 before moving into the starting rotation, and over the next five seasons he started 224 games and won 106, including 20+ wins in 4 straight years, led the league in starts 4 straight years, and finished in the Top 5 in Cy Young voting 3 times. Wood's overall mark in the decade for Chicago was 136-123 with a 3.31 ERA, 113 complete games and 24 shutouts. Jim Kaat was also impressive in a short 2½ year stint with the club, going 45-28 with a 3.10 ERA, winning 20+ games in both full years with the team, and taking three Gold Glove awards. The club's only other Gold Glove winners were shortstop Luis Aparicio in 1970 and first baseman Jim Spencer in 1977. Terry Forster led the team with 75 saves, but Rich Gossage had the top single season of any White Sox relief pitcher in 1975, when he led the AL with 26 saves and had a 1.84 ERA in 142 innings.

Offensive Leaders

Batting Avg		On Base %		Slugging %					
Lamar Johnson	.297	Carlos May	.359	Chet Lemon	.446				
Ralph Garr	.291	Pat Kelly	.357	Lamar Johnson	.434				
Chet Lemon	.284	Chet Lemon	.353	Bill Melton	.433				
Hits		Runs		Stolen Bases					
Jorge Orta	1002	Jorge Orta	442	Pat Kelly	119				
Carlos May	885	Carlos May	420	Carlos May	83				
Bill Melton	730	Bill Melton	376	Jorge Orta	66				
HR		RBI		Doubles		Triples			
Bill Melton	129	Jorge Orta	456	Jorge Orta	162	Jorge Orta	44		
Dick Allen	85	Bill Melton	432	Carlos May	135	Pat Kelly	28		
Jorge Orta	79	Carlos May	416	Chet Lemon	123	Ralph Garr	24		

Pitching Leaders

Wins		Earned Run Average	
Wilbur Wood	136	Tom Bradley	2.97
Stan Bahnsen	55	Jim Kaat	3.10
Jim Kaat	45	Wilbur Wood	3.31
Strikeouts		Shutouts	
Wilbur Wood	1138	Wilbur Wood	24
Bart Johnson	502	Tom Bradley	8
Terry Forster	479	Bart Johnson	6
		Ken Kravec	6
Saves		Stan Bahnsen	6
Terry Forster	75	Tommy John	6
Lerrin LaGrow	42		
Rich Gossage	30		

19. Washington Senators/Texas Rangers – Decade Record: 747-860, 0 Division Titles

In 1972, Senators owner Bob Short moved his franchise to Arlington, Texas, and renamed them the Rangers. Unfortunately, the team continued its downward trend, going from 92 and 96 losses as the Senators in '70-'71 to 100 losses as the Rangers in 1972. Ted Williams stepped down as manager, and Whitey Herzog was brought in, only to be fired before the end of a 1973 season that ended with 105 losses. In those four seasons the team never finished closer than 37 games out of first place. 1974 was a turnaround year under new skipper Billy Martin, and for the remainder of the decade the Rangers were mostly competitive, including two second place finishes and three separate seasons that found them within 5 games of first place.

The Rangers went 84-67 in 1974, finishing in second place, only 5 games behind the soon to be three-time World Champion A's. It was the Rangers' first winning season, and only the second winning season in franchise history, dating back to when the Senators began in 1961. The 27 game improvement was sparked by Martin and led by league MVP Jeff Burroughs, who hit .301 with 25 home runs, 33 doubles, and a league-high 118 RBI. Martin also brought up two rookies, catcher Jim Sundberg, a Gold Glove winner from '1976-'81, and Rookie of the Year first baseman Mike Hargrove, who batted .323. Ferguson Jenkins, acquired from the Cubs in exchange for future 4-time batting champ Bill Madlock, had a 2.82 ERA, 225 strikeouts, and tied for the major league lead with 25 wins.

Texas posted their top record of the decade in 1977, going 94-68, mostly on the strength of much-travelled veteran pitchers Gaylord Perry (15-12), Doyle Alexander (17-11), Bert Blyleven (14-12), and Doc Ellis (10-6), plus excellent team speed (154 steals), and the hitting of Toby Harrah (27 HR, 87 RBI) and Mike Hargrove (.305). As was the case in several years during the 70s, Texas could not break through the Oakland-Kansas City '71-'78 stranglehold on the AL West, and finished 8 games behind the Royals. Two third place finishes followed with strong contributions from newly acquired veterans Al Oliver (.324, 35 doubles) and Bobby Bonds (29 homers, 37 steals) in 1978, and Buddy Bell (200 hits, 42 doubles, 101 RBI, Gold Glove at 3B) and closer Jim Kern (13-5, 1.57 ERA, 29 saves, 136K in 143 innings pitched) in 1979.

The club seemed to suffer from a lack of stability with too many short-stint players - and managers. Following a successful 1974, Texas struggled halfway through 1975, and by July a run-in with new owner Bradford Corbett sealed Billy Martin's fate. He was replaced by third base coach Frank Lucchesi. Less than two years later, Lucchesi had a fist fight with disgruntled second baseman Lenny Randle, and was eventually fired in June 1977. The team went through two interim managers and then finally settled on ex-Baltimore coach Billy Hunter, their fourth manager of the month, who went 60-33 the rest of the way. Hunter then wore out his welcome by the end of 1978, and was replaced by Pat Corrales.

Overall, Toby Harrah was the franchise's top player of the decade; he led the team in games, hits, runs, doubles, triples, and RBI, tied with Burroughs for the lead with 108 home runs, and was second to Dave Nelson with 140 stolen bases. Harrah hit exceptionally well for shortstops of that era, and he made 3 All-Star teams before being moved to third base in 1977. Mike Hargrove's .294 average was second among Rangers with over 1,000 at-bats to Al Oliver (.324 over two seasons), and he led the team with a .399 on-base %. Frank Howard led in slugging (.481) and was second in on-base% (.383) – pitchers wanted no part of Hondo after his monster 1970 (44 HR, 126 RBI, and part of a three year run where he blasted 136 home runs). Howard had only one more productive season after that; he was let go after the 1972 season and was out of the game by October 1973.

The pitching was instable: Fergie Jenkins led the team with a 76-52 record and 17 shutouts over 2 stints with the club. No other pitcher lasted long enough to exceed Gaylord Perry's 42 wins, though starters Jim Bibby (1973) and Bert Blyleven (1977) threw no-hitters.

The bullpen, other than Kern's incredible 1979 performance, was quiet but reliable with Darold Knowles, Paul Linblad, and Steve Faucault.

Offensive Leaders

Batting Avg		On Base %		Slugging %					
Mike Hargrove	.293	Mike Hargrove	.399	Jeff Burroughs	.428				
Bump Wills	.270	Toby Harrah	.351	Mike Hargrove	.409				
Toby Harrah	.258	Bump Wills	.344	Tom Grieve	.408				
Hits		Runs		Stolen Bases					
Toby Harrah	1004	Toby Harrah	526	Dave Nelson	144				
Mike Hargrove	730	Mike Hargrove	380	Toby Harrah	140				
Jim Sundberg	699	Jeff Burroughs	332	Bump Wills	115				
HR		RBI		Doubles		Triples			
Jeff Burroughs	108	Toby Harrah	483	Toby Harrah	151	Toby Harrah	19		
Toby Harrah	108	Jeff Burroughs	412	Mike Hargrove	122	Lenny Randle	18		
Frank Howard	79	Mike Hargrove	295	Jim Sundberg	112	Jim Sundberg	18		

Pitching Leaders

Wins		Earned Run Average	
Fergie Jenkins	76	Gaylord Perry	3.23
Gaylord Perry	42	Fergie Jenkins	3.43
Dick Bosman	38	Dick Bosman	3.49
Strikeouts		Shutouts	
Fergie Jenkins	703	Fergie Jenkins	17
Gaylord Perry	468	Bert Blyleven	11
Dick Bosman	366	Gaylord Perry	10
Saves			
Steve Foucault	35		
Darold Knowles	33		
Jim Kern	29		

20. <u>Montreal Expos</u> – Decade Record: 748-862, 0 Division Titles

The 1970 Montreal Expos, one year removed from expansion, made a nice improvement from their 110 loss debut in 1969 with a 73-89 record, a turnaround of 21 games. The club scored 105 more runs and the pitching solidified under Steve Renko (13-11) and Rookie of the Year Carl Morton (18-11). Unfortunately, the franchise proceeded to languish in the 70 to 79 win range for the next 8 seasons, with the exception of 1976, when the 'Spos staggered to a 55-107 record. They finished 46 games out of first place that season, the furthest off the pace any National League club finished all decade.

Part of the issue was the impatience of the organization in its early years to develop and keep its talent base in place. No Expo played more than 7 seasons with the club during the decade, and no position player more than 6. Rusty Staub, who came to be known as 'Le Grand Orange' to the French Canadian fans, played in 480 games in 3 seasons with Montreal from '69-'71, hitting a combined .296 with 78 home runs and 270 RBI. The 27-year-old Staub was then traded to the Mets in a multi-player deal that included outfielder Ken Singleton, first baseman Mike Jorgenson, and shortstop Tim Foli. The trade was a short-term success, as Singleton had the franchise's best individual season to date in 1973 – he hit .302, led the league with a .425 on-base %, scored 100 runs, and drove in 103 (the first Expo to reach 100 in either category). Jorgenson won a Gold Glove, and Foli became a solid starter. Then after a down year in '74, Singleton was traded away (along with pitcher Mike Torrez, who was coming off a 15-8 season) to Baltimore for two minor leaguers and a washed up Dave McNally. Torrez won 20 games for Baltimore in 1975, and Singleton settled in as one of the American League's best hitters for the next 10 years. Finally, Mike Marshall, one of the decade's best relief aces, who saved 75 games and won 36 for Montreal in 4 seasons, was shipped off in 1973 to the Dodgers for 34 year old Willie Davis. Davis lasted one season in Montreal while Marshall won the Cy Young Award for LA in 1974.

Slowly however, the minor league talent began to pay huge dividends. Steve Rogers went 10-5 with a 1.54 ERA in 1973, struggled for a couple of years, and eventually rounded into form and won 17 games in 1977. For the decade Rogers was the Expos ace, pitching to a 3.13 ERA and winning a team-high 86 games (though he lost 94). Gary Carter hit 17 home runs as a rookie in 1975, playing mostly in the outfield before moving behind the plate the following year and becoming one of the game's best catchers. Third Baseman Larry Parrish finished 3rd in Rookie of the Year voting in 1975, and went on to lead the 70s Expos in doubles (162) and hits (696, tied with Bob Bailey). The outfield of RF Ellis Valentine (71 home runs from '77-'79, Gold Glove in '78 with a league leading 24 assists), LF Warren Cromartie (hit .284 with 536 hits from '77-'79), and Rookie of the Year CF Andre Dawson (.270, 69 HR, 84 SB from '77-'79) was the envy of baseball.

In 1979 the club had its first winning season, going 95-65 under Dick Williams, an improvement of 19 games, and finished only 2 games behind the eventual World Champion Pirates.

Offensive Leaders

Batting Avg		On Base %		Slugging %	
Ellis Valentine	.286	Ken Singleton	.393	Ellis Valentine	.473
Ken Singleton	.285	Ron Hunt	.390	Andre Dawson	.454
Tony Perez	.281	Ron Fairly	.384	Tony Perez	.447

Hits		Runs		Stolen Bases	
Larry Parrish	696	Bob Bailey	366	Andre Dawson	85
Bob Bailey	696	Gary Carter	330	Larry Lintz	79
Gary Carter	642	Larry Parrish	325	Pepe Mangual	57
Tim Foli	642				

HR		RBI		Doubles		Triples	
Bob Bailey	109	Bob Bailey	413	Larry Parrish	162	Andre Dawson	30
Gary Carter	97	Gary Carter	343	Warren Cromartie	120	Warren Cromartie	18
Ellis Valentine	79	Larry Parrish	328	Ellis Valentine	111	Larry Parrish	18

Pitching Leaders

Wins		Earned Run Average	
Steve Rogers	86	Steve Rogers	3.13
Steve Renko	62	Woodie Fryman	3.34
Mike Torrez	40	Mike Torrez	3.75

Strikeouts		Shutouts	
Steve Rogers	980	Steve Rogers	21
Steve Renko	742	Bill Stoneman	10
Bill Stoneman	646	Woodie Fryman	8

Saves	
Mike Marshall	75
Dale Murray	33
Claude Raymond	23

21. <u>Cleveland Indians</u> – Decade Record: 737-866, 0 Division Titles

There was reason for optimism in Cleveland in 1970 – behind the pitching of 6'5" lefty Sam McDowell (20-12, with a league-leading 304 strikeouts) and a promising young lineup that included 1970 and '71 Gold Glove winning catcher Ray Fosse (.307) and third baseman Graig Nettles (26 HR), the Tribe improved 14 games from 1969, though still only good for 76 wins and 5th place in the American League East.

It would take 4 more seasons before Cleveland topped that win total, when in 1974 they went 77-85 and finished 4th, 14 games out of first, the closest they would get to the top all decade. Along the way Nettles, despite slugging 71 home runs with 218 RBI in 3 seasons, was traded away to the Yankees, as was Cleveland's 1971 Rookie of the Year winner, first baseman Chris Chambliss. The two solidified the corners of New York's infield for the rest of the decade, and the Yanks went on to win 3 division titles and 2 World Championships.

One deal that went Cleveland's way was the November 1971 swap that sent hometown boy McDowell to the Giants in exchange for spitballer Gaylord Perry and shortstop Frank Duffy. Perry responded in 1972 with the Indians' best single season of the decade – a 24-16, 1.92 ERA, 234 strikeout performance, capturing the Cy Young Award. Perry was by far the club's best pitcher of the decade, winning a team high 70 games with 17 shutouts and 773 strikeouts from 1972-74. Duffy was a serviceable starting shortstop for six seasons.

Hall of Famer Frank Robinson was acquired in '74, and in 1975 became the Major League's first black manager, leading the Indians to a respectable 79-80 record. On that opening day, April 8, 1975, in Cleveland against the Yankees, player-manager Robinson hit himself fourth, and in dramatic fashion drilled a line drive into the left field seats in his very first at-bat, for a major-league record 8 opening day home runs. Then in 1976, behind the Gold Glove play of center fielder Rick Manning, the slugging of veteran DH Rico Carty (.310, 83 RBI), and Dave LaRoche's 21 saves, the Tribe improved further to 81-78 in 1976, its best record of the 1970s.

Throughout the decade this was a club that despite developing talents such as Chambliss, Manning, Dennis Eckersley, Mike Hargrove, Buddy Bell, and Andre Thornton (33 HR and 105 RBI in 1978), couldn't seem to get out from under front-office moves that rarely worked out. In the 1976 off-season, Cleveland signed Wayne Garland (a 20 game winner for Baltimore in his first season as a major league starter) to a then-unheard of 10 year, $2.3 Million deal. Garland hurt his shoulder in his first spring training start for the Indians and tried to pitch through it en route to a miserable 19 loss 1977. He made just 6 starts in '78 and 14 starts in '79. Garland was finally released in 1981 with 5 more years left on his contract.

Bell, the third baseman who prompted the Nettles trade, was Cleveland's best position player in the 1970s. A brilliant fielder, he also led the Indians in hits (1,016), runs (462), doubles (155), triples (27), and RBI (386). Bell was dealt to Texas before the 1979 season in exchange for Toby Harrah, a solid shortstop-third baseman in his own right. With Texas In 1979 Bell set career highs in batting average, doubles and home runs, while enjoying the only 200 hit and 100 RBI seasons of his career, and winning his first of 5 consecutive Gold Gloves. The following season Bell batted .329 and made his first of four All-Star appearances.

Offensive Leaders

Batting Avg		On Base %		Slugging %	
Chris Chambliss	.282	Chris Chambliss	.339	George Hendrick	.444
Ray Fosse	.277	Graig Nettles	.338	Graig Nettles	.412
Duane Kuiper	.275	Ray Fosse	.331	Chris Chambliss	.397

Hits		Runs		Stolen Bases	
Buddy Bell	1016	Buddy Bell	462	Rick Manning	86
Duane Kuiper	691	Rick Manning	307	John Lowenstein	72
Rick Manning	649	George Hendrick	283	Jim Norris	53

HR		RBI		Doubles		Triples	
George Hendrick	89	Buddy Bell	386	Buddy Bell	155	Buddy Bell	27
Andre Thornton	87	George Hendrick	295	Frank Duffy	96	Duane Kuiper	26
Graig Nettles	71	Andre Thornton	268	Rick Manning	86	Rick Manning	20

Pitching Leaders

Wins		Earned Run Average	
Gaylord Perry	70	Gaylord Perry	2.71
Rick Waits	51	Sam McDowell	3.12
Dennis Eckersley	40	Dennis Eckersley	3.23

Strikeouts		Shutouts	
Gaylord Perry	773	Gaylord Perry	17
Dennis Eckersley	543	Dennis Eckersley	8
Sam McDowell	496	Rick Waits	7

Saves	
Jim Kern	46
Dave LaRoche	42
Sid Monge	28

22. <u>Milwaukee Brewers</u> – Decade Record: 738-873, 0 Division Titles

After their first season as an expansion club in 1969, the Seattle Pilots were formally declared bankrupt on April 1, 1970, six days before opening day. They were immediately moved to Milwaukee as the Brewers, under new owner Bud Selig. The team struggled through the vast majority of the decade, suffering 8 straight losing seasons under 5 different managers, and never finished higher than 5th place. The landscape changed dramatically in 1978-79, as the Brewers improved by 25 games under new manager George Bamberger, fueled by a strong offense. They reeled off 93 and 95 wins respectively.

During the lean years there were some notable individual achievements, such as the speed/power combo displayed by Tommy Harper, who became the major's 5th ever 30-30 man in 1970 with 38 stolen bases and 31 home runs. Harper's speed was no secret; he had led the majors with 73 steals in 1969 as a member of the Pilots. The power display was surprising, though, since Tommy never hit more than 18 homers in any other season during his 15 year career.

Harper was traded to Boston in a 1971 ten-player deal that included first baseman George "Boomer" Scott. Scott won Gold Gloves in all 5 seasons in Milwaukee and was the franchise's first legitimate power threat, with 163 home runs and 463 RBI. In 1973 he became the first Brewer to drive in 100 runs, plating 107 and leading the AL with 295 total bases. In 1975 Scott led the league in homers (36), RBI (109), and total bases (318) while finishing 8th in the MVP vote.

Reliever Ken Sanders earned Fireman of the Year honors with 31 saves and a 1.91 ERA in 1971, and led the Brewers with 61 saves during the decade. Sanders' trade to Philadelphia after the 1972 season brought in third baseman Don Money, who was quietly the team's most consistent player. Money hit .277, played in 4 All-Star games, and led Milwaukee during the 1970s in games (911), runs (495), hits (959), and doubles (172).

In 1974, 18 year old shortstop Robin Yount, who had been the 3rd pick in the 1973 draft, made his debut with the club, and hit .250 in 107 games. Yount steadily improved as a hitter through the remainder of the decade, and would eventually find his power stroke during the 80s en route to a Hall of Fame career. His double play partner by 1978 was rookie Paul Molitor, another future Hall of Famer, who hit .299 with 20 triples and 63 stolen bases over his first two seasons. At first base, Cecil Cooper was acquired from Boston in the George Scott trade; Coop hit .306 from '77-'79 and won a Gold Glove in 1979 while leading the league with 44 doubles. Cooper also drove in 106 runs that year, one of three Brewers to eclipse 100. The others were right fielder Sixto Lezcano (101), and center fielder Gorman Thomas, who knocked in 123 while leading the AL with 45 home runs.

While the franchise was not known for its pitching, the club received solid efforts from Jim Slaton (87-101, 3.83) and Jim Colborn (57-60, 3.65, and the franchise's first 20 win season in 1973). Mike Caldwell must be considered Milwaukee's decade ace, posting a 43-23 record with 41 complete games, 10 shutouts, and a 3.05 ERA in 2½ seasons as a starter.

Offensive Leaders

Batting Avg		On Base %		Slugging %	
Cecil Cooper	.306	Sixto Lezcano	.364	Cecil Cooper	.482
Sixto Lezcano	.283	John Briggs	.358	Gorman Thomas	.459
George Scott	.283	Cecil Cooper	.348	Sixto Lezcano	.457

Hits		Runs		Stolen Bases	
Don Money	959	Don Money	495	Robin Yount	78
Robin Yount	871	George Scott	402	Don Money	66
George Scott	851	Robin Yount	378	Tommy Harper	63

HR		RBI		Doubles		Triples	
George Scott	115	George Scott	463	Don Money	172	Robin Yount	28
Gorman Thomas	99	Don Money	406	Robin Yount	144	Paul Molitor	20
Don Money	98	Sixto Lezcano	319	George Scott	137	Sixto Lezcano	19

Pitching Leaders

Wins		Earned Run Average	
Jim Slaton	87	Mike Caldwell	3.05
Jim Colborn	57	Jim Colborn	3.65
Bill Travers	53	Lary Sorensen	3.73

Strikeouts		Shutouts	
Jim Slaton	781	Jim Slaton	39
Jim Colborn	495	Mike Caldwell	15
Eduardo Rodriguez	404	Bill Travers	14

Saves	
Ken Sanders	61
Tom Murphy	41
Bill Castro	36

23. <u>Atlanta Braves</u> – Decade Record: 725-883, 0 Division Titles

The Braves never seemed to recover during the 1970s after a 3 game NLCS sweep in 1969 at the hands of the Miracle Mets. Atlanta had only 2 winning seasons during the decade and did not come within 8 games of a division title, finishing an average of 25 games out of first place.

While the club struggled, opposing National League pitchers rarely looked forward to facing Atlanta's lineup. Rico Carty won the 1970 batting title with a .366 average, and his 25 HR and 101 RBI were only 3rd best on the team that year behind Hank Aaron (38-118), and Orlando Cepeda (34-111). In 1971, Aaron enjoyed possibly the best season of his storied career, setting highs in home runs (47), slugging % (.669), and on-base % (.410). In 1973, the Braves had 3 players with 40 or more home runs – Dave Johnson (who broke the single season HR record for second baseman with 43), Darrell Evans (41), and Aaron (40).

On April 8th, 1974, all eyes were set on Fulton County Stadium as Hank Aaron smashed his 715th home run, breaking Babe Ruth's career record. The club went on to a decade-high 88 wins that season. Ralph Garr was the NL batting champ with a .353 average, and also paced the league with 214 hits and 17 triples. Buzz Capra had an NL-best 2.28 ERA.

Garr spent 6 years in the 1970s with Atlanta, and was the club leader in runs, hits, doubles, triples, stolen bases, and batting average. Hank Aaron's five year ('70-'74) tally of 179 home runs and 478 RBI led the Braves by a wide margin.

During the decade knuckleballer Phil Niekro was Atlanta's undisputed ace, winning 164 games (including 25 shutouts), and topping 20 wins in a season twice. Side-armer Gene Garber (47 saves, 3.56 ERA), and Tom House (28 saves, 3.06) led the bullpen.

Offensive Leaders							
Batting Avg		On Base %		Slugging %			
Ralph Garr	.318	Hank Aaron	.388	Hank Aaron	.583		
Hank Aaron	.294	Darrell Evans	.375	Gary Matthews	.469		
Gary Matthews	.292	Gary Matthews	.363	Dusty Baker	.441		
Hits		Runs		Stolen Bases			
Ralph Garr	1014	Ralph Garr	461	Ralph Garr	135		
Mike Lum	652	Darrell Evans	419	Jerry Royster	114		
Darrell Evans	649	Hank Aaron	404	Dusty Baker	58		
HR		RBI		Doubles		Triples	
Hank Aaron	179	Hank Aaron	478	Ralph Garr	131	Ralph Garr	40
Darrell Evans	120	Darrell Evans	384	Dusty Baker	111	Jerry Royster	17
Earl Williams	81	Dusty Baker	324	Mike Lum	96	Felix Millan	16

Pitching Leaders			
Wins		Earned Run Average	
Phil Niekro	164	Phil Niekro	3.26
Carl Morton	52	Carl Morton	3.47
Ron Reed	49	Pat Jarvis	3.86
Strikeouts		Shutouts	
Phil Niekro	1866	Phil Niekro	25
Ron Reed	490	Carl Morton	8
Carl Morton	345	Dick Ruthven	7
Saves			
Gene Garber	47		
Cecil Upshaw	30		
Tom House	28		

The Roadrunner

Playing for clubs rarely in post-season contention, and in the shadow of stars like Atlanta Braves teammate and home run king Hank Aaron, Ralph Garr was likely the most under-rated player of the 1970s. Drafted by Atlanta out of Grambling University, where he led the NAIA in 1967 with a .585 average, Garr set an International League record hitting .368 in 1970, and became the Braves starting left fielder in 1971 when Rico Carty was injured in winter ball.

Garr became an immediate sensation in '71 by hitting .400 through mid-May and was tabbed 'Road Runner' for his speed. Aaron once remarked, "Ralph gets down the line as fast as anyone I've ever seen." While he hit only 9 home runs that year and never topped 12 in a season, Garr made like Aaron on May 17th against the Mets. He blasted a game-tying, 2-out 10th inning shot off Tom Seaver (imagine a starting pitcher still out there in the 10th inning!), followed by a 2-out walk off shot to win it in the 12th. Garr finished the season second in the National League with 219 hits and a .342 average, scored 101 runs, stole 30 bases, and led all left fielders with 314 putouts and 15 assists.

In 1972 Garr hit .325, good enough again for second in the National League. Then in 1974 he made his only All-Star appearance and had a career year, leading the NL in batting average (.353), triples (17), and hits (214). After the 1975 season, Garr was traded to the Chicago White Sox, where he enjoyed two more .300 seasons. By 1978 his bat speed and legs had slowed down, and his career came to an end in early 1980 with California.

An infielder in college, Ralph was immediately moved to the outfield after turning pro, and while he displayed excellent range, he was never considered a strong defensive player. Garr was a talented top of the order hitter and an overall offensive force – topping .300 5 times, 200 hits 3 times, and leading the league in triples twice. For the decade Garr ranked 9th among all players with a .307 batting average, was 11th best with 1,546 hits, and #6 with 64 triples. He also tallied 703 runs scored, 201 doubles, and 170 stolen bases. Impressive numbers, though one could argue that Ralph's skill set was not a match for tiny Fulton County Stadium. With his speed and line drive bat who knows what Garr could have hit playing his home games in one of the many large turf ballparks around the National League. And had he not batted ahead of so many sluggers like Aaron, Orlando Cepeda, Dave Johnson, and Darrell Evans, there is no telling what Garr's stolen base totals might have looked like.

As it is, Garr will have to settle for being perhaps the best kept secret of the decade.

24. <u>San Diego Padres</u> – Decade Record: 667-942, 0 Division Titles

The Padres, a 1969 expansion team, easily led the major leagues in losses during the decade. They followed a 110-loss initial season with five more last place finishes to start the 70s. Though San Diego stood out of the National League West cellar for the rest of the decade, they never fared better than 4th place, and enjoyed only one winning season, in 1978.

San Diego's best player during those early years was first baseman Nate Colbert, a three-time All-Star selection and the team leader with 139 70s home runs, in addition to the 24 he hit in 1969. Colbert had two 38 homer seasons, and in 1972 he drove in 22.75% of his teams runs (111 of 488), a record that still stands. Cito Gaston, one of the few additional threats in that Padre lineup, had an All-Star 1970 when he hit .318 with 29 home runs and 93 RBI, and tallied 75 home runs in 5 years with San Diego.

The team's first Hall of Famer came in the form of Dave Winfield, a 6'6" outfielder out of the University of Minnesota who was drafted in 1973 not only by the Padres, but also by the NFL and NBA. By 1977 Winfield was an All-Star, his first of 12 consecutive selections, and in 1979 he finished 3rd in MVP voting, capturing a Gold Glove and leading the league with 118 RBI. Dave was San Diego's decade leader in games, hits, runs, doubles, triples, runs batted in, and walks. Ozzie Smith debuted in 1978, showcasing what became his trademark acrobatic defensive skills, though his bat did not really develop until after he was traded to the Cardinals in 1981. Smith took over for another good field no-hit shortstop, Enzo Hernandez, who had a team leading 129 steals and 83 sacrifices over 7 seasons.

It was so tough to win in San Diego that in 1971 Dave Roberts pitched to a 2.10 ERA and went 14-17. For the decade only one Padres pitcher with 25 or more total decisions managed a winning record - Gaylord Perry, who went 33-17 in two seasons, including a 21-6 2.73 Cy Young Award winning effort in 1978. Randy Jones rebounded from an 8-22 1974 by going 20-12 with a league leading 2.24 ERA in '75, then started the All-Star game in 1976 and finished 22-14, winning the Cy Young Award. Jones never had another winning season, despite pitching well again in 1978 (2.88 ERA), and was 87-92 during the decade with a 3.24 ERA.

In 1976, Butch Metzger was named the National League Rookie of the Year – in 77 games out of the bullpen he went 11-4 with 89 strikeouts, 16 saves, and a 2.92 ERA. He struggled at the start of the 1977 season, was traded to the Cardinals, and was out of baseball by 1979. Metzger became expendable due to the signing of free agent Rollie Fingers in December 1976. Fingers captured two Fireman of the Year awards and saved 85 games with a 3.23 ERA from '77-'79.

Offensive Leaders

Batting Avg		On Base %		Slugging %	
Gene Richards	.292	Johnny Grubb	.363	Nate Colbert	.466
Johnny Grubb	.286	Gene Richards	.363	Dave Winfield	.466
Dave Winfield	.285	Dave Winfield	.356	Cito Gaston	.420

Hits		Runs		Stolen Bases	
Dave Winfield	980	Dave Winfield	510	Enzo Hernandez	129
Nate Colbert	657	Nate Colbert	378	Gene Richards	117
Cito Gaston	582	Cito Gaston	249	Dave Winfield	110

HR		RBI		Doubles		Triples	
Nate Colbert	139	Dave Winfield	539	Dave Winfield	154	Dave Winfield	33
Dave Winfield	134	Nate Colbert	415	Nate Colbert	110	Gene Richards	32
Cito Gaston	75	Cito Gaston	288	Johnny Grubb	101	Cito Gaston	22

Pitching Leaders

Wins		Earned Run Average	
Randy Jones	87	Randy Jones	3.24
Clay Kirby	45	Bob Shirley	3.58
Gaylord Perry	33	Clay Kirby	3.72

Strikeouts		Shutouts	
Clay Kirby	689	Randy Jones	15
Randy Jones	624	Steve Arlin	11
Steve Arlin	434	Clay Kirby	7

Saves	
Rollie Fingers	85
Butch Metzger	16
Vicente Romo	16

25. Seattle Mariners – Decade Record: 187-297, 0 Division Titles

As would be expected of an expansion team, the Mariners struggled through their early years. Darrell Johnson, who had managed Boston for three seasons and won a pennant there in 1975, was hired as the franchise's first manager. Seattle was 66-98 in their initial season in 1977, the same mark as the last MLB team to play in Seattle, the Pilots in 1969. Their opening day pitcher, 39-year old Diego Segui (AKA 'The Ancient Mariner'), was the only man to play for both the Mariners and the Pilots, where he had enjoyed his best season in the majors, going 12-6 with 12 saves and was voted the team's most valuable player. Segui did not enjoy similar success with the Mariners, going 0-7 with a 5.69 ERA.

Segui was not alone in his struggles on the mound - Seattle pitchers were torched for a league-worst 4.83 ERA. Glenn Abbott was the club's closest resemblance to an ace, with a 12-13 record and 4.45 ERA. Enrique Romo did an admirable job out of the bullpen, pitching to a 2.83 ERA and 16 saves. The offense was led by All-Star center fielder Ruppert Jones (26 2B, 8 3B, 22 HR), first baseman Dan Meyer (22 HR, 90 RBI, .273) and ex-Angels outfielder Leroy Stanton (27-90-.275), who established career highs in nearly every offensive category before falling off the map with a .182 average in 1978, his last in the big leagues. For all their struggles, the Ms did manage to avoid last place, finishing a full 13 games ahead of the dismantled Oakland A's, but still 38 games out of first.

Seattle fell to last place in 1978, slipping a bit further with a 56-108 mark. Ex-Astro leftfielder Leon Roberts was one of the club's few bright spots, becoming the first player in the franchise to receive an MVP vote on the strength of team highs of 22 HR, 92 RBI, a.301 batting average, and .515 slugging percentage. The young double play tandem of 2B Julio Cruz (59 steals) and SS Craig Reynolds (.292) was reason for hope, but pitching was again a problem, as the 4.67 team ERA again ranked last in the American League.

In 1979 the Mariners returned to 6th place at 67-95. The offense began to click, as the club boasted its first 100 RBI men, first baseman Bruce Bochte (16 HR-100 RBI-.316 Avg) and DH Willie Horton (29-106-.279). In addition, Meyer contributed 20 home runs, Cruz hit .271 with 49 steals, and Ruppert Jones played all 162 games and set a new team high with 107 runs scored, to go along with 21 homers, 29 doubles, and 33 steals. The pitching began to show signs of progress, improving slightly to 12th in the league, led by the young rotation of Mike Parrott (14-12, 3.77), Rick Honeycutt (11-12, 4.04), and Floyd Bannister (10-15, 4.05).

Offensive Leaders

Batting Avg		On Base %		Slugging %	
Tom Paciorek	.292	Bruce Bochte	.365	Leon Roberts	.484
Bruce Bochte	.291	Leon Roberts	.358	Willie Horton	.458
Leon Roberts	.286	Bob Stinson	.348	Tom Paciorek	.447

Hits		Runs		Stolen Bases	
Ruppert Jones	434	Ruppert Jones	242	Julio Cruz	123
Dan Meyer	406	Dan Meyer	185	Ruppert Jones	68
Bill Stein	311	Julio Cruz	172	Dan Meyer	29

HR		RBI		Doubles		Triples	
Ruppert Jones	51	Dan Meyer	220	Ruppert Jones	79	Ruppert Jones	20
Dan Meyer	50	Ruppert Jones	200	Bruce Bochte	63	Leon Roberts	13
Leon Roberts	37	Bruce Bochte	151	Dan Meyer	63	Dan Meyer	12

Pitching Leaders

Wins		Earned Run Average	
Glenn Abbott	23	Enrique Romo	3.25
Enrique Romo	19	Mike Parrott	4.13
Rick Honeycutt	16	Tom House	4.34

Strikeouts		Shutouts	
Glenn Abbott	192	Mike Parrott	2
John Montague	172	Rick Honeycutt	2
Mike Parrott	168	Floyd Bannister	2
		Paul Mitchell	2

Saves	
Enrique Romo	26
Shane Rawley	15
Byron McLaughlin	14

26. <u>Toronto Blue Jays</u> – Decade Record: 166-318, 0 Division Titles

It was a tough start for Toronto when they began play as an expansion club in 1977. The Blue Jays had the decade's worst overall winning percentage, worst single season record (53-109 in 1979), and finished the furthest out of first place of any team (50½ games behind Baltimore in 1979). Slowly though, the groundwork for success was being put in place. Toronto's draft philosophy was very different from most previous expansion clubs, who generally picked a lot of veteran utility men for fans to recognize as legitimate major leaguers. The Jays, understanding the team would struggle at the outset anyway, focused on drafting other team's young AA and AAA talent. By 1983 the club had its first winning record, and began a stretch of 11 consecutive winning seasons that included consecutive World Series championships.

As expected, Toronto finished in last place in the tough American League East during their initial season, with a 54-107 record. Third baseman Roy Howell led the team in hitting (.316) and on-base % (.383), while Bob Bailor, who played shortstop and the outfield, was the club leader in hits (154), runs (62), and stolen bases (15). Veterans Ron Fairly and Otto Velez provided some power with 19 and 16 home runs respectively. Pete Vuckovich was the Blue Jays best pitcher, pitching mostly out of the bullpen but also starting 8 times, and tallied a 7-7 record with a 3.47 ERA and 8 saves.

The struggles continued in 1978, as Toronto again lost more than 100 games (59-102). DH Rico Carty led the team with a .284 average, and contributed 20 home runs. First baseman John Mayberry hit a team high 22 homers and 70 RBI. Unlike in Kansas City, where Mayberry was acquired, the Jays had few table setters to drive in and finished dead last in the majors with only 28 stolen bases. Young starters Tom Underwood (6-14, 4.10) and Jim Clancy (10-12, 4.09) received no run support but began to show potential. 20-year-old Victor Cruz, acquired from St Louis for Vuckovich, shined in the bullpen, going 7-3 with 9 saves and a 1.71

ERA. Cruz was sent to Cleveland after the season for shortstop Alfredo Griffin, and never had another good year in the big leagues.

In 1979 the Blue Jays were the only AL East team with a losing record; they finished 28½ games behind 6th place Cleveland. Griffin was an immediate success, hitting .287 with 179 hits and 22 doubles, and brought much needed speed with 10 triples and 21 stolen bases (though he was also caught stealing 16 times). But power was still in short supply, as the Jays finished last in the league only 95 home runs. Mayberry again led in homers (21) and RBI (74). While the 39 year-old Carty's number slipped, Otto Velez contributed 15 home runs, 21 doubles, and batted .288 with a .396 OB% in only 325 plate appearances. Underwood again pitched in hard luck (9-16, 3.69), but 21-year-old Dave Stieb went 8-8 with a 4.31 ERA. Stieb joined Vuckovich and Cruz as the only Toronto pitchers to *not* have an overall losing record in the 70s, but more importantly would become a 7-time All-Star and one of the game's best pitchers for the next decade.

Offensive Leaders

Batting Avg		On Base %		Slugging %			
Alfredo Griffin	.287	Otto Velez	.379	Otto Velez	.477		
Roy Howell	.273	John Mayberry	.350	John Mayberry	.437		
Al Woods	.273	Roy Howell	.335	Rico Carty	.432		
Hits		Runs		Stolen Bases			
Bob Bailor	413	Bob Bailor	186	Bob Bailor	34		
Roy Howell	390	Roy Howell	168	Alfredo Griffin	21		
Rick Bosetti	308	Al Woods	134	Rick Bosetti	19		
HR		RBI		Doubles		Triples	
John Mayberry	43	Roy Howell	177	Roy Howell	73	Bob Bailor	17
Otto Velez	40	Otto Velez	148	Bob Bailor	61	Al Woods	11
Roy Howell	33	John Mayberry	144	Rick Bosetti	60	Dave McKay	11

Pitching Leaders

Wins		Earned Run Average	
Dave Lemanczyk	25	Tom Underwood	3.88
Jesse Jefferson	18	Jim Clancy	4.58
Jim Clancy	16	Jesse Jefferson	4.59
Strikeouts		Shutouts	
Tom Underwood	266	Dave Lemanczyk	3
Jesse Jefferson	254	Tom Underwood	2
Dave Lemanczyk	230	Jesse Jefferson	2
Saves			
Mike Willis	12		
Tom Murphy	9		
Victor Cruz	9		

Decade Records

TEAM	W	L	PCT.
Cincinnati Reds	953	657	.592
Baltimore Orioles	944	656	.590
Pittsburgh Pirates	916	695	.569
Los Angeles Dodgers	910	701	.565
Boston Red Sox	895	714	.556
New York Yankees	892	715	.555
Kansas City Royals	851	760	.528
Oakland Athletics	838	772	.520
Minnesota Twins	812	794	.506
Philadelphia Phillies	812	801	.503
St. Louis Cardinals	800	813	.496
San Francisco Giants	794	818	.493
Houston Astros	793	817	.493
Detroit Tigers	789	820	.490
Chicago Cubs	785	827	.487
California Angels	781	831	.484
Texas Rangers	614	672	.477
New York Mets	763	850	.473
Chicago White Sox	752	853	.469
Montreal Expos	748	862	.465
Cleveland Indians	737	866	.460
Milwaukee Brewers	738	873	.458
Atlanta Braves	725	883	.451
San Diego Padres	667	942	.415
Washington Senators	133	188	.414
Seattle Mariners	187	297	.386
Toronto Blue Jays	166	318	.343

Division Winners

	AL East	AL West		NL East	NL West
1970	BALTIMORE	Minnesota		Pittsburgh	Cincinnati
1971	Baltimore	Oakland		PITTSBURGH	San Francisco
1972	Detroit	OAKLAND		Pittsburgh	Cincinnati
1973	Baltimore	OAKLAND		New York	Cincinnati
1974	Baltimore	OAKLAND		Pittsburgh	Los Angeles
1975	Boston	Oakland		Pittsburgh	CINCINNATI
1976	New York	Kansas City		Philadelphia	CINCINNATI
1977	NEW YORK	Kansas City		Philadelphia	Los Angeles
1978	NEW YORK	Kansas City		Philadelphia	Los Angeles
1979	Baltimore	California		PITTSBURGH	Cincinnati

POST SEASON

	ALCS	NLCS	World Series	WS MVP
1970	Baltimore Orioles defeat Minnesota Twins 3 games to 0	Cincinnati Reds defeat Pittsburgh Pirates 3 games to 0	Baltimore Orioles (108-54, AL) defeat Cincinnati Reds (102-60, NL) 4 games to 1	Brooks Robinson 9-21 (.429), 2 2B, 2 HR, 6 RBI
1971	Baltimore Orioles defeat Oakland Athletics 3 games to 0	Pittsburgh Pirates defeat San Francisco Giants 3 games to 1	Pittsburgh Pirates (97-65, NL) defeat Baltimore Orioles (101-57, AL) 4 games to 3	Roberto Clemente 12-29 (.414), 2 2B, 2 HR
1972	Oakland Athletics defeat Detroit Tigers 3 games to 2	Cincinnati Reds defeat Pittsburgh Pirates 3 games to 2	Oakland Athletics (93-62, AL) defeat Cincinnati Reds (95-59, NL) 4 games to 3	Gene Tenace 8-23 (.348), 1 2B, 4 HR, 9 RBI
1973	Oakland Athletics defeat Baltimore Orioles 3 games to 2	New York Mets defeat Cincinnati Reds 3 games to 2	Oakland Athletics (94-68, AL) defeat New York Mets (82-79, NL) 4 games to 3	Reggie Jackson 9-29 (.310), 3 2B, 1 3B, 1 HR, 6 RBI
1974	Oakland Athletics defeat Baltimore Orioles 3 games to 1	Los Angeles Dodgers defeat Pittsburgh Pirates 3 games to 1	Oakland Athletics (90-72, AL) defeat Los Angeles Dodgers (102-60, NL) 4 games to 1	Rollie Fingers 1-0 Rec, 2 Sv, 1.93 ERA
1975	Boston Red Sox defeat Oakland Athletics 3 games to 0	Cincinnati Reds defeat Pittsburgh Pirates 3 games to 0	Cincinnati Reds (108-54, NL) defeat Boston Red Sox (95-65, AL) 4 games to 3	Pete Rose 10-27 (.370), 1 2B, 1 3B, 5 BB
1976	New York Yankees defeat Kansas City Royals 3 games to 2	Cincinnati Reds defeat Philadelphia Phillies 3 games to 0	Cincinnati Reds (102-60, NL) defeat New York Yankees (97-62, AL) 4 games to 0	Johnny Bench 8-15 (.533), 2 HR, 6 RBI
1977	New York Yankees defeat Kansas City Royals 3 games to 2	Los Angeles Dodgers defeat Philadelphia Phillies 3 games to 1	New York Yankees (100-62, AL) defeat Los Angeles Dodgers (98-64, NL) 4 games to 2	Reggie Jackson 9-20 (.450), 5 HR, 8 RBI, 10 R
1978	New York Yankees defeat Kansas City Royals 3 games to 1	Los Angeles Dodgers defeat Philadelphia Phillies 3 games to 1	New York Yankees (100-63, AL) defeat Los Angeles Dodgers (95-67, NL) 4 games to 2	Bucky Dent 10-24 (.417), 7 RBI
1979	Baltimore Orioles defeat California Angels 3 games to 1	Pittsburgh Pirates defeat Cincinnati Reds 3 games to 0	Pittsburgh Pirates (98-64, NL) defeat Baltimore Orioles (102-57, AL) 4 games to 3	Willie Stargell 12-30 (.400), 3 HR, 4 2B, 7 RBI

Top Rivalries

1. Yankees-Royals

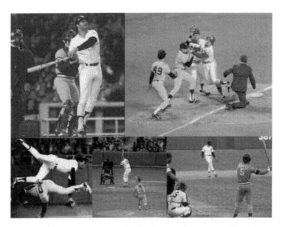

The Yanks and Royals met three straight years in the ALCS from 1976-78. New York came out on top each time, but the matchup was far from one-sided. In fact, each series was a hotly contested pressure-cooker. In '76, the two teams exchanged wins back and forth over the first 4 contests, and in the deciding 5th game at Yankee Stadium, they scored 2 runs each in the 1st inning. KC went up 3-2 in the 2nd, but the Yanks countered with 2 in the 3rd and 2 more in the 6th for what appeared to be a commanding 6-3 lead. Kansas City's George Brett hit a 3-run homer in the 8th inning to tie the game, before New York's Chris Chambliss ended the series with a walk-off homer leading off the 9th.

In 1977 the two teams were the only 100 game winners in baseball and met in the ALCS - again exchanging wins back and forth over the first 4 games. Game 2 included two devastating take-out slides at second base by Kansas City's Hal McRae, one knocking the ball loose from Yankee shortstop Bucky Dent on a tag play, the other a rolling body block on New York second baseman Willie Randolph while breaking up a double play. Both ensured bad blood for the remainder of the series. Game 5 this time was played in Kansas City and again fans were treated to first inning fireworks, including an RBI triple by Brett, who went in hard to Graig Nettles at third. Nettles kicked Brett in the ribs and George came up with fists swinging, the two trading wild hooks as benches emptied. KC went out in front 2-0 and 3-1, only to fall again to a Yankee comeback on RBI singles by Reggie Jackson and Mickey Rivers, followed by a Willie Randolph sac fly which gave New York the lead for good.

The 1978 ALCS did not go 5 games, but the teams once again exchanged wins in the first two games, and got into another see-saw affair in Game 3. Brett smashed 3 solo home runs off Catfish Hunter, but Thurman Munson's 2-run shot in the 8th turned a Royals 4-3 advantage into a 5-4 Yankee win. The next day Nettles and Roy White homered as the Bombers held on 2-1 behind stellar pitching from Ron Guidry and Goose Gossage.

Total runs over the three series: '76: Yanks-23, KC-24, '77: Yanks-21 KC-22, '78: Yanks-19, KC-17. Overall 63-63. Each year the Yankees were the better team, but never by a heck of a lot. While this rivalry didn't extend throughout the entire decade, for sheer intensity and hard-fought competition, nothing was better than the Yankees - Royals.

2. Reds-Pirates

The Reds swept the Bucs in the 1970 National League Championship Series. Flash forward to 1972 - defending World Champion Pittsburgh was leading by 1 in the deciding Game 5 of an NLCS rematch before Johnny Bench led off the 9th with a homer to tie the game. Later in the inning the Pirates' Bob Moose threw a wild pitch, scoring pinch runner George Foster for the deciding run.

In 1974 Pirate pitcher Doc Ellis began a game by purposely hitting Rose, Morgan, and Driessen, and aiming (but missing) the next six pitches at Perez and Bench before being removed. Later in the year Cincinnati's Jack Billingham nailed Pirate pitcher Bruce Kison with a pitch, touching off a bench-clearing brawl.

The Pirates eventually got their revenge over the Big Red Machine in 1979 with an NLCS sweep; league MVP Willie Stargell hit .455 in the Series with 2 home runs and 6 RBI.

Many Pittsburgh fans are still fuming about the MVP award Willie DIDN'T win. That was in 1973, when Stargell led the league with 44 home runs, 43 doubles, 119 RBI, and a .646 Slugging percentage. Cincinnati's Pete Rose took the honor on the strength of 230 hits and a .338 batting average.

Both teams won six division titles and two World Series, and between them they took 6 of the National League's 10 pennants.

3. Pirates-Phillies

The Pennsylvania state rivalry grew as these two teams dominated the National League East with 9 of 10 titles - 6 for Pittsburgh and 3 for Philadelphia. Pittsburgh was the more consistent of the two squads; they finished lower than second place only once all decade - in 1973, when they finished third but still only 2 1/2 games out of first. The Phils struggled with three straight last place seasons from 1971-73 before finding their stride. Physical play was the rule - on opening day 1976 the Pirates' 6-foot-5, 230-pound Dave Parker ran over 5-11, 188-pound Phils' catcher Johnny Oates, breaking his collarbone. Then in 1977, Phillies third baseman Mike Schmidt broke a finger punching the face of Pirates pitcher Bruce Kison after charging the mound.

From 1975-78 Pittsburgh and Philadelphia finished 1-2 each year in the NL East with the Phillies winning three division titles in that span. But while the Pirates won 2 World Championships over the decade, Philadelphia lost in all three of their NLCS appearances.

4. Yankees-Red Sox

Regarded by many as the fiercest rivalry in sports, there was certainly no love lost between the clubs throughout the 70s. How close were the teams during regular season play? Boston won 895 games, 5th best in the majors, and the Yankees won 892, good for 6th best. But New York won three AL pennants and 2 World Series, while Boston managed only one division title and pennant, in 1975.

In the 9th inning of a 1973 game, Yankee catcher Thurman Munson collided with Boston backstop Carlton Fisk, touching off a bench clearing brawl. Then in 1976 Lou Piniella crashed into Fisk at home plate and again punches were exchanged and benches emptied. As order was being finally restored, Sox pitcher Bill Lee was helped off the ground with an injured shoulder and got in Graig Nettles' face before Nettles squared up Lee with a couple more haymakers. In 1978 Boston built a 14 1/2 game lead in August over the two-time defending AL Champs before New York stormed all the way back. The teams finished in a dead tie, forcing a one-game playoff. The Red-Sox led 2-0 in the top 7th when the Yankee's Bucky Dent crushed a three-run homer over the Green Monster, leading the Yanks to a victory and an eventual 2nd straight World Championship.

5. Reds-Dodgers

During the decade these two clubs claimed every National League West title, except in 1971 when the Giants took the division. Cincinnati had 953 regular season wins during the decade, best in the majors, while LA was 4th with 910. The Big Red Machine featured household names like Pete Rose, Joe Morgan, Tony Perez, and Johnny Bench, while the Dodgers were led by first baseman Steve Garvey, third-sacker Ron Cey, speedy second baseman Davey Lopes, and strong pitchers such as Don Sutton and relief ace Mike Marshall.

"I don't think there's a rivalry like ours in either league", said Reds manager Sparky Anderson in 1975.

The Reds captured six division flags, four pennants, and two World Championships. LA won three division titles and three pennants, and the two teams made up all the World Series appearances for the National League in a 5 year stretch from 1974-78.

Most Valuable Player of the Decade

1. Reggie Jackson – Oakland, Baltimore, New York

Success seemed to follow Reginald Martinez Jackson wherever he played during the 1970s. In none of those years did any of Reggie's teams win less than 88 games. Oakland played .586 baseball with Jackson and .423 after he left. New York managed a .537 winning percentage pre-Reggie and .596 with him. The self-proclaimed 'Straw that Stirs the Drink' played on 7 division winning clubs and five World Champions in the decade. And once on the post-season stage, there was nobody better. Jackson hit a torrid .360 with 6 doubles, a triple, 9 HR and 23 RBI in 24 World Series games. He took home two World Series MVP trophies, hitting .310 with 5 extra base hits and 6 RBI for Oakland against the Mets in 1973, and .450 with 5 HR and 8 RBI as a Yankee in taking over the 1977 Series against the Dodgers. "Mr. October" may have been even better in 1978, hitting .462 with 2 HR and 6 RBI in the ALCS and .391 with 2 HR and 8 RBI in the World Series.

Reggie was a 9-time 70s All-Star and won the regular season MVP award in 1973. He finished in the Top 25 in MVP voting 9 times and was a Top 10 finisher 4 times. He led the league in home runs and slugging percentage twice each. For the decade Jackson was tied for the lead among all players with 586 extra-base hits, finished 2nd in HR, 4th in RBI, 8th in runs scored, and 9th in doubles.

Yr	Team	G	AB	R	H	2B	3B	HR	RBI	BB	SO	SB	AVG	OBP	SLG
1970	Oakland	149	426	57	101	21	2	23	66	75	135	26	.237	.359	.458
1971	Oakland	150	567	87	157	29	3	32	80	63	161	16	.277	.352	.508
1972	Oakland	135	499	72	132	25	2	25	75	59	125	9	.265	.350	.473
1973	Oakland	151	539	99	158	28	2	32	117	76	111	22	.293	.383	.531
1974	Oakland	148	506	90	146	25	1	29	93	86	105	25	.289	.391	.514
1975	Oakland	157	593	91	150	39	3	36	104	67	133	17	.253	.329	.511
1976	Baltimore	134	498	84	138	27	2	27	91	54	108	28	.277	.351	.502
1977	New York	146	525	93	150	39	2	32	110	74	129	17	.286	.375	.550
1978	New York	139	511	82	140	13	5	27	97	58	133	14	.274	.356	.477
1979	New York	131	465	78	138	24	2	29	89	65	107	9	.297	.382	.544
Reg Season Tot		1440	5129	833	1410	270	24	292	922	677	1247	183	.275	.363	.508
Total Postseason		53	190	28	58	10	1	14	38	24	44	4	.305	.376	.589
Total World Series		24	102	18	31	6	1	9	23	13	21	1	.360	.431	.767

2. Joe Morgan – Houston, Cincinnati
3. Johnny Bench – Cincinnati
4. Willie Stargell – Pittsburgh
5. Pete Rose – Cincinnati, Philadelphia
6. George Brett – Kansas City
7. Mike Schmidt – Philadelphia
8. Catfish Hunter – Oakland, New York
9. Rollie Fingers – Oakland, San Diego
10. Bert Campaneris – Oakland, Texas, California

Top Individual Seasons

Position Players (GG= Gold Glove)

	Yr	Team	G	AB	R	H	2B	3B	HR	RBI	BB	SO	SB	AVG	OBP	SLG	
Johnny Bench	1970	CIN	158	605	97	177	35	4	45	148	54	102	5	.293	.345	.587	GG
George Foster	1977	CIN	158	615	124	197	31	2	52	149	61	107	6	.320	.382	.631	
Joe Morgan	1976	CIN	141	472	113	151	30	5	27	111	114	41	60	.320	.444	.576	
Fred Lynn	1979	BOS	147	531	116	177	42	1	39	122	82	79	2	.333	.423	.637	GG
Hank Aaron	1971	ATL	139	495	95	162	22	3	47	118	71	58	1	.327	.410	.669	
Joe Morgan	1975	CIN	146	498	107	163	27	6	17	94	132	52	67	.327	.466	.508	GG
Rod Carew	1977	MIN	155	616	128	239	38	16	14	100	69	55	23	.388	.449	.570	
Willie Stargell	1971	PIT	141	511	104	151	26	0	48	125	83	154	0	.295	.398	.628	
Joe Torre	1971	STL	161	634	97	230	34	8	24	137	63	70	4	.363	.421	.555	
Dave Parker	1978	PIT	148	581	102	194	32	12	30	117	57	92	20	.334	.394	.585	GG
Johnny Bench	1972	CIN	147	538	87	145	22	2	40	125	100	84	6	.270	.379	.541	GG
Carlton Fisk	1977	BOS	152	536	106	169	26	3	26	102	75	85	7	.315	.402	.521	
Jim Rice	1979	BOS	158	619	117	201	39	6	39	130	57	97	9	.325	.381	.596	
Carl Yastrzemski	1970	BOS	161	566	125	186	29	0	40	102	128	66	23	.329	.452	.592	
Jim Rice	1978	BOS	163	677	121	213	25	15	46	139	58	126	7	.315	.370	.600	
Rico Carty	1970	ATL	136	478	84	175	23	3	25	101	77	46	1	.366	.454	.584	
Billy Williams	1972	CHC	150	574	95	191	34	6	37	122	62	59	3	.333	.398	.606	
Willie Stargell	1973	PIT	148	522	106	156	43	3	44	119	80	129	0	.299	.392	.646	
Fred Lynn	1975	BOS	145	528	103	175	47	7	21	105	62	90	10	.331	.401	.566	GG
Dick Allen	1972	CHW	148	506	90	156	28	5	37	113	99	126	19	.308	.420	.603	
George Brett	1979	KCR	154	645	119	212	42	20	23	107	51	36	17	.329	.376	.563	
Cesar Cedeno	1972	HOU	139	559	103	179	39	8	22	82	56	62	55	.320	.385	.537	GG
Pete Rose	1973	CIN	160	680	115	230	36	8	5	64	65	42	10	.338	.401	.437	
Greg Luzinski	1977	PHI	149	554	99	171	35	3	39	130	80	140	3	.309	.394	.594	
Jim Rice	1977	BOS	160	644	104	206	29	15	39	114	53	120	5	.320	.376	.593	
Tony Perez	1970	CIN	158	587	107	186	28	6	40	129	83	134	8	.317	.401	.589	
Frank Howard	1970	WSA	161	566	90	160	15	1	44	126	132	125	1	.283	.416	.546	
Willie McCovey	1970	SFG	152	495	98	143	39	2	39	126	137	75	0	.289	.444	.612	
Harmon Killebrew	1970	MIN	157	527	96	143	20	1	41	113	128	84	0	.271	.411	.546	
Dave Parker	1977	PIT	159	637	107	215	44	8	21	88	58	107	17	.338	.397	.531	GG
Dave Kingman	1979	CHC	145	532	97	153	19	5	48	115	45	131	4	.288	.343	.613	
Pete Rose	1976	CIN	162	665	130	215	42	6	10	63	86	54	9	.323	.404	.450	
Bobby Murcer	1971	NYY	146	529	94	175	25	6	25	94	91	60	14	.331	.427	.543	
Orlando Cepeda	1970	ATL	148	567	87	173	33	0	34	111	47	75	6	.305	.365	.543	
Reggie Jackson	1973	OAK	151	539	99	158	28	2	32	117	76	111	22	.293	.383	.531	
Billy Williams	1970	CHC	161	636	137	205	34	4	42	129	72	65	7	.322	.391	.586	
Don Baylor	1979	CAL	162	628	120	186	33	3	36	139	71	51	22	.296	.371	.530	
Ralph Garr	1974	ATL	143	606	87	214	24	17	11	54	28	52	26	.353	.383	.503	
Bobby Bonds	1973	SFG	160	643	131	182	34	4	39	96	87	148	43	.283	.370	.530	
Jim Hickman	1970	CHC	149	514	102	162	33	4	32	115	93	99	0	.315	.419	.582	
Lou Brock	1971	STL	157	640	126	200	37	7	7	61	76	107	64	.313	.385	.425	
Reggie Smith	1977	LAD	148	488	104	150	27	4	32	87	104	76	7	.307	.427	.576	
Dave Parker	1975	PIT	148	558	75	172	35	10	25	101	38	89	8	.308	.357	.541	
Mike Schmidt	1977	PHI	154	544	114	149	27	11	38	101	104	122	15	.274	.393	.574	GG
Hank Aaron	1970	ATL	150	516	103	154	26	1	38	118	74	63	9	.298	.385	.574	
Dave Winfield	1979	SDP	159	597	97	184	27	10	34	118	85	71	15	.308	.395	.558	GG
Cesar Cedeno	1973	HOU	139	525	86	168	35	2	25	70	41	79	56	.320	.376	.537	GG
Mike Schmidt	1979	PHI	160	541	109	137	25	4	45	114	120	115	9	.253	.386	.564	
Johnny Bench	1977	CIN	142	494	67	136	34	2	31	109	58	95	2	.275	.348	.540	GG
Bobby Grich	1979	CAL	153	534	78	157	30	5	30	101	59	84	1	.294	.365	.537	

Starting Pitchers

	Yr	Team	G	CG	IP	W	L	WIN %	ERA	SV	SO	BB	H
Ron Guidry	1978	NYY	35	16	273.2	25	3	.893	1.74	0	248	72	187
Steve Carlton	1972	PHI	41	30	346.1	27	10	.730	1.97	0	310	87	257
Vida Blue	1971	OAK	39	24	312	24	8	.750	1.82	0	301	88	209
Catfish Hunter	1972	OAK	38	16	295.1	21	7	.750	2.04	0	191	70	200
Gaylord Perry	1972	CLE	41	29	342.2	24	16	.600	1.92	1	234	82	253
Tom Seaver	1971	NYM	36	21	286.1	20	10	.667	1.76	0	289	61	210
Wilbur Wood	1971	CHW	44	22	334	22	13	.629	1.91	1	210	62	272
Jim Palmer	1975	BAL	39	25	323	23	11	.676	2.09	1	193	80	253
Jim Palmer	1972	BAL	36	18	274.1	21	10	.677	2.07	0	184	70	219
Tom Seaver	1973	NYM	36	18	290	19	10	.655	2.08	0	251	64	219
Nolan Ryan	1973	CAL	41	26	326	21	16	.568	2.87	1	383	162	238
Don Sutton	1972	LAD	33	18	272.2	19	9	.679	2.08	0	207	63	186
Luis Tiant	1972	BOS	43	12	179	15	6	.714	1.91	3	123	65	128
Gaylord Perry	1978	SDP	37	5	260.2	21	6	.778	2.73	0	154	66	241
Catfish Hunter	1974	OAK	41	23	318.1	25	12	.676	2.49	0	143	46	268
Tom Seaver	1975	NYM	36	15	280.1	22	9	.710	2.38	0	243	88	217
Catfish Hunter	1975	NYY	39	30	328	23	14	.622	2.58	0	177	83	248
Dave McNally	1971	BAL	30	11	224.1	21	5	.808	2.89	0	91	58	188
Jim Palmer	1973	BAL	38	19	296.1	22	9	.710	2.40	1	158	113	225
Steve Carlton	1977	PHI	36	17	283	23	10	.697	2.64	0	198	89	229
Mike Cuellar	1970	BAL	40	21	297.2	24	8	.750	3.48	0	190	69	273
John Candelaria	1977	PIT	33	6	230.2	20	5	.800	2.34	0	133	50	197
Andy Messersmith	1974	LAD	39	13	292.1	20	6	.769	2.59	0	221	94	227
Fergie Jenkins	1971	CHC	39	30	325	24	13	.649	2.77	0	263	37	304
Fergie Jenkins	1974	TEX	41	29	328.1	25	12	.676	2.82	0	225	45	286
Mike Caldwell	1978	MIL	37	23	293.1	22	9	.710	2.36	1	131	54	258
Mickey Lolich	1971	DET	45	29	376	25	14	.641	2.92	0	308	92	336
Gary Nolan	1972	CIN	25	6	176	15	5	.750	1.99	0	90	30	147
Blue Moon Odom	1972	OAK	31	4	194.1	15	6	.714	2.50	0	86	87	164
Phil Niekro	1974	ATL	41	18	302.1	20	13	.606	2.38	1	195	88	249
Randy Jones	1976	SDP	40	25	315.1	22	14	.611	2.74	0	93	50	274
Nolan Ryan	1974	CAL	42	26	332.2	22	16	.579	2.89	0	367	202	221
Frank Tanana	1976	CAL	34	23	288.1	19	10	.655	2.43	0	261	73	212
Jim Palmer	1978	BAL	38	19	296	21	12	.636	2.46	0	138	97	246
Mark Fidrych	1976	DET	31	24	250.1	19	9	.679	2.34	0	97	53	217
Luis Tiant	1974	BOS	38	25	311.1	22	13	.629	2.92	0	176	82	281
Bob Gibson	1972	STL	34	23	278	19	11	.633	2.46	0	208	88	226
Jim Kaat	1974	CHW	42	15	277.1	21	13	.618	2.92	0	142	63	263
Dave McNally	1970	BAL	40	16	296	24	9	.727	3.22	0	185	78	277
Randy Jones	1975	SDP	37	18	285	20	12	.625	2.24	0	103	56	242
Tom Seaver	1972	NYM	35	13	262	21	12	.636	2.92	0	249	77	215
Andy Messersmith	1975	LAD	42	19	321.2	19	14	.576	2.29	1	213	96	244
Steve Blass	1972	PIT	33	11	249.2	19	8	.704	2.49	0	117	84	227
Tom Seaver	1977	TOT	33	19	261.1	21	6	.778	2.58	0	196	66	199
Bob Gibson	1970	STL	34	23	294	23	7	.767	3.12	0	274	88	262
Mickey Lolich	1972	DET	41	23	327.1	22	14	.611	2.50	0	250	74	282
Bob Forsch	1977	STL	35	8	217.1	20	7	.741	3.48	0	95	69	210
Jim Palmer	1976	BAL	40	23	315	22	13	.629	2.51	0	159	84	255
Catfish Hunter	1973	OAK	36	11	256.1	21	5	.808	3.34	0	124	69	222
Buzz Capra	1974	ATL	39	11	217	16	8	.667	2.28	1	137	84	163

Relief Pitchers

	Yr	Team	G	GS	IP	W	L	WIN %	ERA	SV	SO	BB	H
Bruce Sutter	1977	CHC	62	0	107.1	7	3	.700	1.34	31	129	23	69
Mike Marshall	1974	LAD	106	0	208.1	15	12	.556	2.42	21	143	56	191
John Hiller	1973	DET	65	0	125.1	10	5	.667	1.44	38	124	39	89
Bruce Sutter	1979	CHC	62	0	101.1	6	6	.500	2.22	37	110	32	67
Rich Gossage	1977	PIT	72	0	133	11	9	.550	1.62	26	151	49	78
Jim Kern	1979	TEX	71	0	143	13	5	.722	1.57	29	136	62	99
Sparky Lyle	1977	NYY	72	0	137	13	5	.722	2.17	26	68	33	131
Al Hrabosky	1975	STL	65	0	97.1	13	3	.813	1.66	22	82	33	72
Jim Brewer	1972	LAD	51	0	78.1	8	7	.533	1.26	17	69	25	41
Clay Carroll	1972	CIN	65	0	96	6	4	.600	2.25	37	51	32	89
Darold Knowles	1972	OAK	54	0	65.2	5	1	.833	1.37	11	36	37	49
Bob Stanley	1978	BOS	52	3	141.2	15	2	.882	2.60	10	38	34	142
Wayne Granger	1970	CIN	67	0	84.2	6	5	.545	2.66	35	38	27	79
Rollie Fingers	1978	SDP	67	0	107.1	6	13	.316	2.52	37	72	29	84
Sparky Lyle	1972	NYY	59	0	107.2	9	5	.643	1.92	35	75	29	84
Tug McGraw	1972	NYM	54	0	106	8	6	.571	1.70	27	92	40	71
Rollie Fingers	1973	OAK	62	2	126.2	7	8	.467	1.92	22	110	39	107
Mike Marshall	1973	MON	92	0	179	14	11	.560	2.66	31	124	75	163
Sparky Lyle	1974	NYY	66	0	114	9	3	.750	1.66	15	89	43	93
John Hiller	1974	DET	59	0	150	17	14	.548	2.64	13	134	62	127
Lindy McDaniel	1970	NYY	62	0	111.2	9	5	.643	2.01	29	81	23	88
Kent Tekulve	1979	PIT	94	0	134.1	10	8	.556	2.75	31	75	49	109
Joe Sambito	1979	HOU	63	0	91.1	8	7	.533	1.77	22	83	23	80
Rich Gossage	1978	NYY	63	0	134.1	10	11	.476	2.01	27	122	59	87
Doug Bair	1978	CIN	70	0	100.1	7	6	.538	1.97	28	91	38	87
Pedro Borbon	1973	CIN	80	0	121	11	4	.733	2.16	14	60	35	137
Rawly Eastwick	1976	CIN	71	0	107.2	11	5	.688	2.09	26	70	27	93
Mike Marshall	1972	MON	65	0	116	14	8	.636	1.78	18	95	47	82
Mudcat Grant	1970	TOT	80	0	135.1	8	3	.727	1.86	24	58	32	112
Ken Sanders	1970	STL/OAK	50	0	92.1	5	2	.714	1.75	13	64	25	64
Tug McGraw	1971	NYM	51	1	111	11	4	.733	1.70	8	109	41	73
Rich Gossage	1975	CHW	62	0	141.2	9	8	.529	1.84	26	130	70	99
Ron Perranoski	1970	MIN	67	0	111	7	8	.467	2.43	34	55	42	108
Kent Tekulve	1978	PIT	91	0	135.1	8	7	.533	2.33	31	77	55	115
Lerrin LaGrow	1977	CHW	66	0	98.2	7	3	.700	2.46	25	63	35	81
Darold Knowles	1970	WSA	71	0	119.1	2	14	.125	2.04	27	71	58	100
Eddie Watt	1971	BAL	35	0	39.2	3	1	.750	1.82	11	26	8	39
Tom Burgmeier	1971	KCR	67	0	88.1	9	7	.563	1.73	17	44	30	71
Sparky Lyle	1976	NYY	64	0	103.2	7	8	.467	2.26	23	61	42	82
Ramon Hernandez	1972	PIT	53	0	70	5	0	1.000	1.67	14	47	22	50

'Hybrid' Pitcher

	Yr	Team	G	GS	IP	W	L	WIN %	ERA	SV	SO	BB	H
Luis Tiant	1972	BOS	43	19	179	15	6	.714	1.91	3	123	65	128

Top 10 Memorable Moments

1. **Hank Aaron hits 715th Home Run – April 8, 1974**

Babe Ruth's career mark had stood for nearly 40 years before Aaron tied it on his first at-bat of opening day 1974 in Cincinnati. #715 came in the 4th inning of the Braves' home opener, a 2-run shot into the Atlanta bullpen in left field off the Dodgers' Al Downing. '715' flashed in block letters on the scoreboard and Dodger infielders congratulated Aaron as he slowly made his way around the bases with the entire Braves team waiting to greet him at home plate. The consistent, understated Aaron never had a 50 home run season en route to becoming baseball's home run king.

2. **Reggie Jackson hits 3 Home Runs on 3 Consecutive Pitches in World Series – October 18, 1977**

Reggie's flair for the dramatic was on full display in Game 6 of the 1977 World Series. Jackson, who had already homered in Game 4 and in his last at-bat of Game 5, walked his first time up. In the 4th inning Reggie lined a go ahead 2-run homer off Burt Hooten, then followed with a nearly identical shot on the first pitch of his next at-bat with one on off Elias Sosa in the 5th, making the score 7-3. The final blow came against Charlie Hough: a long bomb to dead center on the first pitch of the 8th, giving him 4 home runs in his last 4 swings, and securing MVP honors for Mr. October, to go along with his 1973 award.

3. **Carlton Fisk hits walkoff homerun in 12th inning to win Game 6 of 1975 World Series – October 22, 1975**

Down 3 games to 2, the Red Sox took an early 3-0 lead on a Fred Lynn home run, fell behind 6-3, and then tied it in the 8th on Bernie Carbo's second pinch hit homer of the series. From there, the Reds' George Foster nailed Denny Doyle at home in the bottom 9th, followed by a brilliant Dwight Evans catch to rob Joe Morgan in the 11th. Finally, Fisk led off the 12th against rookie Pat Darcy with a long fly down the left field line, then shuffled toward first while waving his arms to body English the ball fair. The drive hit the foul pole, tying the series as Fenway erupted to celebrate the ending of one of baseball's classic contests.

4. **Chris Chambliss ends 1976 ALCS with Game 5 homer in 9th – October 13, 1976**

Yankee fans long used to success were suffering through a 12 year pennant drought. On a frigid night at Yankee Stadium, New York led 6-3 in the 8th inning of the ALCS' deciding game, then watched George Brett tie the score on a three-run homer off Grant Jackson. Leading off the 9th, Chris Chambliss faced right hander Mark Littell, and belted a high fastball over the right field fence. Fans stormed the field, and despite Chambliss' best efforts, he never reached third base and made a beeline for the clubhouse, helmet in his arm, alternately spinning away and barreling over revelers who were mobbing him.

5. **Pete Rose breaks NL record with hit in 38th straight game – July 25, 1978**

Fresh off his 3,000th hit in May, Rose went 2 for 4 on June 14, and matched that in the two games that followed. His hot streak extended into July, and by July 24th he had tied the modern National League record set by Tommy Holmes of the Boston Braves in 1945 by hitting in 37 consecutive games. The next night Rose singled off Craig Swan at Shea Stadium to set a new modern record, which he extended to 44 games, tying Willie Keeler's all-time NL mark set in 1897.

6. **Brooks Robinson (1970 World Series) and Graig Nettles (1978 World Series) star at the Hot Corner**

Baltimore third baseman Brooks Robinson did it all in the 1970 World Series, hitting .429 with 2 home runs, and making perhaps the play of the decade in Game 1 – backhanding a Lee May 3 hopper behind third base, and with his momentum taking him about four steps into foul territory, planted and heaved a throw that skidded on the turf and into first baseman Boog Powell's mitt to nail May by a step. In the 1st inning of Game 3 Robinson made a leaping grab of Tony Perez's hopper, stepped on third and fired to first for a double play. In the 2nd frame, Robinson snagged a slow grounder and barely threw out a sprinting Tommy Helms. And in the sixth, Robinson made a diving catch of a line drive by Johnny Bench.

In Game 3 of the '78 Fall Classic Nettles single-handedly saved at least 4 runs with the Yankees down 2 games to none and clinging to a 2-1 lead. With 2 out in the 3rd and a runner on he robbed Reggie Smith of a double with a diving backhand snag and a strong throw to first. Then he ended the 5th by starting a force play on a tough chopper hit by Steve Garvey with bases loaded. Finally, in the next inning with bases loaded again, Dave Lopes hit a hard one-hopper that Nettles snared on a backhand, and with his body falling toward the line, whirled in a 360 and rifled a strike to second to barely force the runner and end another threat.

7. **Bucky Dent hits 3-run Home Run in one-game playoff – October 2, 1978**

The Yankees had already battled back from 14½ games down in August to overtake the Sox, but by season's end the teams finished in a tie. It was only fitting that Boston pulled ahead 2-0 in the one-game playoff at Fenway Park. The light-hitting Dent came up with 2 on in the bottom of the 7th inning, and after fouling a ball off his ankle and limping around for 5 minutes, took Mike Torrez' next pitch over the Green Monster, giving the Yankees a lead they would never surrender in a 5-4 victory.

8. **Willie Stargell closes out decade with 4 for 5 Game 7 performance in 1979 World Series clincher – October 17, 1979**

The 1979 season co-MVP hit .455 in a 3-game sweep of Cincinnati, going 5 for 11 with 2 doubles and 2 home runs and taking NLCS MVP Honors. Then in the World Series against Baltimore, 'Pops' saved his best for last, with a 4-5 performance that included the go ahead 2-run home run, plus 2 doubles and a single. At 39, Stargell became the oldest World Series MVP, tying Reggie Jackson's 1977 mark of 25 total bases, finishing 12 for 30 with a record 7 extra base hits (4 doubles, 3 home runs), and 7 RBI.

9. **Nolan Ryan throws record-tying 4th no-hitter – June 1, 1975**

Ryan fought through elbow pain that would require off-season surgery, fanning 9 Baltimore Orioles en route to his fourth career no-hitter in 109 starts, tying Sandy Koufax's record of 4 no-hitters. Two years earlier, in 1973, Ryan tossed his first two no-hitters and broke Koufax's strikeout record of 382 by one. In 1974 he followed with another no-hitter, and twice that season tied a record with 19 strikeouts in a 9 inning game.

10. **Lou Brock steals record 105th Base – September 10, 1974**

One steal behind Maury Wills' record of 104 steals in the last game of a home stand at Busch Stadium, the 35 year old Brock swiped second off the Phillies' Dick Ruthven and Bob Boone in two consecutive times on base. He went on to steal 118 bases, winning his 8th stolen base crown in 9 years while enjoying one of his finest all-around seasons, batting .306 with 194 hits and 105 runs scored. Brock eventually broke Ty Cobb's all-time record of 892 steals in 1977, and finished his career with 938 swipes.

Honorable Mention-

- Tom Seaver strikes out 19 batters to tie MLB record, including last 10 in a row – April 22, 1970
- Pete Rose bowls over Ray Fosse to win 1970 All-Star game for National League – July 14, 1970
- Reggie Jackson hits light tower on roof in 1971 All-Star game blast off Doc Ellis at Tiger Stadium– July 13, 1971
- Pete Rose and Bud Harrelson fight at second base in Game 3 of 1973 NLCS – October 8, 1973

The Midsummer Classic

1970 All-Star Game – Riverfront Stadium (CIN)
National League 5, American League 4

The NL trailed 4-1 going into the 9th before a Dick Dietz home run and three more hits sent the game into extra innings. In the 12th Jim Hickman singled, and Pete Rose raced around from second base, bowling over and injuring Ray Fosse to score the winning run. Carl Yastrzemski went 4 for 6.

WP: Claude Osteen   LP: Clyde Wright
HR: Dick Dietz (NL)   MVP: Carl Yastrzemski (AL)

1971 All-Star Game – Tiger Stadium (DET)
American League 6, National League 4

Reggie Jackson's 520 foot 2-run blast off the Tiger Stadium roof began an American League comeback from a 3-0 deficit. They snapped a 9 game NL winning streak in a game that featured home runs from six future Hall of Famers.

WP: Vida Blue   LP: Dock Ellis
HR: Johnny Bench (NL), Hank Aaron (NL), Reggie Jackson (AL), Frank Robinson (AL), Harmon Killebrew (AL), Roberto Clemente (NL)   MVP: Frank Robinson (AL)

1972 All-Star Game – Atlanta Fulton County Stadium (ATL)
National League 4, American League 3

The NL tied a back-and-forth affair against Wilbur Wood in the 9th inning, and Joe Morgan's single won it in the 10th.

WP: Tug McGraw   LP: Dave McNally
HR: Hank Aaron (NL), Cookie Rojas (AL)
MVP: Joe Morgan (NL)

1973 All-Star Game – Royals Stadium (KC)
National League 7, American League 1

Bobby Bonds went 2-2 with a 2-run homer and hustling double as the NL coasted in the last of Willie Mays' 24 All-Star appearances.

WP: Rick Wise   LP: Bert Blyleven
HR: Johnny Bench (NL), Bobby Bonds (NL), Willie Davis (NL)
MVP: Bobby Bonds (NL)

1974 All-Star Game – Three Rivers Stadium (PIT)
National League 7, American League 2

The game featured defensive gems by Cesar Cedeno, Joe Morgan, and write-in starter Steve Garvey, who added a single and RBI double. Mike Marshall closed the door with two hitless innings as the AL was held to only four hits.

WP: Ken Brett   LP: Luis Tiant
HR: Reggie Smith (NL)
MVP: Steve Garvey (NL)

1975 All-Star Game – County Stadium (MIL)
National League 6, American League 3

Hank Aaron made his final All-Star appearance in front of his home town fans. Carl Yastrzemski tied the game in the 6th with a 3-run homer off Tom Seaver, but Bill Madlock's 2-run single in the 9th off Goose Gossage broke the deadlock.

WP: Ken Brett   LP: Luis Tiant
HR: Steve Garvey (NL), Jimmy Wynn (NL), Carl Yastrzemski (AL)
MVP: Bill Madlock (NL) / Jon Matlack (NL)

1976 All-Star Game – Veterans Stadium (PHI)
National League 7, American League 1

A Pete Rose single and Steve Garvey triple led to 2 first inning runs off starter Mark 'The Bird' Fidrych. That would prove to be all the National League needed as the AL managed only 1 hit past the 5th inning. George Foster had 3 RBI and Cesar Cedeno closed the scoring with a 2-run homer.

WP: Randy Jones LP: Mark Fidrych
HR: George Foster (NL), Cesar Cedeno (NL)
MVP: George Foster (NL)

1977 All-Star Game – Yankee Stadium (NYY)
National League 7, American League 5

Starting pitcher Jim Palmer surrendered 5 runs in 2 innings. A late AL comeback fell short as the NL continued its dominance, paced by 2 RBI each from Greg Luzinski and Dave Winfield.

WP: Don Sutton LP: Jim Palmer
HR: Joe Morgan (NL), Greg Luzinski (NL), Steve Garvey (NL), George Scott(AL)
MVP: Don Sutton (NL)

1978 All-Star Game – San Diego Stadium (SD)
National League 7, American League 3

The American League built an early 3-0 lead on 2 triples by Rod Carew, but the NL rallied for 3 in the third. They broke a 3-3 tie in the bottom 8th, keyed by Steve Garvey's lead-off- triple, a wild pitch, and a two-run single by Bob Boone.

WP: Bruce Sutter LP: Rich Gossage
HR: None
MVP: Steve Garvey (NL)

1979 All-Star Game – The Kingdome (SEA)
National League 7, American League 6

Lee Mazzilli's 8th inning homer tied the game, and his 9th inning bases loaded walk off Ron Guidry was the difference. In a game that featured 20 hits, 9 for extra bases, the game's highlight was a bottom of the 8th cannon throw on a fly from right-fielder Dave Parker to catcher Gary Carter, who blocked the plate to nail Brian Downing.

WP: Bruce Sutter LP: Jim Kern
HR: Fred Lynn (AL), Lee Mazzilli (NL)
MVP: Dave Parker (NL)

Selected All-Star Starters

1970

Pos	American League		National League	
P	Jim Palmer	Baltimore	Tom Seaver	New York
C	Bill Freehan	Detroit	Johnny Bench	Cincinnati
1B	Boog Powell	Baltimore	Dick Allen	St. Louis
2B	Rod Carew	Minnesota	Glenn Beckert	Chicago
3B	Harmon Killebrew	Minnesota	Tony Perez	Cincinnati
SS	Luis Aparicio	Chicago	Don Kessinger	Chicago
OF	Frank Howard	Washington	Rico Carty	Atlanta
OF	Carl Yastrzemski	Boston	Willie Mays	San Francisco
OF	Frank Robinson	Baltimore	Hank Aaron	Atlanta

1971

Pos	American League		National League	
P	Vida Blue	Oakland	Dock Ellis	Pittsburgh
C	Ray Fosse	Cleveland	Johnny Bench	Cincinnati
1B	Boog Powell	Baltimore	Willie McCovey	San Francisco
2B	Rod Carew	Minnesota	Glenn Beckert	Chicago
3B	Brooks Robinson	Baltimore	Joe Torre	St. Louis
SS	Luis Aparicio	Boston	Bud Harrelson	New York
OF	Tony Oliva	Minnesota	Willie Stargell	Pittsburgh
OF	Carl Yastrzemski	Boston	Willie Mays	San Francisco
OF	Frank Robinson	Baltimore	Hank Aaron	Atlanta

1972

Pos	American League		National League	
P	Jim Palmer	Baltimore	Bob Gibson	St. Louis
C	Bill Freehan	Detroit	Johnny Bench	Cincinnati
1B	Dick Allen	Chicago	Lee May	Houston
2B	Rod Carew	Minnesota	Joe Morgan	Cincinnati
3B	Brooks Robinson	Baltimore	Joe Torre	St. Louis
SS	Luis Aparicio	Boston	Don Kessinger	Chicago
OF	Carl Yastrzemski	Boston	Willie Stargell	Pittsburgh
OF	Bobby Murcer	New York	Roberto Clemente	Pittsburgh
OF	Reggie Jackson	Oakland	Hank Aaron	Atlanta

1973

Pos	American League		National League	
P	Catfish Hunter	Oakland	Rick Wise	St. Louis
C	Carlton Fisk	Boston	Johnny Bench	Cincinnati
1B	Dick Allen	Chicago	Hank Aaron	Atlanta
2B	Rod Carew	Minnesota	Joe Morgan	Cincinnati
3B	Brooks Robinson	Baltimore	Ron Santo	Chicago
SS	Bert Campaneris	Oakland	Chris Speier	San Francisco
OF	Bobby Murcer	New York	Cesar Cedeno	Houston
OF	Amos Otis	Kansas City	Billy Williams	Chicago
OF	Reggie Jackson	Oakland		

1974

Pos	American League		National League	
P	Gaylord Perry	Cleveland	Andy Messersmith	Los Angeles
C	Carlton Fisk	Boston	Johnny Bench	Cincinnati
1B	Dick Allen	Chicago	Steve Garvey	Los Angeles
2B	Rod Carew	Minnesota	Joe Morgan	Cincinnati
3B	Brooks Robinson	Baltimore	Ron Cey	Los Angeles
SS	Bert Campaneris	Oakland	Larry Bowa	Philadelphia
OF	Jeff Burroughs	Texas	Pete Rose	Cincinnati
OF	Bobby Murcer	New York	Jimmy Wynn	Los Angeles
OF	Reggie Jackson	Oakland	Hank Aaron	Atlanta

1975

Pos	American League		National League	
P	Vida Blue	Oakland	Jerry Reuss	Pittsburgh
C	Thurman Munson	New York	Johnny Bench	Cincinnati
1B	Gene Tenace	Oakland	Steve Garvey	Los Angeles
2B	Rod Carew	Minnesota	Joe Morgan	Cincinnati
3B	Graig Nettles	New York	Ron Cey	Los Angeles
SS	Bert Campaneris	Oakland	Dave Concepcion	Cincinnati
OF	Joe Rudi	Oakland	Lou Brock	St. Louis
OF	Bobby Bonds	New York	Jimmy Wynn	Los Angeles
OF	Reggie Jackson	Oakland	Pete Rose	Cincinnati

1976

Pos	American League		National League	
P	Mark Fidrych	Detroit	Randy Jones	San Diego
C	Thurman Munson	New York	Johnny Bench	Cincinnati
1B	Rod Carew	Minnesota	Steve Garvey	Los Angeles
2B	Bobby Grich	Baltimore	Joe Morgan	Cincinnati
3B	George Brett	Kansas City	Pete Rose	Cincinnati
SS	Toby Harrah	Texas	Dave Concepcion	Cincinnati
OF	Ron LeFlore	Detroit	Greg Luzinski	Philadelphia
OF	Fred Lynn	Boston	George Foster	Cincinnati
OF	Rusty Staub	Detroit	Dave Kingman	New York

1977

Pos	American League		National League	
P	Jim Palmer	Baltimore	Don Sutton	Los Angeles
C	Carlton Fisk	Boston	Johnny Bench	Cincinnati
1B	Rod Carew	Minnesota	Steve Garvey	Los Angeles
2B	Willie Randolph	New York	Joe Morgan	Cincinnati
3B	George Brett	Kansas City	Ron Cey	Los Angeles
SS	Rick Burleson	Boston	Dave Concepcion	Cincinnati
OF	Richie Zisk	Chicago	Greg Luzinski	Philadelphia
OF	Carl Yastrzemski	Boston	George Foster	Cincinnati
OF	Reggie Jackson	New York	Dave Parker	Pittsburgh

1978

Pos	American League		National League	
P	Jim Palmer	Baltimore	Vida Blue	San Francisco
C	Carlton Fisk	Boston	Johnny Bench	Cincinnati
1B	Rod Carew	Minnesota	Steve Garvey	Los Angeles
2B	Don Money	Milwaukee	Joe Morgan	Cincinnati
3B	George Brett	Kansas City	Pete Rose	Cincinnati
SS	Freddie Patek	Kansas City	Larry Bowa	Philadelphia
OF	Jim Rice	Boston	Greg Luzinski	Philadelphia
OF	Reggie Jackson	New York	George Foster	Cincinnati
OF	Richie Zisk	Texas	Rick Monday	Los Angeles

1979

Pos	American League		National League	
P	Nolan Ryan	California	Steve Carlton	Philadelphia
C	Darrell Porter	Kansas City	Ted Simmons	St. Louis
1B	Rod Carew	Minnesota	Steve Garvey	Los Angeles
2B	Frank White	Kansas City	Davey Lopes	Los Angeles
3B	George Brett	Kansas City	Mike Schmidt	Philadelphia
SS	Roy Smalley	Minnesota	Larry Bowa	Philadelphia
OF	Jim Rice	Boston	George Foster	Cincinnati
OF	Fred Lynn	Boston	Dave Winfield	San Diego
OF	Carl Yastrzemski	Boston	Dave Parker	Pittsburgh

Injury Replacements

1970: Dave Johnson (Balt) started in place of Rod Carew
1971: Bill Freehan (Det) started in place of Ray Fosse, Norm Cash (Det) started in place of Boog Powell, Bobby Murcer (NYY) started in place of Tony Oliva
1972: Bobby Grich (Balt) started in place of Luis Aparicio
1972: Willie Mays (NY) started in place of Roberto Clemente
1973: John Mayberry (KC) started in place of Dick Allen
1974: Thurman Munson (NYY) started in place of Carlton Fisk
1978: Fred Lynn (Bos) started in place of Reggie Jackson
1978: Ted Simmons (Stl) started in place of Johnny Bench
1979: Don Baylor (Cal) started in left field for Carl Yastrzemski (Bos) who had moved to 1B to start for Rod Carew
1979: Bob Boone (Phi) started in place of Ted Simmons

3000 Hits

In all 52 Hall of Famers played in the Major Leagues at some point during the 1970s. Many elusive milestones were reached, including the 3,000 hits plateau. Going into the decade only 8 hitters had reached that magic number - Cap Anson, Honus Wagner, Nap Lajoie, Ty Cobb, Tris Speaker, Eddie Collins, Paul Waner, and Stan Musial.

On May 7, 1970, Atlanta's Hank Aaron became the 9th player in Major League history and the first since Musial in 1958 to reach 3000 hits. He was just getting started. In 1974 Aaron broke Babe Ruth's career home run mark of 714; his total of 755 was a record that stood for 33 years. Then in 1975 Hank broke Ruth's all-time RBI record. Aaron retired in 1976, and is still the Major League career leader in runs batted in (2,297), extra base hits (1,477), and total bases (6,856). Although most well-known for his power, Hank was a lifetime .305 hitter and ranks third all time with 3,771 hits.

By the time 1980 rolled around the exclusive club of 8 had almost doubled, to 15. Here are the other players to reach the 3000 hit mark during the 1970s:

- On July 18th, 1970, only two months after Aaron had done so, San Francisco's Willie Mays, the Sporting News' 1960s Player of the Decade, reached 3000 hits. In 1972 Willie was traded to the Mets, and retired after the New York's pennant winning 1973 season, where at age 42 he became the oldest position player to appear in a World Series. Mays finished with a .302 lifetime average and 660 home runs.

- Roberto Clemente was the 1971 World Series MVP in the Pirates' 7 game win over Baltimore. In 1972 the 38-year-old struggled through an injury-plagued season where he still managed to hit .312 in 102 games. On September 30, 1972, Clemente doubled off New York's Jon Matlack for his 3000th hit in what would be his final regular season at-bat. Roberto was tragically killed in a plane crash later that year.

-Like Clemente, Al Kaline played an entire career with the same team and was a right fielder known for his rifle arm. "Mr. Tiger" was an 18-time All-Star and won 10 Gold Gloves. On September 24, 1974 he doubled off Baltimore's Dave McNally for his 3000th hit, and retired when the season ended as Detroit's leading home run hitter with 399.

-On May 5, 1978, Pete Rose of the Reds, en route to eventually becoming the Major League all-time hit leader, singled against Montreal ace Steve Rogers for his 3000th hit. Later that season Rose embarked on a National League record-tying 44 game hitting streak. He retired in 1986 with a record 4,256 hits.

-Like Hank Aaron, the Cardinals' Lou Brock hit several milestones during the 1970s. Brock's 3000th hit took place on August 13, 1979 against his former team, the Chicago Cubs. In 1974 Lou shattered Maury Wills' single-season record of 104 stolen bases, finishing with 118. Then in 1977 he broke Ty Cobb's lifetime mark of 892 steals. Brock retired after the 1979 season with a .293 average, 3,023 hits, 938 stolen bases, and 900 RBI.

-Carl Yastrzemski played his entire 23 year career for the Boston Red Sox. Less than a month after Brock accomplished the feat, Yaz singled for his 3000th hit on September 12th. He retired in 1983 as Boston's all-time leader with 3,419 hits, 1,844 RBI, 646 doubles, and 3,308 games played. Yastrzemski also hit 452 home runs and won 7 Gold Gloves, 3 batting titles, and a triple crown.

In all, the 1970s is tied with the 1990s as the decade with the most players reaching the 3,000 hit plateau (7). No other decade has seen more than 4 men accomplish this.

500 Home Run Club

In 2014 Albert Pujols entered the 500 Home Run Club, becoming the 26th player to reach the milestone.

Going into the 1970s only 8 players had accomplished the feat - Babe Ruth, Jimmie Foxx, Mel Ott, Ted Williams, Willie Mays, Eddie Matthews, Mickey Mantle, and Hank Aaron. Four more players, all eventual Hall of Famers, joined the 500 HR club during the decade.

"Mr Cub" Ernie Banks was the first player to reach the plateau in the '70s, on May 12, 1970 at his hometown Wrigley Field in Chicago. Banks retired after the 1971 season with 512 home runs, and played his entire career as a Cub. He still holds team records for games played (2,528), at-bats (9,421), extra-base hits (1,009), and total bases (4,706). The shortstop/first baseman was a 14-time All-Star and 2-time Most Valuable Player.

On August 10, 1971 Harmon Killebrew became the 10th member of the 500 HR club with a first inning bomb in Minnesota off Baltimore's Mike Cuellar, then added a second homer off Cuellar later in the game. Killebrew played for the Washington Senators, who later moved to Minnesota as the Twins, and one year for Kansas City. When he retired in 1975, his 573 career home runs were the most in American League by a right handed hitter and second in the AL overall to Babe Ruth. Killebrew led the league in home runs 6 times and was the 1969 AL Most Valuable Player.

Later that same year, on September 13, Frank Robinson hit his 500th homer as a member of the Baltimore Orioles. He retired in 1976 with 586 home runs, 4th at the time behind only Ruth, Aaron, and Mays. Robbie did it all in the major leagues, capturing the Rookie of the Year Award in 1956, NL Gold Glove Award in 1958, NL MVP in 1961, and a 1966 season with Baltimore where he won the Triple Crown, AL MVP, and World Series MVP. He was also the 1971 All-Star Game MVP, won over 1,000 games as baseball's first black manager, and was the 1989 Manager of the Year

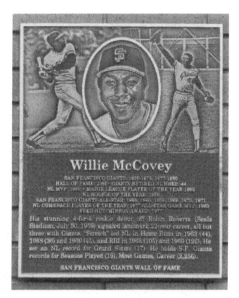

The Giants' Willie 'Stretch' McCovey became the last man to join the 500 homer club in the 1970s when he went deep against the Braves in Atlanta Fulton County Stadium on June 30, 1978. McCovey retired in 1980 with home runs in 4 different decades, 521 overall, and led the National League 3 times. He was a 6-time All-Star, 1959 Rookie of the Year, 1969 NL Most Valuable Player, and 1977 Comeback Player of the Year.

Statistical Leaders

Home Runs
Year by Year League Leaders

| National League | | | American League | |
Player (Team)	HR	Year	Player (Team)	HR
Johnny Bench (CIN)	45	1970	Frank Howard (WSA)	44
Willie Stargell (PIT)	48	1971	Bill Melton (CHW)	33
Johnny Bench (CIN)	40	1972	Dick Allen (CHW)	37
Willie Stargell (PIT)	44	1973	Reggie Jackson (OAK)	32
Mike Schmidt (PHI)	36	1974	Dick Allen (CHW)	32
Mike Schmidt (PHI)	38	1975	Reggie Jackson (OAK)	36
			George Scott (MIL)	36
Mike Schmidt (PHI)	38	1976	Graig Nettles (NYY)	32
George Foster (CIN)	52	1977	Jim Rice (BOS)	39
George Foster (CIN)	40	1978	Jim Rice (BOS)	46
Dave Kingman (CHC)	48	1979	Gorman Thomas (MIL)	45

Top Decade Total

Player	Team	HR
Willie Stargell	PIT	296
Reggie Jackson	OAK-BAL-NYY	292
Johnny Bench	CIN	290
Bobby Bonds	SF-NYY-Cal-CHW-Tex-Cle	280
Lee May	CIN-HOU-BAL	270
Dave Kingman	SF-NYM-SD-Cal-NYY-CHC	252
Graig Nettles	CLE-NYY	252
Mike Schmidt	PHI	235
Tony Perez	CIN-MON	226
Reggie Smith	BOS-STL-LA	225
Willie McCovey	SF-SD	207
George Scott	BOS-MIL-KC-NYY	206
Greg Luzinski	PHI	204
Carl Yastrzemski	BOS	202
George Foster	SF-CIN	201
Hank Aaron	ATL-MIL	201
John Mayberry	HOU-KC-TOR	198
Bobby Murcer	NYY-SF-CHC	198
Sal Bando	OAK-MIL	195
Darrell Evans	ATL-SF	184
Rusty Staub	MON-NYM-DET	184

Top Single Season

Player	Team	Year	HR
George Foster	CIN	1977	52
Dave Kingman	CHC	1979	48
Willie Stargell	PIT	1971	48
Hank Aaron	ATL	1971	47
Jim Rice	BOS	1978	46
Gorman Thomas	MIL	1979	45
Mike Schmidt	PHI	1979	45
Johnny Bench	CIN	1970	45
Willie Stargell	PIT	1973	44
Frank Howard	WSH	1970	44
Davey Johnson	ATL	1973	43
Billy Williams	CHC	1970	42
Jeff Burroughs	ATL	1977	41
Darrell Evans	ATL	1973	41
Harmon Killebrew	MIN	1970	41
George Foster	CIN	1978	40
Hank Aaron	ATL	1973	40
Johnny Bench	CIN	1972	40
Carl Yastrzemski	BOS	1970	40
Tony Perez	CIN	1970	40

Runs Batted In
Year by Year League Leaders

National League			American League	
Player (Team)	RBI	Year	Player (Team)	RBI
Johnny Bench (CIN)	148	1970	Frank Howard (WSA)	126
Joe Torre (STL)	137	1971	Harmon Killebrew (MIN)	119
Johnny Bench (CIN)	125	1972	Dick Allen (CHW)	113
Willie Stargell (PIT)	119	1973	Reggie Jackson (OAK)	117
Johnny Bench (CIN)	129	1974	Jeff Burroughs (TEX)	118
Greg Luzinski (PHI)	120	1975	George Scott (MIL)	109
George Foster (CIN)	121	1976	Lee May (BAL)	109
George Foster (CIN)	149	1977	Larry Hisle (MIN)	119
George Foster (CIN)	120	1978	Jim Rice (BOS)	139
Dave Winfield (SDP)	118	1979	Don Baylor (CAL)	139

Top Decade Total

Player	Team	RBI
Johnny Bench	CIN	1013
Tony Perez	CIN-MON	954
Lee May	CIN-HOU-BAL	936
Reggie Jackson	OAK-BAL-NYY	922
Willie Stargell	PIT	906
Rusty Staub	MON-NYM-DET	860
Bobby Bonds	SF-NYY-Cal-CHW-Tex-Cle	856
Carl Yastrzemski	BOS	846
Bobby Murcer	NYY-SF-CHC	840
Graig Nettles	CLE-NYY	831
Ted Simmons	STL	828
Bob Watson	HOU	822
Sal Bando	OAK-MIL	812
Al Oliver	PIT-TEX	812
George Scott	BOS-MIL-KC-NYY	802
Greg Luzinski	PHI	755
Amos Otis	KC	753
Reggie Smith	BOS-STL-LA	750
Steve Garvey	LA	736
Willie Montanez	Phi-Atl-SF-NYM-Tex	730

Top Single Season

Player	Team	Year	RBI
George Foster	CIN	1977	149
Johnny Bench	CIN	1970	148
Don Baylor	CAL	1979	139
Jim Rice	BOS	1978	139
Joe Torre	STL	1971	137
Jim Rice	BOS	1979	130
Greg Luzinski	PHI	1977	130
Johnny Bench	CIN	1974	129
Billy Williams	CHC	1970	129
Tony Perez	CIN	1970	129
Willie McCovey	SF	1970	126
Frank Howard	WSH	1970	126
Johnny Bench	CIN	1972	125
Willie Stargell	PIT	1971	125
Gorman Thomas	MIL	1979	123
Fred Lynn	BOS	1979	122
Billy Williams	CHC	1972	122
Rusty Staub	DET	1978	121
George Foster	CIN	1976	121
George Foster	CIN	1978	120
Greg Luzinski	PHI	1975	120

Doubles
Year by Year League Leaders

National League		Year	American League	
Player (Team)	2B		Player (Team)	2B
Wes Parker (LAD)	47	1970	Tony Oliva (MIN)	36
			Amos Otis (KCR)	36
			Cesar Tovar (MIN)	36
Cesar Cedeno (HOU)	40	1971	Reggie Smith (BOS)	33
Cesar Cedeno (HOU)	39	1972	Lou Piniella (KCR)	33
Willie Montanez (PHI)	39			
Willie Stargell (PIT)	43	1973	Sal Bando (OAK)	32
			Pedro Garcia (MIL)	32
Pete Rose (CIN)	45	1974	Joe Rudi (OAK)	39
Pete Rose (CIN)	47	1975	Fred Lynn (BOS)	47
Pete Rose (CIN)	42	1976	Amos Otis (KCR)	40
Dave Parker (PIT)	44	1977	Hal McRae (KCR)	54
Pete Rose (CIN)	51	1978	George Brett (KCR)	45
Keith Hernandez (STL)	48	1979	Cecil Cooper (MIL)	44
			Chet Lemon (CHW)	44

Top Decade Total				Top Single Season			
Player	Team	2B		Player	Team	Year	2B
Pete Rose	CIN-PHI	394		Hal McRae	KC	1977	54
Al Oliver	PIT-TEX	320		Pete Rose	CIN	1978	51
Tony Perez	CIN-MON	303		Keith Hernandez	STL	1979	48
Ted Simmons	STL	299		Fred Lynn	BOS	1975	47
Cesar Cedeno	HOU	292		Pete Rose	CIN	1975	47
Amos Otis	KC	286		Wes Parker	LA	1970	47
Hal McRae	CIN-KC	285		Warren Cromartie	MON	1979	46
Joe Morgan	HOU-CIN	275		Jack Clark	SF	1978	46
Reggie Jackson	OAK-BAL-NYY	270		Dave Parker	PIT	1979	45
Willie Montanez	Phi-Atl-SF-NYM-Tex	266		George Brett	KC	1978	45
Johnny Bench	CIN	264		Pete Rose	CIN	1974	45
Rusty Staub	MON-NYM-DET	263		Chet Lemon	CHW	1979	44
Bobby Bonds	SF-NYY-Cal-CHW-Tex-Cle	255		Cecil Cooper	MIL	1979	44
Willie Stargell	PIT	253		Dave Parker	PIT	1977	44
Chris Chambliss	CLE-NYY	252		Willie Stargell	PIT	1973	43
Joe Rudi	OAK-CAL	251		Fred Lynn	BOS	1979	42
Bob Watson	HOU	250		George Brett	KC	1979	42
Steve Garvey	LA	248		Buddy Bell	TEX	1979	42
Reggie Smith	BOS-STL-LA	247		Dave Cash	MON	1977	42
Carl Yastrzemski	BOS	247		Pete Rose	CIN	1976	42

Triples
Year by Year League Leaders

National League		Year	American League	
Player (Team)	3B		Player (Team)	3B
Willie Davis (LAD)	16	1970	Cesar Tovar (MIN)	13
Roger Metzger (HOU)	11	1971	Freddie Patek (KCR)	11
Joe Morgan (HOU)	11			
Larry Bowa (PHI)	13	1972	Carlton Fisk (BOS)	9
			Joe Rudi (OAK)	9
Roger Metzger (HOU)	14	1973	Al Bumbry (BAL)	11
			Rod Carew (MIN)	11
Ralph Garr (ATL)	17	1974	Mickey Rivers (CAL)	11
Ralph Garr (ATL)	11	1975	George Brett (KCR)	13
			Mickey Rivers (CAL)	13
Dave Cash (PHI)	12	1976	George Brett (KCR)	14
Garry Templeton (STL)	18	1977	Rod Carew (MIN)	16
Garry Templeton (STL)	13	1978	Jim Rice (BOS)	15
Garry Templeton (STL)	19	1979	George Brett (KCR)	20

Top Decade Total		
Player	Team	3B
Rod Carew	MIN-CAL	80
Larry Bowa	PHI	74
George Brett	KC	73
Roger Metzger	CHC-HOU-SF	71
Willie Davis	LA-MON-TEX-STL-SD-CAL	70
Ralph Garr	ATL-CHW	64
Pete Rose	CIN-PHI	64
Al Oliver	PIT-TEX	63
Mickey Rivers	CAL-NYY	61
Lou Brock	STL	56
Don Kessinger	CHC-STL-CHW	55
Dave Cash	PIT-PHI-MON	53
Garry Maddox	SF-PHI	53
Amos Otis	KC	53
Garry Templeton	STL	52
Bobby Bonds	SF-NYY-Cal-CHW-Tex-Cle	51
Dave Parker	PIT	51
Manny Sanguillen	PIT-OAK	51
Jim Rice	BOS	49
Cesar Cedeno	HOU	47
Jose Cruz	STL-HOU	47
Joe Morgan	HOU-CIN	47

Top Single Season			
Player	Team	Year	3B
George Brett	KC	1979	20
Garry Templeton	STL	1979	19
Garry Templeton	STL	1977	18
Ralph Garr	ATL	1974	17
Paul Molitor	MIL	1979	16
Rod Carew	MIN	1977	16
Willie Davis	LA	1970	16
Jim Rice	BOS	1978	15
Jim Rice	BOS	1977	15
Al Cowens	KC	1977	14
George Brett	KC	1976	14
Roger Metzger	HOU	1973	14
Don Kessinger	CHC	1970	14
Willie Wilson	KC	1979	13
Willie Randolph	NYY	1979	13
Garry Templeton	STL	1978	13
George Brett	KC	1977	13
Mickey Rivers	CAL	1975	13
George Brett	KC	1975	13
Larry Bowa	PHI	1972	13
Cesar Tovar	MIN	1970	13

Hits
Year by Year League Leaders

National League			American League	
Player (Team)	H	Year	Player (Team)	H
Pete Rose (CIN)	205	1970	Tony Oliva (MIN)	204
Billy Williams (CHC)	205			
Joe Torre (STL)	230	1971	Cesar Tovar (MIN)	204
Pete Rose (CIN)	198	1972	Joe Rudi (OAK)	181
Pete Rose (CIN)	230	1973	Rod Carew (MIN)	203
Ralph Garr (ATL)	214	1974	Rod Carew (MIN)	218
Dave Cash (PHI)	213	1975	George Brett (KCR)	195
Pete Rose (CIN)	215	1976	George Brett (KCR)	215
Dave Parker (PIT)	215	1977	Rod Carew (MIN)	239
Steve Garvey (LAD)	202	1978	Jim Rice (BOS)	213
Garry Templeton (STL)	211	1979	George Brett (KCR)	212

Top Decade Total		
Player	Team	H
Pete Rose	CIN-PHI	2045
Rod Carew	MIN-CAL	1787
Al Oliver	PIT-TEX	1686
Lou Brock	STL	1617
Bobby Bonds	SF-NYY-CAL-CLE	1565
Tony Perez	CIN-MON	1560
Larry Bowa	PHI	1552
Ted Simmons	STL	1550
Amos Otis	KC	1549
Bobby Murcer	NYY-SF-CHC	1548
Ralph Garr	ATL-CHW-CAL	1546
Thurman Munson	NYY	1536
Bob Watson	HOU	1507
Carl Yastrzemski	BOS	1492
Rusty Staub	MON-NYM-DET	1487
George Scott	BOS-MIL-KC-NYY	1475
Steve Garvey	LA	1469
Dave Cash	PIT-PHI-MON	1464
Lee May	CIN-HOU-BAL	1461
Joe Morgan	HOU-CIN	1451

Top Single Season			
Player	Team	Year	H
Rod Carew	MIN	1977	239
Pete Rose	CIN	1973	230
Joe Torre	STL	1971	230
Ralph Garr	ATL	1971	219
Rod Carew	MIN	1974	218
Dave Parker	PIT	1977	215
Pete Rose	CIN	1976	215
George Brett	KC	1976	215
Ralph Garr	ATL	1974	214
Jim Rice	BOS	1978	213
Dave Cash	PHI	1975	213
George Brett	KC	1979	212
Ron LeFlore	DET	1977	212
Garry Templeton	STL	1979	211
Keith Hernandez	STL	1979	210
Pete Rose	CIN	1975	210
Steve Garvey	LA	1975	210
Pete Rose	PHI	1979	208
Jim Rice	BOS	1977	206
Willie Montanez	SF-Atl	1976	206
Dave Cash	PHI	1974	206

Extra Base Hits
Year by Year League Leaders

National League			American League	
Player (Team)	XBH	Year	Player (Team)	R
Johnny Bench (CIN)	84	1970	Tommy Harper (MIL)	70
Willie Stargell (PIT)	74	1971	Reggie Smith (BOS)	65
Billy Williams (CHI)	77	1972	Dick Allen (CHI)	70
			Bobby Murcer (NYY)	70
Willie Stargell (PIT)	90	1973	Sal Bando (OAK)	64
Johnny Bench (CIN)	73	1974	Joe Rudi (OAK)	65
Mike Schmidt (PHI)	75	1975	Reggie Jackson (OAK)	78
Mike Schmidt (PHI)	73	1976	Graig Nettles (NYY)	63
George Foster (CIN)	85	1977	Hal McRae (KC)	86
Jack Clark (SFG)	79	1978	Jim Rice (BOS)	86
Dave Parker (PIT)	77	1979	George Brett (KC)	85

Top Decade Total

Player	Team	XBH	2B	3B	HR
Bobby Bonds	SF-NYY-CAL-CHW-Tex-Cle	586	255	51	280
Reggie Jackson	OAK-BAL-NYY	586	270	24	292
Johnny Bench	CIN	572	264	18	290
Tony Perez	CIN-MON	572	303	43	226
Willie Stargell	PIT	568	253	19	296
Pete Rose	CIN-PHI	537	394	64	79
Al Oliver	PIT-TEX	527	320	63	144
Lee May	CIN-HOU-BAL	514	224	20	270
Reggie Smith	BOS-STL-LAD	511	247	39	225
Amos Otis	KCR	498	286	53	159
Joe Morgan	HOU-CIN	495	275	47	173
Cesar Cedeno	HOU	487	292	47	148
George Scott	BOS-MIL-KC-NYY	486	239	41	206
Ted Simmons	STL	484	299	34	151
Graig Nettles	CLE-NYY	480	212	16	252
Rusty Staub	MON-NYM-DET	475	263	28	184
Bobby Murcer	NYY-SFG-CHC	473	237	38	198
Carl Yastrzemski	BOS	468	247	19	202
Greg Luzinski	PHI	453	234	20	204
Mike Schmidt	PHI	449	183	31	235

Top Single Season

Player	Team	Year	XBH	2B	3B	HR
Willie Stargell	PIT	1973	90	43	3	44
Jim Rice	BOS	1978	86	25	15	46
Hal McRae	KCR	1977	86	54	11	21
George Brett	KCR	1979	85	42	20	23
George Foster	CIN	1977	85	31	2	52
Jim Rice	BOS	1979	84	39	6	39
Johnny Bench	CIN	1970	84	35	4	45
Jim Rice	BOS	1977	83	29	15	39
Fred Lynn	BOS	1979	82	42	1	39
Billy Williams	CHC	1970	80	34	4	42
Willie McCovey	SFG	1970	80	39	2	39
Jack Clark	SFG	1978	79	46	8	25
Reggie Jackson	OAK	1975	78	39	3	36
Dave Parker	PIT	1979	77	45	7	25
Greg Luzinski	PHI	1977	77	35	3	39
Bobby Bonds	SFG	1973	77	34	4	39
Billy Williams	CHC	1972	77	34	6	37
Mike Schmidt	PHI	1977	76	27	11	38
Fred Lynn	BOS	1975	75	47	7	21
Mike Schmidt	PHI	1975	75	34	3	38

Runs Scored
Year by Year League Leaders

National League		Year	American League	
Player (Team)	R	Year	Player (Team)	R
Billy Williams (CHC)	137	1970	Carl Yastrzemski (BOS)	125
Lou Brock (STL)	126	1971	Don Buford (BAL)	99
Joe Morgan (CIN)	122	1972	Bobby Murcer (NYY)	102
Bobby Bonds (SFG)	131	1973	Reggie Jackson (OAK)	99
Pete Rose (CIN)	110	1974	Carl Yastrzemski (BOS)	93
Pete Rose (CIN)	112	1975	Fred Lynn (BOS)	103
Pete Rose (CIN)	130	1976	Roy White (NYY)	104
George Foster (CIN)	124	1977	Rod Carew (MIN)	128
Ivan de Jesus (CHC)	104	1978	Ron LeFlore (DET)	126
Keith Hernandez (STL)	116	1979	Don Baylor (CAL)	120

Top Decade Total				Top Single Season			
Player	Team	R		Player	Team	Year	R
Pete Rose	CIN-PHI	1068		Billy Williams	CHC	1970	137
Bobby Bonds	SF-NYY-Cal-CHW-Tex-Cle	1020		Bobby Bonds	SF	1970	134
Joe Morgan	HOU-CIN	1005		Bobby Bonds	SF	1973	131
Amos Otis	KC	861		Pete Rose	CIN	1976	130
Carl Yastrzemski	BOS	845		Rod Carew	MIN	1977	128
Lou Brock	STL	843		Ron LeFlore	DET	1978	126
Rod Carew	MIN-CAL	837		Lou Brock	STL	1971	126
Reggie Jackson	OAK-BAL-NYY	833		Carl Yastrzemski	BOS	1970	125
Bobby Murcer	NYY-SF-CHC	816		George Foster	CIN	1977	124
Johnny Bench	CIN	792		Joe Morgan	CIN	1972	122
Cesar Cedeno	HOU	777		Jim Rice	BOS	1978	121
Reggie Smith	BOS-STL-LA	776		Don Baylor	CAL	1979	120
Graig Nettles	CLE-NYY	773		Pete Rose	CIN	1970	120
Al Oliver	PIT-TEX	767		Cesar Tovar	MIN	1970	120
Sal Bando	OAK-MIL	759		George Brett	KC	1979	119
Roy White	NYY	752		Bobby Bonds	SF	1972	118
Tony Perez	CIN-MON	740		Jim Rice	BOS	1979	117
Rusty Staub	MON-NYM-DET	732		Ken Griffey	CIN	1977	117
Larry Bowa	PHI	725		Jim Wynn	HOU	1972	117
George Scott	BOS-MIL-KC-NYY	724		Fred Lynn	BOS	1979	116

Batting Average
Year by Year League Leaders

National League				American League	
Player (Team)	Avg	Year	Player (Team)	Avg
Rico Carty (ATL)	.366	**1970**	Alex Johnson (CAL)	.329
Joe Torre (STL)	.363	**1971**	Tony Oliva (MIN)	.337
Billy Williams (CHC)	.333	**1972**	Rod Carew (MIN)	.318
Pete Rose (CIN)	.338	**1973**	Rod Carew (MIN)	.350
Ralph Garr (ATL)	.353	**1974**	Rod Carew (MIN)	.364
Bill Madlock (CHC)	.354	**1975**	Rod Carew (MIN)	.359
Bill Madlock (CHC)	.339	**1976**	George Brett (KCR)	.333
Dave Parker (PIT)	.338	**1977**	Rod Carew (MIN)	.388
Dave Parker (PIT)	.334	**1978**	Rod Carew (MIN)	.333
Keith Hernandez (STL)	.344	**1979**	Fred Lynn (BOS)	.333

Top Decade Total

Player	Team	Avg
Rod Carew	MIN-CAL	.343
Bill Madlock	TEX-CHC-SF-PIT	.320
Dave Parker	PIT	.317
Pete Rose	CIN-PHI	.314
George Brett	KC	.310
Ken Griffey	CIN	.310
Jim Rice	BOS	.310
Fred Lynn	BOS	.309
Ralph Garr	ATL-CHW-CAL	.307
Steve Garvey	LA	.304
Al Oliver	PIT-TEX	.303
Joe Torre	STL-NYM	.303
Bob Watson	HOU	.301
Tony Oliva	MIN	.299
Lou Brock	STL	.298
Bake McBride	STL-PHI	.298
Ron LeFlore	DET	.297
Manny Sanguillen	PIT-OAK	.297
Ted Simmons	STL	.297
Cecil Cooper	BOS-MIL	.296

Top Single Season

Player	Team	Year	Avg
Rod Carew	MIN	1977	.388
Rico Carty	ATL	1970	.366
Rod Carew	MIN	1974	.364
Joe Torre	STL	1971	.363
Rod Carew	MIN	1975	.359
Bill Madlock	CHC	1975	.354
Ralph Garr	ATL	1974	.353
Rod Carew	MIN	1973	.350
Keith Hernandez	STL	1979	.344
Ralph Garr	ATL	1971	.343
Glenn Beckert	CHC	1971	.342
Roberto Clemente	PIT	1971	.341
Bill Madlock	CHC	1976	.339
Dave Parker	PIT	1977	.338
Pete Rose	CIN	1973	.338
Tony Oliva	MIN	1971	.337
Lyman Bostock	MIN	1977	.336
Ken Griffey	CIN	1976	.336
Dave Parker	PIT	1978	.334
Fred Lynn	BOS	1979	.333

On Base Percentage
Year by Year League Leaders

National League			American League	
Player (Team)	OB%	Year	Player (Team)	OB%
Rico Carty (ATL)	.454	1970	Carl Yastrzemski (BOS)	.452
Willie Mays (SFG)	.425	1971	Bobby Murcer (NYY)	.427
Joe Morgan (CIN)	.417	1972	Dick Allen (CHW)	.420
Ken Singleton (MON)	.425	1973	John Mayberry (KCR)	.417
Joe Morgan (CIN)	.427	1974	Rod Carew (MIN)	.433
Joe Morgan (CIN)	.466	1975	Rod Carew (MIN)	.421
Joe Morgan (CIN)	.444	1976	Hal McRae (KCR)	.407
Reggie Smith (LAD)	.427	1977	Rod Carew (MIN)	.449
Jeff Burroughs (ATL)	.432	1978	Rod Carew (MIN)	.411
Pete Rose (PHI)	.418	1979	Fred Lynn (BOS)	.423

Top Decade Total		
Player	Team	OB%
Rod Carew	MIN-CAL	.408
Joe Morgan	HOU-CIN	.404
Mike Hargrove	TEX	.400
Ken Singleton	NYM-MON-BAL	.398
Pete Rose	CIN-PHI	.389
Bernie Carbo	CIN-STL-BOS-MIL-CLE	.388
Gene Tenace	OAK-SD	.386
Carl Yastrzemski	BOS	.384
Fred Lynn	BOS	.383
Bill Madlock	TEX-CHC-SF-PIT	.381
Ken Griffey	CIN	.377
Dick Allen	Phi-STL-LA-CHW-Oak	.377
Ron Fairly	MON-STL-OAK-TOR-CAL	.376
Mike Schmidt	PHI	.374
Reggie Smith	BOS-STL-LA	.374
Willie Stargell	PIT	.374
Joe Torre	STL-NYM	.374
Boog Powell	BAL-CLE-LA	.373
Hank Aaron	ATL-MIL	.373
Steve Braun	MIN-SEA-KC	.372

Top Single Season			
Player	Team	Year	OB%
Joe Morgan	CIN	1975	.466
Rico Carty	ATL	1970	.454
Carl Yastrzemski	BOS	1970	.452
Rod Carew	MIN	1977	.449
Joe Morgan	CIN	1976	.444
Willie McCovey	SF	1970	.444
Ken Singleton	BAL	1977	.438
Rod Carew	MIN	1974	.433
Jeff Burroughs	ATL	1978	.432
Reggie Smith	LA	1977	.427
Joe Morgan	CIN	1974	.427
Bobby Murcer	NYY	1971	.427
Dick Dietz	SF	1970	.426
Ken Singleton	MON	1973	.425
Willie Mays	SF	1971	.425
Fred Lynn	BOS	1979	.423
Ron Fairly	MON	1973	.422
Merv Rettenmund	BAL	1971	.422
Darrell Porter	KC	1979	.421
Rod Carew	MIN	1975	.421

Slugging Percentage
Year by Year League Leaders

National League		Year	American League	
Player (Team)	SLG%		Player (Team)	SLG%
Willie McCovey (SFG)	.612	1970	Carl Yastrzemski (BOS)	.592
Hank Aaron (ATL)	.669	1971	Tony Oliva (MIN)	.546
Billy Williams (CHC)	.606	1972	Dick Allen (CHW)	.603
Willie Stargell (PIT)	.646	1973	Reggie Jackson (OAK)	.531
Mike Schmidt (PHI)	.546	1974	Dick Allen (CHW)	.563
Dave Parker (PIT)	.541	1975	Fred Lynn (BOS)	.566
Joe Morgan (CIN)	.576	1976	Reggie Jackson (BAL)	.502
George Foster (CIN)	.631	1977	Jim Rice (BOS)	.593
Dave Parker (PIT)	.585	1978	Jim Rice (BOS)	.600
Dave Kingman (CHC)	.613	1979	Fred Lynn (BOS)	.637

Top Decade Total		
Player	Team	SLG%
Willie Stargell	PIT	.555
Jim Rice	BOS	.552
Hank Aaron	ATL-MIL	.527
Fred Lynn	BOS	.526
Dave Parker	PIT	.521
George Foster	SF-CIN	.517
Dick Allen	Phi-STL-LA-CHW-Oak	.513
Mike Schmidt	PHI	.511
Reggie Jackson	OAK-BAL-NYY	.508
Reggie Smith	BOS-STL-LA	.507
Dave Kingman	SF-NYM-SD-Cal-NYY-CHC	.504
Greg Luzinski	PHI	.493
Johnny Bench	CIN	.491
Billy Williams	CHC-OAK	.491
Carlton Fisk	BOS	.484
Bobby Bonds	SF-NYY-Cal-CHW-Tex-Cle	.483
Willie McCovey	SF-SD	.478
Tony Perez	CIN-MON	.478
Bill Robinson	PHI-PIT	.476
George Brett	KC	.475

Top Single Season			
Player	Team	Year	SLG%
Hank Aaron	ATL	1971	.669
Willie Stargell	PIT	1973	.646
Fred Lynn	BOS	1979	.637
George Foster	CIN	1977	.631
Willie Stargell	PIT	1971	.628
Dave Kingman	CHC	1979	.613
Willie McCovey	SF	1970	.612
Billy Williams	CHC	1972	.606
Dick Allen	CHW	1972	.603
Jim Rice	BOS	1978	.600
Jim Rice	BOS	1979	.596
Greg Luzinski	PHI	1977	.594
Jim Rice	BOS	1977	.593
Carl Yastrzemski	BOS	1970	.592
Tony Perez	CIN	1970	.589
Johnny Bench	CIN	1970	.587
Billy Williams	CHC	1970	.586
Dave Parker	PIT	1978	.585
Rico Carty	ATL	1970	.584
Jim Hickman	CHC	1970	.582

Stolen Bases
Year by Year League Leaders

National League Player (Team)	SB	Year	American League Player (Team)	SB
Bobby Tolan (CIN)	57	1970	Bert Campaneris (OAK)	42
Lou Brock (STL)	64	1971	Amos Otis (KCR)	52
Lou Brock (STL)	63	1972	Bert Campaneris (OAK)	52
Lou Brock (STL)	70	1973	Tommy Harper (BOS)	54
Lou Brock (STL)	118	1974	Bill North (OAK)	54
Davey Lopes (LAD)	77	1975	Mickey Rivers (CAL)	70
Davey Lopes (LAD)	63	1976	Bill North (OAK)	75
Frank Taveras (PIT)	70	1977	Freddie Patek (KCR)	53
Omar Moreno (PIT)	71	1978	Ron LeFlore (DET)	68
Omar Moreno (PIT)	77	1979	Willie Wilson (KCR)	83

Top Decade Total

Player	Team	SB
Lou Brock	STL	551
Joe Morgan	HOU-CIN	488
Cesar Cedeno	HOU	427
Bobby Bonds	SF-NYY-Cal-CHW-Tex-Cle	380
Davey Lopes	LA	375
Freddie Patek	PIT-KC	344
Bert Campaneris	OAK-TEX-CAL	336
Bill North	CHC-OAK-LA-SF	324
Ron LeFlore	DET	294
Amos Otis	KC	294
Rod Carew	MIN-CAL	253
Larry Bowa	PHI	251
Frank Taveras	PIT	248
Don Baylor	BAL-OAK-CAL	240
Mickey Rivers	CAL-NYY	226
Dave Concepcion	CIN	220
Omar Moreno	PIT	217
Tommy Harper	MIL-BOS-CAL-OAK-BAL	200
Garry Maddox	SF-PHI	193
Pat Kelly	KC-CHW-BAL	192

Top Single Season

Player	Team	Year	SB
Lou Brock	STL	1974	118
Willie Wilson	KC	1979	83
Ron LeFlore	DET	1979	78
Omar Moreno	PIT	1979	77
Davey Lopes	LA	1975	77
Bill North	OAK	1976	75
Omar Moreno	PIT	1978	71
Frank Taveras	PIT	1977	70
Mickey Rivers	CAL	1975	70
Lou Brock	STL	1973	70
Ron LeFlore	DET	1978	68
Joe Morgan	CIN	1975	67
Joe Morgan	CIN	1973	67
Lou Brock	STL	1971	64
Davey Lopes	LA	1976	63
Lou Brock	STL	1972	63
Cesar Cedeno	HOU	1977	61
Joe Morgan	CIN	1976	60
Julio Cruz	SEA	1978	59
Davey Lopes	LA	1974	59

Wins
Year by Year League Leaders

National League			American League	
Player (Team)	W	Year	Player (Team)	W
Gaylord Perry (SFG)	23	**1970**	Mike Cuellar (BAL)	24
Bob Gibson (STL)	23		Dave McNally (BAL)	24
			Jim Perry (MIN)	24
Fergie Jenkins (CHC)	24	**1971**	Mickey Lolich (DET)	25
Steve Carlton (PHI)	27	**1972**	Gaylord Perry (CLE)	24
			Wilbur Wood (CHW)	24
Ron Bryant (SFG)	24	**1973**	Wilbur Wood (CHW)	24
Andy Messersmith (LAD)	20	**1974**	Catfish Hunter (OAK)	25
Phil Niekro (ATL)	20		Fergie Jenkins (TEX)	25
Tom Seaver (NYM)	22	**1975**	Catfish Hunter (NYY)	23
			Jim Palmer (BAL)	23
Randy Jones (SDP)	22	**1976**	Jim Palmer (BAL)	22
Steve Carlton (PHI)	23	**1977**	Dave Goltz (MIN)	20
			Dennis Leonard (KCR)	20
			Jim Palmer (BAL)	20
Gaylord Perry (SDP)	21	**1978**	Ron Guidry (NYY)	25
Joe Niekro (HOU)	21	**1979**	Mike Flanagan (BAL)	23
Phil Niekro (ATL)	21			

Top Decade Total		
Player	Team	W
Jim Palmer	BAL	186
Gaylord Perry	SF-CLE-TEX-SD	184
Steve Carlton	STL-PHI	178
Fergie Jenkins	CHC-TEX-BOS	178
Tom Seaver	NYM-CIN	178
Catfish Hunter	OAK-NYY	169
Don Sutton	LA	166
Phil Niekro	ATL	164
Vida Blue	OAK-SF	155
Nolan Ryan	NYM-CAL	155
Bert Blyleven	MIN-TEX-PIT	148
Luis Tiant	MIN-BOS-NYY	142
Wilbur Wood	CHW	136
Jack Billingham	HOU-CIN-DET	135
Mike Torrez	STL-MON-BAL-OAK-BOS	134
Tommy John	CHW-LA-NYY	133
Rick Wise	PHI-STL-BOS-CLE	133
Ken Holtzman	CHC-OAK-BAL-NYY	126
Jerry Koosman	NYM-MIN	124
Paul Splittorff	KC	123

Top Single Season			
Player	Team	Year	W
Steve Carlton	1972	PHI	27
Ron Guidry	1978	NYY	25
Catfish Hunter	1974	OAK	25
Fergie Jenkins	1974	TEX	25
Mickey Lolich	1971	DET	25
Wilbur Wood	1973	CHW	24
Ron Bryant	1973	SF	24
Wilbur Wood	1972	CHW	24
Gaylord Perry	1972	CLE	24
Fergie Jenkins	1971	CHC	24
Vida Blue	1971	OAK	24
Mike Cuellar	1970	BAL	24
Dave McNally	1970	BAL	24
Jim Perry	1970	MIN	24
Mike Flanagan	1979	BAL	23
Steve Carlton	1977	PHI	23
Jim Palmer	1975	BAL	23
Catfish Hunter	1975	NYY	23
Joe Coleman	1973	DET	23
Gaylord Perry	1970	SF	23
Bob Gibson	1970	STL	23

Strikeouts
Year by Year League Leaders

National League		Year	American League	
Player (Team)	SO		Player (Team)	SO
Tom Seaver (NYM)	283	1970	Sam McDowell (CLE)	304
Tom Seaver (NYM)	289	1971	Mickey Lolich (DET)	308
Steve Carlton (PHI)	310	1972	Nolan Ryan (CAL)	329
Tom Seaver (NYM)	251	1973	Nolan Ryan (CAL)	383
Steve Carlton (PHI)	240	1974	Nolan Ryan (CAL)	367
Tom Seaver (NYM)	243	1975	Frank Tanana (CAL)	269
Tom Seaver (NYM)	235	1976	Nolan Ryan (CAL)	327
Phil Neikro (ATL)	262	1977	Nolan Ryan (CAL)	341
J.R. Richard (HOU)	303	1978	Nolan Ryan (CAL)	260
J.R. Richard (HOU)	313	1979	Nolan Ryan (CAL)	223

Top Decade Total				Top Single Season			
Player	Team	SO		Player	Team	Year	SO
Nolan Ryan	NYM-CAL	2678		Nolan Ryan	1973	CAL	383
Tom Seaver	NYM-CIN	2304		Nolan Ryan	1974	CAL	367
Steve Carlton	STL-PHI	2097		Nolan Ryan	1977	CAL	341
Bert Blyleven	MIN-TEX-PIT	2082		Nolan Ryan	1972	CAL	329
Gaylord Perry	SF-CLE-TEX-SD	1907		Nolan Ryan	1976	CAL	327
Phil Niekro	ATL	1866		J.R. Richard	1979	HOU	313
Fergie Jenkins	CHC-TEX-BOS	1841		Steve Carlton	1972	PHI	310
Don Sutton	LA	1767		Mickey Lolich	1971	DET	308
Vida Blue	OAK-SF	1600		Sam McDowell	1970	CLE	304
Jerry Koosman	NYM-MIN	1587		J.R. Richard	1978	HOU	303
Jim Palmer	BAL	1559		Vida Blue	1971	OAK	301
Mickey Lolich	DET-NYM-SD	1496		Tom Seaver	1971	NYM	289
J.R. Richard	HOU	1374		Tom Seaver	1970	NYM	283
Andy Messersmith	CAL-LA-ATL-NYY	1340		Fergie Jenkins	1970	CHC	274
Joe Coleman	WSH-DET-OAK	1319		Bob Gibson	1970	STL	274
Catfish Hunter	OAK-NYY	1309		Frank Tanana	1975	CAL	269
Rudy May	CAL-NYY-BAL-MON	1238		Fergie Jenkins	1971	CHC	263
Luis Tiant	MIN-BOS-NYY	1229		Phil Niekro	1977	ATL	262
Jon Matlack	NYM-TEX	1215		Frank Tanana	1976	CAL	261
Fred Norman	LA-STL-SD-CIN	1208		Nolan Ryan	1978	CAL	260

Earned Run Average
Year by Year League Leaders

National League			American League	
Player (Team)	ERA	Year	Player (Team)	ERA
Tom Seaver (NYM)	2.82	1970	Diego Segui (OAK)	2.56
Tom Seaver (NYM)	1.76	1971	Vida Blue (OAK)	1.82
Steve Carlton (PHI)	1.97	1972	Luis Tiant (BOS)	1.91
Tom Seaver (NYM)	2.08	1973	Jim Palmer (BAL)	2.40
Buzz Capra (ATL)	2.28	1974	Catfish Hunter (OAK)	2.49
Randy Jones (SDP)	2.24	1975	Jim Palmer (BAL)	2.09
John Denny (STL)	2.52	1976	Mark Fidrych (DET)	2.34
John Candelaria (PIT)	2.34	1977	Frank Tanana (CAL)	2.54
Craig Swan (NYM)	2.43	1978	Ron Guidry (NYY)	1.74
J.R. Richard (HOU)	2.71	1979	Ron Guidry (NYY)	2.78

Top Decade Total			Top Single Season			
Player	Team	ERA	Player	Team	Year	ERA
Jim Palmer	BAL	2.58	Ron Guidry	NYY	1978	1.74
Tom Seaver	NYM-CIN	2.61	Tom Seaver	NYM	1971	1.76
Bert Blyleven	MIN-TEX-PIT	2.88	Vida Blue	OAK	1971	1.82
Rollie Fingers	OAK-SD	2.89	Luis Tiant	BOS	1972	1.91
Gaylord Perry	SF-CLE-TEX-SD	2.92	Wilbur Wood	CHW	1971	1.91
Frank Tanana	CAL	2.93	Gaylord Perry	CLE	1972	1.92
Andy Messersmith	CAL-LA-ATL-NYY	2.93	Steve Carlton	PHI	1972	1.97
Jon Matlack	NYM-TEX	2.97	Gary Nolan	CIN	1972	1.99
Mike Marshall	HOU-MON-LA-ATL-TEX-MIN	2.98	Catfish Hunter	OAK	1972	2.04
Don Wilson	HOU	3.01	Jim Palmer	BAL	1972	2.07
Don Sutton	LA	3.07	Tom Seaver	NYM	1973	2.08
Vida Blue	OAK-SF	3.07	Roger Nelson	KC	1972	2.08
Tommy John	CHW-LA-NYY	3.09	Don Sutton	LA	1972	2.08
Mel Stottlemyre	NYY	3.11	Jim Palmer	BAL	1975	2.09
Don Gullett	CIN-NYY	3.11	Dave Roberts	SD	1971	2.10
Dennis Eckersley	CLE-BOS	3.12	Mike Paul	TEX	1972	2.17
Steve Rogers	MON	3.13	Randy Jones	SD	1975	2.24
Nolan Ryan	NYM-CAL	3.14	Jon Matlack	TEX	1978	2.27
Catfish Hunter	OAK-NYY	3.17	Buzz Capra	ATL	1974	2.28
Ken Forsch	HOU	3.18	Nolan Ryan	CAL	1972	2.28

Saves
Year by Year League Leaders

National League Player (Team)	Sv	Year	American League Player (Team)	Sv
Wayne Granger (CIN)	35	1970	Ron Perranoski (MIN)	34
Dave Giusti (PIT)	30	1971	Ken Sanders (MIL)	31
Clay Carroll (CIN)	37	1972	Sparky Lyle (NYY)	35
Mike Marshall (MON)	31	1973	John Hiller (DET)	38
Mike Marshall (LAD)	21	1974	Terry Forster (CHW)	24
Rawly Eastwick (CIN)	22	1975	Rich Gossage (CHW)	26
Al Hrabosky (STL)	22			
Rawly Eastwick (CIN)	26	1976	Sparky Lyle (NYY)	23
Rollie Fingers (SDP)	35	1977	Bill Campbell (BOS)	31
Rollie Fingers (SDP)	37	1978	Rich Gossage (NYY)	27
Bruce Sutter (CHC)	37	1979	Mike Marshall (MIN)	32

Top Decade Total Player	Team	Sv
Rollie Fingers	OAK-SD	209
Sparky Lyle	BOS-NYY-TEX	190
Mike Marshall	HOU-MON-LA-ATL-TEX-MIN	177
Dave Giusti	PIT	140
Tug McGraw	NYM-PHI	132
Dave LaRoche	CAL-MIN-CHC-CLE	122
John Hiller	DET	115
Gene Garber	PIT-KC-PHI-ATL	110
Clay Carroll	CIN-CHW-PIT	106
Bruce Sutter	CHC	105
Rich Gossage	CHW-PIT-NYY	101
Terry Forster	CHW-PIT-LA	100
Darold Knowles	Wsh-Oak-CHC-Tex-Mon-Stl	99
Bill Campbell	MIN-BOS	95
Jim Brewer	LA-CAL	92
Al Hrabosky	STL-KC	90
Randy Moffitt	SF	83
Kent Tekulve	PIT	83
Ken Sanders	MIL-NYM	82
Pedro Borbon	CIN	79

Top Single Season Player	Team	Year	Sv
John Hiller	DET	1973	38
Bruce Sutter	CHC	1979	37
Rollie Fingers	SD	1978	37
Clay Carroll	CIN	1972	37
Rollie Fingers	SD	1977	35
Sparky Lyle	NYY	1972	35
Wayne Granger	CIN	1970	35
Ron Perranoski	MIN	1970	34
Mike Marshall	MIN	1979	32
Kent Tekulve	PIT	1979	31
Kent Tekulve	PIT	1978	31
Bill Campbell	BOS	1977	31
Bruce Sutter	CHC	1977	31
Mike Marshall	MON	1973	31
Ken Sanders	MIL	1971	31
Dave Giusti	PIT	1971	30
Jim Kern	TEX	1979	29
Terry Forster	CHW	1972	29
Lindy McDaniel	NYY	1970	29
Doug Bair	CIN	1978	28

Winning Percentage

Top Decade Total					Top Single Season					
Player	Team	Wn%	W	L	Player	Team	Year	Wn%	W	L
Don Gullett	CIN-NYY	.686	109	50	Ron Guidry	NYY	1978	.893	25	3
John Candelaria	PIT	.648	70	38	Bob Stanley	BOS	1978	.882	15	2
Pedro Borbon	CIN	.647	66	36	Ron Davis	NYY	1979	.875	14	2
Jim Palmer	BAL	.644	186	103	Roger Moret	BOS	1973	.867	13	2
Tom Seaver	NYM-CIN	.638	178	101	Roger Moret	BOS	1975	.824	14	3
Catfish Hunter	OAK-NYY	.624	169	102	Wayne Simpson	CIN	1970	.824	14	3
Tommy John	CHW-LA-NYY	.613	133	84	Al Hrabosky	STL	1975	.813	13	3
Gary Nolan	CIN	.612	79	50	Tommy John	LAD	1974	.813	13	3
Clay Carroll	CIN-CHW-PIT	.610	61	39	Catfish Hunter	OAK	1973	.808	21	5
Luis Tiant	MIN-BOS-NYY	.607	142	92	Dave McNally	BAL	1971	.808	21	5
Dennis Eckersley	CLE-BOS	.606	77	50	Larry Gura	KC	1978	.800	16	4
Mike Cuellar	BAL-CAL	.606	120	78	John Candelaria	PIT	1977	.800	20	5
Don Sutton	LA	.601	166	110	Rick Rhoden	LAD	1976	.800	12	3
Mike Flanagan	BAL	.600	60	40	George Stone	NYM	1973	.800	12	3
Dave McNally	BAL-MON	.595	94	64	Don Gullett	CIN	1975	.789	11	3
Bill Lee	BOS-MON	.592	109	75	Don Gullett	CIN	1976	.786	11	3
J.R. Richard	HOU	.591	97	67	Steve Hargan	CLE	1970	.786	11	3
Vida Blue	OAK-SF	.587	155	109	Gaylord Perry	SD	1978	.778	21	6
Steve Carlton	STL-PHI	.586	178	126	Tom Seaver	TOT	1977	.778	21	6
Dennis Leonard	KC	.584	87	62	Don Gullett	NYY	1977	.778	14	4

Shutouts

Top Decade Total			Top Single Season			
Player	Team	SHO	Player	Team	Year	SHO
Jim Palmer	BAL	44	Jim Palmer	BAL	1975	10
Nolan Ryan	NYM-CAL	42	Ron Guidry	NYY	1978	9
Tom Seaver	NYM-CIN	40	Bert Blyleven	MIN	1973	9
Bert Blyleven	MIN-TEX-PIT	39	Nolan Ryan	CAL	1972	9
Don Sutton	LA	39	Don Sutton	LA	1972	9
Gaylord Perry	SF-CLE-TEX-SD	36	Wilbur Wood	CHW	1972	8
Fergie Jenkins	CHC-TEX-BOS	33	Steve Carlton	PHI	1972	8
Vida Blue	OAK-SF	32	Vida Blue	OAK	1971	8
Steve Carlton	STL-PHI	32	Tom Seaver	TOT	1977	7
Catfish Hunter	OAK-NYY	30	Frank Tanana	CAL	1977	7
Jon Matlack	NYM-TEX	28	Nolan Ryan	CAL	1976	7
Luis Tiant	MIN-BOS-NYY	28	Andy Messersmith	LA	1975	7
Jack Billingham	HOU-CIN-DET	27	Catfish Hunter	NYY	1975	7
Phil Niekro	ATL	25	Luis Tiant	BOS	1974	7
Mike Cuellar	BAL-CAL	25	Jon Matlack	NYM	1974	7
Andy Messersmith	CAL-LA-ATL-NYY	24	Jack Billingham	CIN	1973	7
Frank Tanana	CAL	24	Gaylord Perry	CLE	1973	7
Wilbur Wood	CHW	24	Mel Stottlemyre	NYY	1972	7
Ken Holtzman	CHC-OAK-BAL-NYY	22	Wilbur Wood	CHW	1971	7
Rudy May	CAL-NYY-BAL-MON	22	Mel Stottlemyre	NYY	1971	7
Jerry Reuss	STL-HOU-PIT-LA	22				
Rick Wise	PHI-STL-BOS-CLE	22				

Awards

Most Valuable Player Award

National League

YEAR	Player (Team)	Pos	HR	RBI	AVG	MISC
1970	Johnny Bench (CIN)	C	45	148	.293	.587 SLG%, 35 2B, Gold Glove, Pennant Winner
1971	Joe Torre (STL)	3B	24	137	.363	230 Hits, 352 TB, 34 2B, .555 SLG%
1972	Johnny Bench (CIN)	C	40	125	.270	100 BB, .379 OB%, Gold Glove, Pennant Winner
1973	Pete Rose (CIN)	LF	5	64	.338	230 Hits, 115 Runs, 36 2B, Division Winner
1974	Steve Garvey (LA)	1B	21	111	.312	200 Hits, 95 Runs, 32 2B, Gold Glove, Pennant Winner
1975	Joe Morgan (CIN)	2B	17	94	.327	.466 OB%, 67 SB, Gold Glove, World Champion
1976	Joe Morgan (CIN)	2B	27	111	.320	.444 OB%, 60 SB, Gold Glove, World Champion
1977	George Foster (CIN)	LF	52	149	.320	.631 SLG%, 124 Runs, 197 Hits
1978	Dave Parker (PIT)	RF	30	117	.334	.585 SLG%, 194 Hits, Gold Glove
1979	Willie Stargell (PIT)	1B	32	82	.281	.552 SLG%, World Champion
	Keith Hernandez (STL)	1B	11	105	.344	48 2B, 116 Runs, 210 Hits, Gold Glove

American League

YEAR	Player (Team)	Pos	HR	RBI	AVG	MISC
1970	Boog Powell (BAL)	1B	35	114	.297	104 BB, .412 OB%, .549 SLG%, World Champion
1971	Vida Blue (OAK)	P				24-8, 1.82 ERA, 301K, 8 SHO, .952 WHIP
1972	Dick Allen (CHW)	1B	37	113	.308	.603 SLG%, .420 OB%, 99 BB, 19 SB
1973	Reggie Jackson (OAK)	RF	32	117	.293	99 Runs, .531 SLG%, World Champion
1974	Jeff Burroughs (TEX)	RF	25	118	.301	33 2B, .504 SLG%, 91 BB, .397 OB%
1975	Fred Lynn (BOS)	CF	21	105	.331	47 2B, 103 Runs, Gold Glove, Pennant Winner
1976	Thurman Munson (NYY)	C	17	105	.302	27 2B, .432 SLG%, 14 SB, Pennant Winner
1977	Rod Carew (MIN)	1B	14	100	.388	128 Runs, 239 Hits, .449 OB%, 16 3B, 38 2B
1978	Jim Rice (BOS)	LF	46	139	.315	213 Hits, .600 SLG%, 15 3B
1979	Don Baylor (CAL)	LF/DH	36	139	.296	120 Runs, 33 2B, .530 SLG%, Division Winner

Cy Young Award

National League

YEAR	Player (Team)	ERA	W	L	SO	MISC
1970	Bob Gibson (STL)	3.12	23	7	274	23 CG
1971	Fergie Jenkins (CHI)	2.77	24	13	263	
1972	Steve Carlton (PHI)	1.97	27	10	310	30 CG, 8 SHO
1973	Tom Seaver (NYM)	2.08	19	10	251	18 CG, .976 WHIP
1974	Mike Marshall (LA)	2.42	15	12	143	21 Saves, 106 Games, 83 Games Finished
1975	Tom Seaver (NYM)	2.38	22	9	243	15 CG, 5 SHO
1976	Randy Jones (SD)	2.74	22	14	93	25 CG, 5 SHO, 1.027 WHIP
1977	Steve Carlton (PHI)	2.64	23	10	198	
1978	Gaylord Perry (SD)	2.73	21	6	154	
1979	Bruce Sutter (CHI)	2.22	6	6	110	37 Saves, .977 WHIP

American League

YEAR	Player (Team)	ERA	W	L	SO	MISC
1970	Jim Perry (MIN)	3.04	24	12	168	
1971	Vida Blue (OAK)	1.82	24	8	301	8 SHO, .952 WHIP
1972	Gaylord Perry (CLE)	1.92	24	16	234	29 CG, 5 SHO, .978 WHIP
1973	Jim Palmer (BAL)	2.40	22	9	158	19 CG, 6 SHO
1974	Catfish Hunter (OAK)	2.49	25	12	143	.986 WHIP
1975	Jim Palmer (BAL)	2.09	23	11	193	25 CG, 10 SHO
1976	Jim Palmer (BAL)	2.51	22	13	159	23 CG, 6 SHO
1977	Sparky Lyle (NYY)	2.17	13	5	68	26 Saves, 72 Games, 60 Games Finished
1978	Ron Guidry (NYY)	1.74	25	3	248	9 SHO, .946 WHIP
1979	Mike Flanagan (BAL)	3.08	23	9	190	5 SHO

Rookie of the Year Award

National League

YEAR	Player (Team)	Pos	HR	RBI	AVG	MISC
1970	Carl Morton (MON)	P				18-11, 3.60 ERA, 154 SO
1971	Earl Williams (ATL)	C	33	87	.260	
1972	Jon Matlack (NYM)	P				15-10, 2.32 ERA, 169 SO
1973	Gary Matthews (SF)	LF	12	58	.300	
1974	Bake McBride (STL)	CF	6	56	.309	30 SB
1975	John Montefusco (SF)	P				15-9, 2.88 ERA, 215 SO
1976	Butch Metzger (SD)	P				11-4, 2.92 ERA, 89 SO, 16 Sv
	Pat Zachry (CIN)	P				14-7, 2.74 ERA, 143 SO
1977	Andre Dawson (MON)	CF	19	65	.282	26 2B, 21 SB
1978	Bob Horner (ATL)	3B	23	63	.266	
1979	Rick Sutcliffe (LA)	P				17-10, 3.46 ERA, 117 SO

American League

YEAR	Player (Team)	Pos	HR	RBI	AVG	MISC
1970	Thurman Munson (NYY)	C	6	53	.302	25 2B
1971	Chris Chambliss (CLE)	1B	9	48	.275	
1972	Carlton Fisk (BOS)	C	22	61	.293	9 3B, 28 2B, Gold Glove
1973	Al Bumbry (BAL)	LF	7	34	.337	11 3B, 23 SB
1974	Mike Hargrove (TEX)	1B	4	66	.323	
1975	Fred Lynn (BOS)	CF	21	105	.331	47 2B, 103 Runs, Gold Glove
1976	Mark Fidrych (DET)	P				19-9, 2.34 ERA, 97 SO
1977	Eddie Murray (BAL)	DH/1B	27	88	.283	29 2B, 173 Hits
1978	Lou Whitaker (DET)	2B	3	58	.285	
1979	Alfredo Griffin (TOR)	SS	2	31	.287	22 2B, 10 3B
	John Castino (MIN)	3B	5	52	.285	